On print at $18.5

Tradition and Politics in South Asia

BY THE SAME AUTHOR

Sir Charles Wood's Indian Policy, 1853-66
Liberalism and Indian Politics, 1872-1922
The Crisis of Indian Unity, 1917-40
Churchill, Cripps, and India, 1939-45

Tradition and Politics in South Asia

Edited by

R. J. Moore

VIKAS PUBLISHING HOUSE PVT LTD
New Delhi Bombay Bangalore Calcutta Kanpur

VIKAS PUBLISHING HOUSE PVT LTD
5 Ansari Road, New Delhi 110002
Savoy Chambers, 5 Wallace Street, Bombay 400001
10 First Main Road, Gandhi Nagar, Bangalore 560009
8/1-B Chowringhee Lane, Calcutta 700016
80 Canning Road, Kanpur 208004

ISBN 0 7069 0608 X

1VO2M6001

Printed at National Printing Works, 10 Daryaganj, New Delhi-110002.

Preface

This volume grew out of a seminar and conference that were held at the School of Oriental and African Studies, University of London. The seminar began with the modest purpose of providing a context for the analysis of the meaning and importance of tradition for the various disciplines represented in the School's Centre of South Asian Studies. On the basis of the interest that the seminar aroused the Centre secured the support of the Nuffield Foundation for an international conference. In June-July 1969 some fifty scholars, half of them invited from other British universities and abroad, assembled to consider the nature of tradition in South Asia and its role in the politics and society of the subcontinent from earliest times to the present.

While it was never intended to publish all of the conference papers a small group of scholars at the School was asked to consider a publication that would reflect some of the project's main concerns. The present work on the nature and function of tradition, especially the Hindu Great Tradition, in the political history of South Asia was planned accordingly. The revision of papers in the light of discussion, and the commissioning of further contributions, has taken longer than anticipated. The delay has not affected the essential value of the present volume, but because of it some contributors would have welcomed the opportunity for a further revision of their papers, had it been feasible, prior to publication. I have appreciated the contributors' patience and their understanding of the practical difficulties inherent in the project. I have preserved the conventions of transliteration and referencing that they have observed as most appropriate to their respective disciplines. My thanks are due to Robin Radford for her work on the index.

I wish to acknowledge the substantial support of Professor Sir Cyril Philips, Professor Adrian Mayer, Professor Kenneth Ballhatchet and Professor Hugh Tinker at the several stages of the project.

R. J. MOORE

The Flinders University
of South Australia

Introduction

While the myth of the unchanging East has long been abandoned many scholars still believe that Asian civilizations have been distinguished by their great traditions or world views. While the various academic disciplines concentrate upon different aspects of a great tradition they probably believe it to possess a coherence. Few would insist that the aspects of a tradition that are their primary concern amount only to phenomena observed once to exist. Most would regard them as related to a comprehensive value system.

The merits of the individual contributions to the present volume will be readily apparent to the authors' specialist colleagues. Taken together the papers acquire the added significance of an attempt by authorities from a variety of disciplines to define the world view that is encapsulated in Indian tradition and to trace its importance for political change over three millennia.

The first four papers are concerned with the concept of tradition, its methodological utility for South Asian studies and the quintessence of the Hindu Great Tradition.

Miss Cantlie analyzes the usage of "tradition" and finds that the term has been commonly applied in antithesis to concepts enjoying approval. Advocates of change have often regarded tradition as antagonistic. In politics tradition has been cast as the enemy of revolution and liberty. However, recent reappraisals have suggested that tradition "may generate attacks on a part of itself as a method of evolution," while liberty depends upon the traditions of a free society. In the field of science tradition has been viewed as hostile to rationality, though a quarter of a century ago Sir Karl Popper argued the importance of a tradition of scientific inquiry. With regard to society Weber considered tradition as inimical to rational calculation, particularly to the ethos characteristic of modern bourgeois capitalism. During the last twenty years Weberian sociology has been reformulated and American comparativists have defined the attributes of a tradition/modernity paradigm. Predictably, perhaps, one scholarly response has been the assertion that successful innovation depends upon the development of a "tradition of modernity."

It has become commonplace to regard change as dependent upon tradition, to speak of traditions of liberty, scientific thought and modernity. Concepts that seemed to emerge as and embody antitheses to tradition have become institutionalized within the traditional order in the course of time. The notion of tradition as unchanging has yielded to that of tradition as dynamic, as an adaptive or absorptive process. The Great Tradition ceases to seem a closed canon and appears open to influence and redirection in response to the context in which a civilization finds itself.

In terms of the modernity/tradition paradigm the task of social science has been to study how traditions update themselves to meet the demands of the modern world. In South Asia Mr. and Mrs. Rudolph have made empirical analyses of ways in which aspects of tradition have operated as media of modernization. Their case studies have included the contribution of caste associations to mass mobilization in a democratic polity; the importance of Gandhi, the traditional leader *par excellence,* in the growth of a nationalist ethic; and the suppression of local custom by the uniform processes of Brahmanical law. In each case Indian tradition developed in a direction characteristic of the modernity side of the paradigm, but the modernity achieved remains in a traditional matrix and deviates from the western liberal model of modernity. In important respects Indian tradition has adapted to new opportunities without yielding its autonomy.

Mrs Rudolph's paper surveys some of the methodological implications of such findings. She develops the point that the attributes of the comparativists' Weberian-Parsonian model of modernity should not be expected to appear wherever modernization occurs. Social scientists should attach to modernity the notion of inherent plurality rather than that of necessary singularity. The complement of the several Great Traditions may be the diversity of modernities. Of course, the modernity/tradition paradigm may still be useful for heuristic or comparative purposes, but it may do more harm than good unless the long concomitant assumption of uni-directional evolutionary development is discarded. The paradigm may constrain the scientific imagination, encouraging a deterministic prejudice and obscuring the developmental potentialities of traditions.

It is ironical that Mr. and Mrs. Rudolph's *The Modernity of Tradition* (1967), which asserted the autonomy of Indian tradition and its modernizing propensities, should have suffered criticism on the grounds, first, that to reveal the adaptive tendencies of tradition is to uphold reactionary Hinduism; and secondly, that to reveal the autonomy of tradition is to concede the inadequacy of Western categories for the study of social and political change in South Asia. The first criticism implies a suspicion that Mr and Mrs Rudolph are too ready to accept the superiority for India of a Hindu as against a Western liberal world view. The second implies the need for social scientists in South Asia to deduce apposite analytical categories from the indigenous world view. Both criticisms suggest the need to define the latter. However Mrs Rudolph doubts whether it could provide an adequate dynamic model for social scientists in South Asia. Among her caveats is the view that even if a model comprehended the Hindu ethic it would leave the non-Hindus out of account.

Professor Derrett's paper seeks to define the inherited tradition of modern India, particularly as it concerns Indian law. For Professor Derrett "tradition is that element in the present which represents (and re-presents) the past; ... a people's past when represented in their present is their tradition.... Tradition is a living phenomenon." The paper is concerned not with the fossilized past, existing after its function has ceased, as in a ceremony, but with that form of tradition wherein "the old is continued functionally in the current, and thus grows and moves in keeping with the needs and general growth of the society." Its concern is the Great Tradition of "pervasive Hindu civilization." Professor Derrett finds a strong desire among Indians to believe that their legal system is founded on tradition and he accepts it as reflecting a sound pragmatic presupposition: "that elements in Indian law which are traditional have in a sense stood the test of time and are likely to work," whereas non-traditional elements will either be distorted or fail. Legal traditions introduced by the British are now part of Indian tradition. If this were not so they would not have survived. Even the British tradition of an independent judiciary is pressed into service to answer the needs of the Indian social order. The autonomy of the Hindu world view is asserted.

While Professor Derrett finds ample evidence of the consonance of modern Indian law with particular Indian traditions, even where appearances are to the contrary, perhaps the major contribution of his paper to the study of tradition lies in the significance that he attaches to the ubiquity of litigation in India. He finds the key to this phenomenon in the fierce competition of castes for scarce resources, which has given rise to interminable appeals for legal arbiters to balance claims and determine status. The fundamental fact of Indian life appears as institutionalized caste conflict, once controlled by kings but now regulated by politicians or by the law courts. The appeal of Indian society is characteristically to an authority beyond itself: to a tradition-oriented system of law that will legitimize *de facto* power as status or prestige. However, there is an order beyond that of competition and law. Its name is religion, "the counterpart and concomitant of family and public life."

Professor Heesterman's paper is concerned primarily with the relationship between levels of reality in the world view of Hinduism, between the order of society and politics and that of religion. Professor Heesterman discerns a characteristically Indian conflict between the immanent order of social relations, which depends upon transactions between pure and impure castes, and the higher order of transcendence. The function of the Great Tradition is to provide an unchanging model to which present social and political realities seek to conform. The process of re-presenting the past to justify the present, or of defending the present as representing the past, is essentially a legitimizing process. The Great Tradition is the referent for legitimation. This is the background to the process that Srinivas has called "sanskritization," and to the contrast between the ideal society's caste system—the harmony of the *varnas* —and the evident reality of *jati* competition.

In the realm of politics Professor Heesterman analyzes the key relationship between *de facto* power and legitimizing authority: in Indian terms, between the king, a Kshatra, and the Brahman. From a study of the royal consecration ceremony (*rajasuya*) he concludes that the ancient Indian state of the Brahmanas was not a territorial unit over which the king presided. Rather, it was a clan system. Membership of the state depended not upon residence but upon membership of the clan, with the king's position deriving from a contract between clans: "his position remains embedded in the constituent relations of the community, whose unity he should represent." The king does not transcend the community or rule by divine transcendent right. However powerful he may be his authority is derived from the community. This concept of kingship ushers in the world of *realpolitik*, with royal authority dependent upon the shifting relationships, rivalry and factionalism within the community. The king is a conqueror; the royal consecration ceremony bespeaks the recognition of his authority's dependence upon institutionalized conflict. When Indian civilization attacked the problem of "lifting authority from the continually shifting ground of personal relations and [of establishing] a fixed order sustained by it" there was involved "a fundamental change of 'weltanschauung'...that set the terms of Indian tradition."

Professor Heesterman finds the most coherent reflection of the change in the *shrauta* ritual. As against the earlier *rajasuya* ceremony, the ritual concerns not institutionalized conflict but individual sacrifice, divorced from the community. The sacrificer is elevated above the transactions of the social order. He is a world renouncer. The change implied "a dichotomy of the universe. On the one hand the worldly sphere of social relations, on the other the outerworldly sphere of the individual, cut off from society and transcending it." The effect of the segregation was, however, to leave the social order unreformed: "Authority having been siphoned off, the state lacked the means to rise above the essential instability of personal relations." The state was atrophied in its development, at the mercy of the impermanence of power, the rise and fall of kings.

Professor Heesterman concludes that the essence of Indian tradition is "the continued co-existence of a social reality with a transcendent theory that denies reality not as a consequence of insufficient understanding but as a matter of principle." The *leitmotif* of Indian tradition is the continuing attempt, under different influences, to bridge the gap. Thus the modern caste association stands between the local *jati* and the supra local *varna*. An even more significant example of the quest for legitimation is the tenor of Gandhi's leadership of the nationalist movement. Gandhi's "extraordinary capacities were cast in the mould of the classical renouncer." Furthermore, Gandhi's leadership of the Congress was remarkable for his insistence upon the separation between the power of the parliamentary party as a participant in factional politics and the authority of the Congress at large as a truly national organization proceeding by consensus.

Professors Derrett and Heesterman seem to share the view that the Indian *weltanschauung* is characterized by a dualistic conception of reality. The immanent order of social and political relations is one of conflict and competition. Its arrangements are justified or legitimized by appeal to their consistency with the transcendent order of a Great Tradition. Professor Derrett's notion that Indian tradition is characterized by the re-presentation of the ideal past consistently with the real present (a process whose inevitable concomitant he regards as "humbug") is similar to Professor Heesterman's theme that *de facto* power seeks legitimation by appealing for authority to a court of a higher order. Together they provide a theoretical context for the main findings of Mr. and Mrs. Rudolph: that caste associations, the national leadership of a world renouncer and the extension of Brahmanic law have been important traditional conductors of modernization. All three examples fit in more or less happily with the argument that the Indian spirit strives to accommodate present reality to a Great legitimizing Tradition. India develops by assimilating changes to the logic of her Great Tradition. The dynamics of development would seem to include competition, conflict and a dialogue between the orders of immanence and transcendence. The dialogue is almost bound to be constructive. The ways of accommodating the worldly order to the outerworldly are limited only by the Indian imagination, which has often been stimulated by foreign influences or the impact of foreign invasion. Individuals, groups or regions have, as it were, a high court of appeal sitting permanently to endorse claims resting on self interest but expressed in terms of transcendent authority or authoritative tradition. When modern Western institutions were imposed upon or adopted by India and assimilated to prevailing social contexts, the dialogue was bound to involve the attributes of "modernity" and the transcendent order. In this way the relationship between modernity and tradition has indeed been dialectical rather than dichotomous.

These conclusions have methodological implications for students of Indian politics and society. No simple model is likely to comprehend the plurality of orders characteristic of Indian thought and practice or the tension between them. The student of law or politics or administration needs models that include the terms and relations of ongoing caste competition, the ideal forms to which the competitors are referring and the ostensible structure of rights and obligations.

The remaining eight papers in this volume are concerned with tradition and politics at various stages in the history of South Asia. The first two reveal some of the implications of Indian civilization's world view for the theory and practice of kingship in ancient times. The next two consider aspects of the relationships between the Mughal and British imperial regimes and Indian tradition. The final four analyse particular Indian responses, each in its way reflecting the *weltanschauung*, to the intellectual and institutional innovations of Islam and the West.

The segregation of the orders of power and authority, which Professor Heesterman deduces from the *shrauta* ritual of late Vedic times, could have radical implications in the realm of politics. Carried ruthlessly to its logical conclusion, segregation cleared the way for the cynical development of politics as an autonomous craft. The end of politics might become the achievement and consolidation of individual power; the means might be calculated by reference only to that end. In his paper on statecraft in ancient India, Professor Trautmann writes of an "arthashastra tradition." He finds that Kautiliya's famous *Arthashastra* was probably compiled in A.D. second or third century from earlier monographs on the science of politics: it is "not an extreme or peculiar work but a somewhat more advanced yet very faithful representative of the tradition within which it was formed." Its concern is a science of politics adequate to a world in which "hostility open or concealed is the normal relation between states,...peace is merely the temporary cessation of hostilities, and the limits of the sub-continent are the only bounds placed upon the ambition of the king." Its spirit is the "cool calculation of risk and the conservation of energy with which the quest for power is to be conducted;...a preference for the devious, the cunning, the crooked or deceitful."

Professor Trautmann dates the *Arthashastra* tradition to the early Buddhist period and associates its development with the Brahman ministers of the usurping conquerors, the Nandas and the Mauryas. He contrasts it with an older, more general and more enduring tradition that goes back to the period of the epics: the tradition of the *Dharmashastras,* which seeks to define kingship in the context of *dharma* or the great chain of doing. The power of the king is justified by reference to his duties. This, too, is a Brahman tradition and, like most Hindu justifications of the state, it is an extension of the theory of the sacrifice. Only through the order provided by the king "can religion be secured for the gods do not accept the sacrifices performed in an anarchic or ill-ruled land." In the *Dharmashastra* tradition kingship is given a religious function and if its instruments are morally questionable they are justified by claims to kingly divinity and fears of anarchy. Even a bad king merits obedience.

Professor Trautmann draws attention to a third tradition in ancient Indian politics, the tradition of the royal mystique, enunciated not in treatises but in courtly epics and royal biographies and inscriptions. Its spirit is archaising, preserving a Vedic ideal of kingship throughout the ancient period. It obscures the historical realities of ancient Indian politics by projecting the king in ideal terms: as a hero, a conqueror, a universal emperor who holds the four corners of the subcontinent under his sway and who celebrates certain Vedic royalr ites. Professor de Casparis sums up this point in his paper on inscriptions and dynastic traditions: "The king, as depicted in the inscriptions, is by definition a conqueror reducing all his rivals to submission. His conquest of the four corners of the earth is commonplace. The inscriptions normally describe the traditional picture of the ideal king—more or less adapted to the particular ruler with which the court poet is concerned."

Professor de Casparis's paper is of particular interest because of conclusions that it draws from epigraphic evidence of the relationship between power and authority, from the time of Asoka until *c.* A.D. 1300: "The most important traditions are those relating to the origins and beginnings of dynasties. They had the important function of providing the ruling classes with some kind of legitimacy." While this function frequently undermined the historical accuracy of inscriptions, they do show that legitimacy was sought in various ways. Some inscriptions were thoroughly sanskritized by the inclusion of genealogies linking the dynasty with "the solar and lunar dynasties of the Epics and Puranas via endless lists of mostly mythical, partly entirely fictitious names." But these are fewer than the prestige of scriptural authority would lead one to suppose. Many inscriptions accommodate the epic or *puranic* traditions to local traditions or eliminate them almost entirely, their purpose often being to root regional supremacy in the approval of a deity or great king. Other inscriptions reveal two further sources of legitimation: the law of *karman* is held to justify deviations from the normal rules of royal succession, and the goddess Laksmi-sri, who symbolizes royal majesty and favours the strong, is held to "condone serious irregularities elsewhere attributed to *karman* or fate (*daiva*)." Professor de Casparis concludes, however, that with the passage of time inscriptions became increasingly sanskritized. In the inscriptions of the later ancient period scriptural tradition predominated, and rulers sought legitimacy by associating their dynasties with the sun or the moon dynasties of the epics and *puranas*. He also suggests that the conception of the kingdom that is found in the inscriptions contrasts with the *Arthashastra's* secular *mandala* theory, which holds that the kingdom is surrounded by circles of other kingdoms in different relations with it. The inscriptions reflect a conception of the kingdom in which the king's *tejas* or divine energy radiates like the light of the sun. Kingly power is represented as strongest at the centre and extending with diminishing strength through concentric circles. The similarity to the sun stands as evidence for the claim of legitimate descent from the solar dynasties of authoritative scriptures.

The royal mystique of the Hindu kings provided a context favourable to the imposition of autocratic rule by Muslim invaders. Professor Rashid's paper traces the gradual refinement of a Muslim theory of kingship by divine right to its ultimate exposition by Abul Fazl in the age of Akbar. Though kingship was unknown to the *sharia* and at odds with the idea of the *imamat*, Muslims developed a theory to justify the concentration of power required to govern conquered peoples. Muslim jurists expounded the doctrine that God chose the king to mitigate the anarchy caused by the wickedness of man. The doctrine is consistent with the *Dharmashastra* tradition, and the pious sultan succeeded logically to the estate of the pious king. The very success of the Mughal dynasty and its effective operation as the sole source of power, controlling all appointments in the empire, encouraged the exaltation of the emperor as God's regent. His divine aura was further enhanced by the magnificence of his durbar and the effusions of his academic courtiers. For Abul Fazl royalty was "the brilliant light emanating from God, and a ray from the sun."

The Muslims did not perpetuate the theory of divine right without change. Their jurists held the king to be bound by Islamic law, to be answerable to God for dispensing justice among men and defending the faith. Whereas Hindu kings claimed descent from the gods to legitimize their position as conquerors in a world of endemic conflict, the Muslims regarded themselves as chosen by God to govern according to His law and to impose peace. However, with the Mughals the ethical purpose of government combined with a pragmatic theory of kingship to weaken the Islamic character of the dynasty, and in Akbar's time religious toleration developed into eclecticism.

The Hindu and Muslim theories of divine right inhibited the emergence of the concept of the territorial state as an entity independent of its ruler. In consequence, they also inhibited the emergence of a ruling class or an administration exercising power independently of the royal will. In these respects Indian political theory contrasted dramatically with the political traditions of the British merchants who began to acquire territorial rights in the late 18th century.

Dr Spear's paper reveals the profound reluctance of the British to transplant elements of their own political tradition in Indian soil in the late 18th and early 19th centuries. Indeed, Dr Spear writes of the British observing at first a "principle of apartness" towards Indian society. With regard to Bengal, the first region to be brought under the control of the East India Company, there was "no desire to take over the state..., to impose western moulds upon it, or to absorb elements of its tradition." Acquisition and eventual direct rule by British administrators were accomplished reluctantly and for the sake of trade and economy. Even then, British governors shrank from a consistent policy of innovation and tempered change with respect for what they regarded as traditional institutions. Dr Spear argues that until the 1830s policy in India generally was characterized by a "dual approach of basic acceptance of the Indian state structure and the addition of improvements based on western ideas," that early British India was "really Mughal India writ large." Moreover, though more and more Indian states were annexed and placed under direct British rule, towards those that were not assimilated the "principle of apartness" remained: "princely India was politically outcaste India." It may be added that the ultimate culmination of this policy was Lord Minto's famous declaration in 1909 at Udaipur, whose dynasty traced its descent from the sun:

> I have always been opposed to anything like pressure on Durbars with a view to introducing British methods of administration. I have preferred that reforms should emanate from Durbars themselves and grow up in harmony with the traditions of the state....The methods sanctioned by tradition in states are usually well adapted to the needs and relations of the ruler and his people. The loyalty of the latter to the former is generally a personal loyalty which administrative efficiency, if carried

out on lines unsuited to local conditions, would lessen or impair.

Dr Spear's analysis of the traditionalist emphasis of early British rule might be extended with profit to the constitutional development of India from the Mutiny to Independence. The major reforms frequently reveal a concern to integrate the "natural" or "traditional" leaders of the people within the predominantly Western institutions that were introduced. Dispute still exists among scholars over the extent to which British reformers envisaged the introduction of a parliamentary system until 1935, when responsible government was conceded subject to the accession of the princes. The India Act of 1935 was a curious eleventh-hour attempt to bring British India and "outcaste" princely India together under a constitution that accommodated the principles of responsible government and unlimited autocracy. Until the last, advance towards a modern Indian state was tied to the wheels of the princes' chariots.

Meanwhile, stimulated by contact with the West, the mind of India produced a series of fresh rapprochements between the power and authority components of the legitimation syndrome.

Dr Mukherjee's paper traces India's first major creative response to the challenge of Western thought, from its emergence in the social reformism of Ram Mohan Roy, through the Brahma movement, to the little studied political writing of Rabindranath Tagore. Ram Mohan's unitarianism and social reformism were produced by a synthesis of several influences: the monotheism and ethical teachings of Islam and Cristianity, European rationalism and the rediscovery by British Orientalists of the scriptures on which ancient Indian culture had rested. While Ram Mohan and his Bengali followers rejected Christian proselytism they embraced Western learning and reappraised their own tradition by its light: "The excitement of the Bengalis by western education was...the excitement about the replacement of convention by rationalism and blind faith by individual conscience." Their concern was "a reinterpretation of the old tradition in the spirit of rationalism." They found a tradition of reason and humanism in the *upanishads*. The aim of the Brahma movement under Debendranath Tagore was to sever the dead hand of Hinduism, with its idolatry and social injustice, "to absorb and assimilate and, to an extent, sustain the Western impact at all levels of society while at the same time maintaining the continuity of tradition." Debendranath's son, Rabindranath, imbibed this rejection of the ossified aspects of Hinduism, "the numerous rituals and ceremonials, the worship of gods and goddesses." He recalled his youthful imagination being fired by the English literary embodiment of the spirit of revolutionary humanism, "Wordsworth's sonnets about human liberty" and Shelley's "immature productions [that] declared against the tyranny of priestcraft and preached the overthrow of all despotisms."

In the late 19th and early 20th centuries social reformism was worsted by Hindu orthodoxy, which was enlisted to the support of Hindu nationalism. When Rabindranath turned his hand to political writing during the agitation against the partition of Bengal (1905-11) he linked his opposition to Hindu convention with an attack upon Indian nationalism, both of which were inimical to individual liberty and true humanism. Convention and orthodoxy "foiled our manly advent" and "emasculated" the Hindu mind, while they "created irreconcilable divisions between Hindus and Muslims." Similarly, nationalism meant the supersession of individual reason and morality, "of higher humanity, in crowd minds. For the crowd mind is essentially primitive; its forms are elemental." Tagore condemned nationalism as foreign to Indian tradition: "Our history, our religion, our society, our family, none have recognised the ascendancy of the cult of the Nation." Tagore's reinterpretation of tradition involved the rejection of the idea of nation, the banishment of the social and superstitious accretions with which Hinduism had become overlaid, the opening of communications between the educated and the masses and between Hindus and Muslims in lieu of the existing barriers between castes and communities, and the organization of society into local self-governing units. Political power was legitimized by its contribution to individual freedom.

Tagore's political voice was small compared with those of the Hindu nationalists. Professor Rothermund's paper is concerned with those nationalists who summoned tradition to their aid, who wanted "to build the national solidarity of the present and of the future on the implied solidarity of the past." They confronted British imperialism with an affirmation of the self-sufficiency of an Indian ethical community. Their technique was to filter tradition, to discard those elements that made for schisms and emphasize those productive of unity. This approach made them political radicals but often also social conservatives, for the rejection of cherished privileges or beliefs would alienate support. As the existing harmony of Indian society was imperfect traditionalists were faced with dissidents whom it did not accommodate satisfactorily, notably the untouchables and the Muslims. Their major problem therefore became the resolution of conflicts. Professor Rothermund perceives elements of "solidarity traditionalism" in Nehru and Gandhi, and he comments upon their approaches to conflict resolution. While Nehru produced a "synthesis of Marxism and tradition...[that] is amazing," Gandhi converted the Congress into an organization that transcended the limits of an ordinary political party governed by majority rule to become a microcosm of Indian society guided by consensus. The Congress itself was accommodated to the tradition of national solidarity. Perhaps the clearest example of the Congress operating on two levels occurred between 1937 and 1939, when the central Congress Working Committee controlled the activities of individual provincial Congress governments. The authority-conferring consensus of the organization legitimized the power exercised by its elected parliamentary representatives. However, as Professor Rothermund concludes, neither Nehru's synthesis nor Gandhi's experiments in solidarity (whether constitutional or agitational) provided the Indian nation with a solution to the problem of conflict resolution. Dissident movements became, and remain, a threat to Indian unity.

Notwithstanding the enormous contribution of Vivekananda, Aurobindo Ghose and Gandhi to the nationalist movement, Dr Dalton's paper argues that their reappraisal of Indian tradition led all three to adopt a political theory that was essentially anarchistic. For Dr Dalton anarchism means the acceptance of a cluster of beliefs: the goodness and perfectibility of man; the oppressiveness and superfluousness of order resting on political power; and the ability of liberated man to create an harmonious social order. Dr Dalton argues that Vivekenanda, Aurobindo and Gandhi responded to the impact of British imperialism and Western cultural imperialism by reconstructing "the meaning of their Hindu tradition to...provide India with the spirit of nationalism." Unlike Western anarchists the Indians based their view of man's perfectibility upon his spiritual nature. They began from the basic Hindu doctrine that man was part of the infinite. His growth and social harmony depended upon freedom from external control: "Liberty allows growth of individual self awareness, and beyond that it leads to a realization of human solidarity and social harmony." As man moved towards spiritual freedom he necessarily moved towards spiritual oneness. Service to the community was the inevitable corollary of freedom.

Dr Dalton would argue that the Indian anarchists, confronted by foreign rule, found in the individualistic premises of Hinduism a firm basis for denying the need for political institutions. In ancient times Indian political theorists had shrunk from such a radical extension of spiritual premises, which they would have considered appropriate only in some past legendary Golden Age, Satya Yuga or Age of Truth, when the world was more pure. Of the three nationalist anarchists only Gandhi put his mature theories to the test in practical politics, seeking to purge politics of their impurities. His weapon was *satyagraha*, truth force. Gandhi's experiments in truth, his fasts and self-sufferings in the face of oppression from above and disunity within society, were attempts to set up chain reactions consistent with *dharma* or the true law of being in the universe. If, as Dr Dalton argues, the experimental anarch regarded his experiments as more than nationalist revolutionary techniques then he was surely a millenarian, believing in the achievement of a new Age of Truth. His was the most creative expression of the Indian spirit in modern times. He bridged the gap between power and authority by denying the former and finding the principle of *dharma* immanent in human situations. Ultimately power could not be legitimized. Authority was not transcendent. Sacrifice was not only a relationship between one man and God but involved other men. Individual sacrifice set up responses in other men, responses consonant with truth or *dharma*. Sacrifice linked men to the great chain of being.

In the concluding paper, Dr Boulton suggests that within the Great Tradition of Hinduism there has always existed a confrontation between "an authoritarian right and a reforming left." In the age of nationalism the traditional religious conflict between the quasi-legitimate establishment and reformists who were often influenced by monotheism or eclecticism was continued in political form. In other words, power was always susceptible to challenge when the mind of India was exposed to fresh stimuli. Such observations upon the frangibility of power and a tradition of dissent ought perhaps to be seen as further evidence of the straining to bridge the gap between power and authority.

Dr Boulton considers briefly the right wing conformist orientation of Bankim and the left wing orientation of Gandhi. However, his main concern is to place the Oriya movement for provincial autonomy, and the political writings of Orissa's leading poet, Phakirmohana Senapati, within his conceptual framework. He regards the movement as a left wing protest against right wing domination by Bengal, which was acting as a conductor of Western materialism. Phakirmohana reaffirms the spiritual values of Hinduism and attacks the Brahmans' growing materialism and pride of status, reminding them that their true social function was the propagation of *dharma*. He advocates a type of "religious socialism," in which "all would dedicate themselves to the performance of *dharma*, either through the service of each other, or, when their physical powers failed, through worship in a religious retreat for ascetics." However, there would be a king and a ruling class, whose power would derive from their moral superiority. As a patriot of Orissa Phakirmohana appealed to the values of traditional Oriya society and employed Oriya language and literature as symbols. The foreign stimuli to the Oriya movement were Bengali imperialism and Western materialism. The legitimation of the quest for Oriya autonomy was provided by the true spirit of Hinduism, which would be embodied in an ideal society worthy of the highest traditions of Orissa. Here is an example of the re-presentation of Hindu tradition in the service of a regional movement for political power.

The unity of the present volume derives from the contribution that the papers make collectively to an understanding of the nature and political significance of the dominant world view of South Asia. The world view is remarkable for its preoccupation with the relationships between the orders of transcendence and immanence, between authority and power, between the ideal society of the *varnas* and the real society of the *jati*, between ritual status and economic status, between pure and impure, between an idealized past and a real present. As it accepts a developing *de facto* world order of competition and conflict the latter series in the relationship is likely to be engaged in a constructive dialogue with the former or legitimizing series. The Weberian-Personian model of tradition suffers, in the case of South Asia, from its failure to appreciate the dialogue. It embodies the uncritical acceptance of the pretensions of a *de facto* social establishment, appealing to authoritative tradition in order to insulate itself against the contrapuntal tendencies of the *weltanschauung*. The present volume emphatically denies the fossilizing influence of tradition in South Asian politics. It suggests that throughout history tradition has acted as a conductor of political change.

R. J. MOORE

Contributors

R.J. Moore, Professor of History, Flinders University of South Australia.

Audrey Cantlie, Lecturer in Sociology with reference to South Asia, School of Oriental and African Studies, University of London.

Susanne Hoeber Rudolph, Professor and Chair of Department of Political Science, University of Chicago.

J. Duncan M. Derrett, Professor of Oriental Laws in the University of London.

J.C. Heesterman, Professor of Indology at Leiden University.

Thomas R. Trautmann, Professor of History, University of Michigan.

J.G. de Casparis, Professor of South and South East Asian, Archaeology and Ancient History, London University.

Shaikh Abdur Rashid, formerly Professor of History and Director of Historical Research, Muslim University, Aligarh.

Percival Spear, Fellow of Selwyn College, Cambridge.

T.P. Mukherjee, Lecturer in Bengali, School of Oriental and African Studies, University of London.

Dietmar Rothermund, Professor of Modern History, South Asian Institute of Heidelberg University.

Dennis Dalton, Associate Professor of Political Science, Barnard College, Columbia University.

John Boulton, Lecturer in Bengali and Oriya, School of Oriental and African Studies, University of London.

Contents

1. The Concept of Tradition
   AUDREY CANTLIE 1

2. Beyond Modernity and Tradition: Theoretical and Ideological Aspects of Comparative Social Sciences
   SUSANNE HOEBER RUDOLPH 17

3. Tradition and Law in India
   J. DUNCAN M. DERRETT 32

4. Power and Authority in Indian Tradition
   J.C. HEESTERMAN 60

5. Traditions of Statecraft in Ancient India
   THOMAS R. TRAUTMANN 86

6. Inscriptions and South Asian Dynastic Traditions
   J.G. DE CASPARIS 103

7. The Mughal Imperial State
   SHAIKH ABDUR RASHID 128

8. The British and the Indian State to 1830
   PERCIVAL SPEAR 151

9. Rabindranath Tagore's Political Writings and Indian Tradition
   T.P. MUKHERJEE 172

10. Traditionalism and National Solidarity in India
    DIETMAR ROTHERMUND 191

11. The Theory of Anarchism in Modern India—An Analysis of the Political Thought of Vivekananda, Aurobindo and Gandhi
    DENNIS DALTON 198

12. Nationalism and Tradition in Orissa, with Special Reference to the Works of Phakirmohana Senapati
    JOHN BOULTON 228

Index 261

   ANTHONY CANTOR 1

   J. DUNCAN M. DERRETT [illegible]

   J. C. HEESTERMAN [illegible]

   THOMAS R. TRAUTMANN [illegible]

   J. G. DE CASPARIS 102

   [illegible] [illegible]

   [illegible] [illegible]

   [illegible] [illegible]

    DENNIS DALTON [illegible]

    JOHN BOULTON [illegible]

Index [illegible]

1 The Concept of Tradition

AUDREY CANTLIE

1. Concepts of Tradition

In his paper on "Tradition and Some Other Forms of Order" (1952) Professor Acton defines a tradition by three criteria:

> A belief or practice becomes a tradition when (a) it persists over several generations, (b) if it changes at all, it changes only slightly and gradually, and (c) it is not questioned by its adherents nor thought by them to need justification. More briefly still, we may say that traditions are chronic, continuous and authoritative.

In this sense the concept of tradition is itself a tradition. Its origin is lost in the distant past. Its history is one of continuous change and extensions in meaning, but because these changes are effected slightly and gradually by imperceptible shifts of meaning over time, they have the highest degree of continuity. And its authority derives from the precedents of accepted usage. Words unquestionably mean what they have been used to mean.

The concept of tradition, like other traditions, has become a reservoir of accumulated experience which always contains more elements than are present in any individual formulation. Different disciplines according to the bias of their interests have tended to select certain of these aspects to the neglect of others and to present them in a dichotomous relationship with some other concept viewed as non-traditional.

Tradition and Modernity

Probably the commonest use of the words "tradition" and "traditional" today is found in the context of the sociology of development where they are contrasted with "modernity," a word used interchangeably with industrialization, westernization, development and progress. The model of modernity is given by the self-image of the West, more particularly perhaps of the United States, and its main characteristics are described by the Rudolphs (1967) as follows:

> Modernity assumes that local ties and parochial perspectives give way to universal commitments and cosmopolitan attitudes; that the truths of utility, calculation, and science take precedence over those of the emotions, the sacred, and the non-rational; that the individual rather than the group be the primary unit of society and politics; that the associations in which men live and work be based on choice not birth; that mastery rather than fatalism orient their attitude towards the material and human environment; that identity be chosen and achieved, not ascribed and affirmed; that work be separated from family, residence, and community in bureaucratic organizations; that manhood be delayed while youth prepares for its tasks and responsibilities; that age, even when it is prolonged, surrender much of its authority to youth and men some of theirs to women; that mankind cease to live as races apart by recognizing in society and politics its common humanity; that government cease to be a manifestation of powers beyond man and out of the reach of ordinary men by basing itself on participation, consent, and public accountability.

Tradition by implication is what modernity is not. Traditional societies are typically referred to as stagnant, unprogressive, fatalistic and irrational. They exist, as Minogue puts it (1968), "like the destined victim in a murder novel, merely to be destroyed by the process of modernization." Development is conceived as the substitution of modernity for tradition. "Whoever wants progress must get rid of tradition" (Hoselitz, 1961).

This view is in process of reappraisal. Social theorists are beginning to examine the potential contribution of tradition to the process of modernization and to discuss the two in a dialectical rather than a dichotomous relationship. For instance, Bert F. Hoselitz points out (1961) that tradition is little studied and tentatively suggests that it may have its uses:

> Are all traditions the same in their impact on economic growth? If it is granted that the prevalence of tradition makes for stability

> or stationariness, can we not find some uses for tradition in a situation of rapid economic development when the threat of widespread social disorganization is ever present? And finally, is it reasonable to stipulate any traditionless society, and may we not even say that at a certain stage of social and economic development the exercise of rationality itself in given fields of social action becomes a tradition?

In *The Modernity of Tradition* (1967)—a title that itself challenges the conventional antithesis—the Rudolphs argue that the opposition between tradition and modernity is misconceived and misleading. They analyze three areas of India's political development—the role of caste in the working of democracy, the charismatic leadership of Gandhi, and the creation of an all-India system of law—in terms of the adaptive functions of tradition for the process of modernization. Traditional institutions are reinterpreted to meet modern needs and modern institutions in turn are transformed in the process of assimilation to Indian tradition. Modernity and tradition "infiltrate and inform each other."

In a similar vein Rajni Kothari (1968) has recently suggested that the development of tradition is a precondition of successful modernization:

> The legitimation of the new and innovational elements depends precisely on the dynamism of the old and established forms of behaviour....No society can live without traditions, and the challenge of modernization is to build and develop traditions of modernity.

The dichotomy between tradition and modernity could not have been more completely abandoned.

Tradition and Rationality

The opposition between "traditional" and "rational" owes much to the work of Weber. Weber took the view that sociological categories or ideal types were temporary formulations useful for stimulating theories and for understanding the causes of social phenomena in some of their aspects. His own central concern was with the causes of the emergence of modern capitalism and many of his ideal types were formulated with this in mind. The trend towards a rational, methodical ordering of life was, in his view, the feature of modern capitalism that distinguished it from all earlier types of capitalist enterprise and to this he opposed the traditional way of life as an impediment.

Weber classifies social action according to its mode of orientation and types of authority according to the grounds on which they are considered legitimate. Social action is classed as "traditional" in so far as it is oriented to accepted usage, and "rational" in so far as it involves deliberate consideration of the most efficient means to an end. Similarly authority is "traditional" in so far as it is based on a belief in the sanctity of an order as it has been handed down from the past, "has always existed," and it is "rational" in so far as it is based on a belief in the legality of a set of rules. Because Weber's classification of types of social action is in terms of subjective motivation, it follows that adherence to a tradition is traditional action when it springs from unthinking acquiescence, but it shades over into rational action when it is self-consciously embraced as an end. Acton makes the same point when he argues that those who accept a traditional belief on evidence after investigation are no longer adherents of a tradition: they no longer accept the belief on its own authority, but because of the evidence that supports it. Conversely—although Weber does not develop this point—it would seem that those who assist in the application of a set of rationally-devised rules are acting traditionally if their adherence to these rules becomes based on their long continuance. In any particular action both traditional and rational elements may well be present, but conceptually the distinction is quite clear.

The separation and opposition of traditional and rational becomes more difficult to maintain when they are conceived not as subjectively determined categories of action, but as objectively different types of beliefs and practices. Under this view traditional practices are usually taken to be those which are handed down more or less unchanged from the past, irrespective of the motive of the actor. For example, Coleman (1968), who rejects the subjective approach, defines traditional as "static, the opposite of innovatory, or new, or unique." But he also says:

> There is also a tradition of innovation, where what is perennial is change itself in a given social item. The tradition calls for changes

in women's clothes and the annual models of automobiles in Detroit. Even the changes themselves seem to follow a tradition.

He says:

> Traditional behaviour is behaviour by some maxim, formulated or not, that one has learned. It implies some normative power in the tradition.

But he also says:

> The 'rational' can be repetitive, taught, and normative, in other words, the traditional thing to do.

The nature of modern rationalism is discussed by Michael Oakeshott in his essay, *Rationalism in Politics* (1967). To the rationalist, he says, nothing is of value merely because it exists (and certainly not because it has existed for many generations). He believes that all institutions should be reviewed in the light of reason unclouded by the fumes of tradition. He has no sense of the cumulation of experience and cuts himself off from the traditional knowledge of his society. The conduct of public affairs is assimilated to the technique of engineering, and destruction and creation is always considered preferable to repair and reform. The errors of the rationalist, according to Oakeshott, are many.

Firstly, the whole notion of the mind as an independent apparatus for thinking is an error. The mind does not exist in advance of the thoughts which are its constitutive elements, and rationality cannot therefore be the quality of having independently premeditated propositions about an activity before it begins."Good" English, for example, is not something that exists in advance of how English is written. Secondly, rationalism falsely asserts that there is no knowledge which is not technical knowledge. Oakeshott divides knowledge into two types: technical knowledge, which is susceptible of formulation in rules or directions which can be written down; and practical or traditional knowledge, which cannot be reduced to rules and therefore cannot be taught, but only acquired by association with someone who practises it. Both types of knowledge are involved in every human activity, and one cannot substitute for the other. No one, for example, would suppose that the whole of the knowledge of how to play the piano, or manage a farm, or engage in politics, can be comprehended as a set of rules. The rationalist fails to recognize that part of knowledge which consists of a customary or traditional way of doing things, and his knowledge in consequence is never more than half-knowledge. Thirdly, because the rationalist mistakes the nature of knowledge, he mistakes the nature of education. His morality is the morality of the self-conscious pursuit of moral ideals rather than the unselfconscious following of a tradition of moral behaviour, and the appropriate form of moral education is accordingly exhortation in moral principles rather than the acquisition of a habit of moral behaviour. His politics is the realization of premeditated abstract principles rather than the activity of attending to the general arrangements of society, and political education in consequence is instruction in techniques necessary for the success of the chosen political ideology. Moral and political behaviour does not in fact follow on moral and political principles. On the contrary, these principles are abridgements of a tradition of behaviour.

Oakeshott's criticism of the rationalist position is further developed in his own concept of rationality.

Oakeshott does not see the rationality of conduct in an independent premeditation that has taken place in advance of the conduct. He holds that it is impossible to project a purpose for activity in advance of the activity itself. For example, without having participated in the activities of a scientific tradition, a scientist not only has no knowledge of how to set about solving a scientific problem, but he cannot even formulate a scientific project. Both the problems and the means of solving them are drawn out of a tradition of scientific activity by a process of abstraction. Equally the rationality of conduct is not something contributed to the conduct by its consequences. Behaviour ordinarily seen as highly irrational and even insane can on occasion be singularly successful (e.g. some types of political leadership). Oakeshott therefore concludes that the rationality of conduct must be a characteristic of the conduct itself and he finds this in

> ...faithfulness to the knowledge of how to conduct the specific activity we are engaged in.... The conduct of a scientist may properly be called 'rational' in respect of its faithfulness to the traditions of scientific inquiry. ... 'Rationality' is the certificate we give to any conduct which can maintain a place in the flow of

> sympathy, the coherence of activity, which composes a way of living. . . . Practical human conduct may be accounted 'rational' ...in respect of its faithfulness to its tradition of moral activity.

For Oakeshott, ultimately, only the traditional can be rational.

Tradition and Revolution

The antithesis between tradition and revolution resolves itself into the problem of whether the past is best understood as a continuous process or a series of starting points. In his discussion of this problem Minogue (1968) points out that up to the 17th century the word "revolution" was understood literally as a return to an earlier state, and that the first revolution in the modern sense was the French Revolution of 1789, which became the prototype of all subsequent revolutions. The French revolutionaries did not think they were simply turning the wheel of fortune to restore an earlier, better condition, but creating something new, and it is this sense of novelty that decisively marks off the French Revolution from any other precedent of political turbulence.

Minogue describes tradition as follows:

> It has no beginning and no end. A tradition can be designated, but it cannot be defined, because any definition would be a formulation of the tradition, and there are any number of possible formulations, none of which can limit or explain its future career. It is both complex and continuous over time, with the consequence that many discernible elements of it will exhibit discontinuity. And like an electrical charge, it may jump over gaps.

He then asks:

> Given such a flexible idea, can we find any kind of situation which would prohibit us from assimilating a political revolution to tradition? Can we, in other words, discover in revolution a discontinuity so complete that we might conclude that a political tradition has come to an end?

He suggests that there are a number of difficulties involved in any formulation of revolution implying complete discontinuity with the past. In the first place, every revolution since 1789 has modelled itself on the French Revolution so that we can now appropriately speak of a revolutionary tradition:

> The whole idea of tradition is a cannibal, it will eat up any concept of political change....Time is tradition's ally, for what today seems strikingly new tomorrow will have sunk to familiarity; each passing year makes the purges of Stalin more of a piece with the *oprichnina* of Ivan IV.

It is also difficult to show that revolutions produce unique kinds of social consequences for similar transformations have been achieved without revolutionary means. Revolution can be used to mean the illegal overthrow of a government resulting in widespread social transformation, or the idea of a revolutionary process can be incorporated into our account of how tradition works:

> That British politics during the nineteenth century were, in certain respects, 'revolutionized' will therefore not contradict the fact that the British political tradition remained intact and unviolated throughout the period. But the fact that we have these alternatives illustrates well the aggressive way in which the ideas of revolution and tradition invade each other's territory.

Minogue concludes that the self-transformation of man through a revolutionary break with the past is a romantic and impossible endeavour. He sees tradition broadly as "a bundle of diverse elements" in continuous interaction—in Oakeshottian terms as a conversation—with the result that attacks on a tradition usually come from *within* the tradition itself. Tradition, he suggests, may generate attacks on a part of itself as a method of evolution: revolution is one way that tradition works.[1]

[1]Editor's note: This notion resembles W.F. Wertheim's conception of counterpoint in tradition (*East-West Parallels: Sociological Approaches to Modern Asia*, The Hague, 1964), the Rudolphs' analysis of Western influences releasing tradition's marginal propensities to change (*The Modernity of Tradition*) and Boulton's account of the left/right dialectic in Hinduism (below, 236-239). See also below, 17-31.

Tradition and Liberty

Edward Shils (1955) begins an article on the relationship between tradition and liberty by pointing out that liberal thought holds that tradition is antagonistic to liberty:

> Rationalistic liberalism, which ascribed validity only to what the individual himself had decided in the light of his own perceptions and reason, criticized tradition as the mindless repetition of inherited lines of thought and conduct into which individuality did not enter.

Shils questions this antithesis. The political system of liberty, he says, cannot be conducted on the basis of rational calculation: it must be made part of the traditions of a free society. Our apprecia- tion of the value of the individual is itself based on a long tradition, and free institutions can flourish only if the values underlying these institutions—the worth of the individual, reluctance to submit to authority, aspiration to rational self-determination, etc.—are accepted unreflectingly as part of our sacred heritage. Further, a free political system requires a matrix of stable non-political insti- tutions for which the best guarantee is an effective reception of tradition. Liberty lives in a context of order maintained by tradition. Shils contrasts the rigidity of traditionalism with the vagueness and flexibility of tradition, and concludes that liberty is at an optimum when tradition is neither so rigid as to inhibit rational criticism of its parts nor so dilapidated that it cannot provide liberal institutions with a stable matrix. "The free society must rest on tradition."

* * * *

I find it remarkable that so many writers start from an initial anti- thesis between tradition and some other concept and, after present- ing a variety of arguments, conclude that the two are in no way antithetical. This is of course partly the result of stylistic conve- nience but something more may be involved. If the concept of tra- dition were of a different order from the concepts to which it is usu- ally opposed, this would explain why the initial antithesis cannot on examination be maintained. At the beginning of the argument tra- dition typically starts out as one concept among many. At the end it has usually absorbed the concept to which it was originally opposed: "traditions of modernity" (Kothari); "tradition of innovation" (Coleman); "revolutionary tradition" (Minogue); rational conduct is conduct faithful to a tradition of activity (Oakeshott); revolution may be the way that a tradition works (Minogue); liberty cannot survive without a tradition of liberty (Shils). It is clearly impossible to take the view that tradition is opposed to modernization, revolution, innovation, liberty and rationality, and at the same time to speak of a tradition of modernity, revolution, innovation, and so forth. The unfolding of the argument in each case seems to repeat the life-history of the concepts themselves. They originated as challenges to the accepted traditions of the existing order. They became in course of time institutionalized as part of that order: they became absorbed in tradition.

2. The Nature of Tradition

Of the three criteria by which Professor Acton distinguishes tradition, its continuity with the past, its unchanging nature and its authoritativeness, only the first is true and it is true by definition. So far from being resistant to change, the necessity of maintaining continuity with the past involves tradition in an endless process of change, and although tradition claims authority, the basis of its authority has been misunderstood.

Tradition and Authority

The authority of tradition is asserted to rest on the sanctity of immemorial custom, a belief in the legitimacy, as Weber puts it, of what has "always existed." This is not so.

In the first place, not all ancient customs are authoritative. The customs of the Japanese, for example, carry no weight in England. We consider as binding upon ourselves only the customs of our own society, for it is from society that authority ultimately derives. In the second place, the fact that certain ways of acting have existed from remote antiquity does not in itself provide a justification for them. No thief or murderer would seek to justify his action in court on the grounds that after all men have stolen and killed from time immemorial. A precedent can only be established by the action of someone already invested by society with authority. Authority does not follow on precedent: it creates it.

Out of the totality of social arrangements at any one time society consecrates certain values and usages which are passed on in the binding form of tradition. Through these traditions society perpetuates itself. They therefore partake of the sacred moral quality that Durkheim attributes to society itself. The mistaken belief that traditions are not subject to change probably derives in part from the same association. Many societies, like many traditions, are conceived in a timeless way as having no beginning or end. Occasionally there is a myth of sacred origin, but this too is placed outside time. Because they exist outside time, they do not change.

Tradition and Differentiation

In simple undifferentiated societies tradition also tends to be undifferentiated. The different areas of social life, such as politics, law, kinship, economics and religion, are scarcely to be distinguished from the totality of arrangements of a society and remain embedded in tradition. With increasing complexity, certain areas of social life tend to differentiate themselves out of the whole and to take on a more independent existence. At this point there is a change in the relationship to tradition which can be illustrated from de Casparis's paper on "Inscriptions and South Asian Dynastic Traditions."

De Casparis is chiefly interested in inscriptions as a source for dynastic history. He says, however, that their historical content can only be assessed if one knows the expected traditional forms in which the inscriptions are cast; that is, one must know and discount traditional forms in order to arrive at history. Tradition may provide clues to history, but it is not itself history.[2]

In the same way a specialist in ancient Hindu law would, I think, take the view that the sacred written law, customary law and legislation, together with some notion of equity not entirely identical with them, might all contribute to a legal decision in a particular case. He might perhaps speak of traditional sources of law, traditional elements within law, traditional influences on law, or even of traditional law, but in the last resort he would not, I think, see law as

[2]Editor's note: Professor Trautmann makes a similar point in his discussion of the distortion of history by the tradition of the 'royal mystique" (pp. 99-102).

exhausted by tradition. Tradition may be a set of principles or precepts that inform and enter into the law, but they are not law themselves.

With the development of subsystems within society there is a tendency to use tradition to refer only to those central values originally attached to society as a whole. The activities of the subsystems are not seen as traditions, although they usually contain traditional elements, but as history, politics, law, religion, and so forth. From another point of view of course it can be argued that these differentiated systems develop traditions of their own so that we can speak of the political, legal, or moral traditions of a particular society. This is a matter of terminology. A distinction, however, has arisen between the traditions of behaviour found in the subsystems and the increasingly normative quality of the central tradition which formerly governed the totality of social arrangements.

Tradition and Change

Traditions, if they are to survive, necessarily undergo modifications over time in response to changing circumstances. These changes may be recognized or unrecognized. In the first case, which commonly holds among scientific and to a lesser extent political traditions, changes are typically presented as developments faithful to the spirit of the tradition. Psycho-analysts or Marxists, for example, may claim to remain truer to the spirit of Freud or Marx by carrying forward his work than by petrifying it. In the second case, which applies with particular force to religions based on a closed canonical collection, tradition must change without appearing to change. In such cases there arises the particular dilemma of tradition. Its survival depends on its capacity to change, and its legitimacy depends on its appearance of remaining unchanged. The problem is typically resolved by matching changes in the present with corresponding changes in the image of the past.

Tradition shares with history a passionate interest in the past. It is not, however, interested in the whole of the past but only in those past events that have an immediate relevance for the present. The historian regards the past as more or less fixed, according to the limits of his knowledge, and the actual course of events is for him crucial. Tradition, on the other hand, like a lover who idealizes his mistress in the image he has made her, combines the utmost veneration for the past with an almost complete disregard for its real nature. It is continually casting back into the past and reordering events to bring them into line with the needs of the moment. From one point of view tradition can be seen as originating in the past and continuing downwards into the present. From another point of view it can be seen as a set of beliefs and practices in the present which project themselves backwards into the past.

In societies without writing men are free to remember the past in terms of the present. Societies with written traditions must get over the inconvenience of having a bible and re-interpretation has to substitute for re-remembering. There are a number of well-established methods by which a given set of texts can be accommodated to changing social situations. Professor Derrett discusses these in the field of Hindu law under the bold heading, "Expedients for Circumventing the Written Text" (1968). The orthodox Hindu starts from the premise that all knowledge, past, present and future, is to be found in the Veda and all *śāstric* injunctions are for him equally binding. A number of these texts are now almost 3,000 years old and their literal application to contemporary life is in some cases inappropriate. The *Kalivarjya* theory, that certain items of the civil law are valid for each of the four ages, has proved useful in ridding the law of archaisms. The distinction between rules binding in conscience and directory only and rules binding in law and therefore mandatory, particularly in the absence of any key as to how the two are to be distinguished, enabled the courts to circumvent a number of injunctions by holding them to be moral rather than legal obligations. Similarly the introduction of a distinction between *vidhis* or injunctions and *arthavadas* or illustrations provided an avenue by which inconvenient rules could be subordinated as explanatory material. The possibility of using conflicting texts to influence interpretation and of treating rules as illustrative rather than exhaustive were further sources of variation. Hinduism, indeed, is rich in such expedients, necessitated both by the long continuance of its tradition and the many different peoples to which it has spread. As Professor Derrett puts it, "The umbrella of the *śāstra* was desired to cast the largest possible shadow."

Analogous mechanisms are found in the Christian Church. Canon law has always been distinguished as containing two parts, one of divine origin and therefore immutable, and the other as mutable and adjustable to the social conditions of a particular age. The difficulty lies in determining whether a particular law is of divine origin or not, and the history of canon law shows a continuous shifting of the dividing line between the two parts. The early church took the view that scriptural injunctions were binding on all men for all time, but the canonists of the later Middle Ages held that, in respect of some injunctions, God was speaking for all men at all times, but in respect of others he was speaking only of the Jews in the circumstances of that period (Cf. the *Kalivarjya* theory). Part of the Mosaic law was therefore universal and part transitory. On this basis it was possible to effect a change in the applicability of an injunction by judging it of one category rather than the other. The treatment of prohibitions as illustrative rather than exhaustive provided, as in the case of Hindu law, another source of flexibility.

On the other hand, a sacred literature in varying degrees can survive the activities of its adherents and provide a reservoir of ideas for the strategy of return. It is always open to the reformer to reject the developments of tradition as corruptions of the original message and to make a fresh beginning on the basis of the texts that speak directly to him across time. Literate traditions, as Pocock points out (1968), are never wholly "traditional" in that part of their message escapes the changes inherent in transmission and remains fixed in the text. Recent reformers in India have been active in calling up images from the past although these have been often reworked in the direction of Western models.

Few definitions of tradition can rival Professor Derrett's succinct formulation in his paper on "Tradition and Law in India": "...tradition is that element in the present which represents (and re-presents) the past." The notion of representation implies that the present is never the past unchanged and that the whole concept of an unchanging tradition is mistaken: at best the present is "a lineally derived representative" of the past. When representation is absent, a tradition can still maintain consistency with its past by re-presenting it. Commentators who extract new meanings from old texts, professional genealogists in the service of new dynasties, and socially mobile castes elaborating myths of origin are all engaged in legitimation through re-presentation. Continuity may, however, take the form of an apparent break with the past when it is represented by its opposite in the present. Certain parts of Indian tradition are related by reversal and opposition so that the tradition itself evolves through a series of oscillations. To take one example, the history of Hinduism, viewed from one possible perspective, can be seen as an alternation between Brahmanical and anti-Brahmanical movements. The hegemony of the Brahmans has regularly generated counter-attacks in the form of heterodoxies and sects which rejected the Brahman's monopoly of worship and denied the relevance of caste distinctions for salvation. The founders of these movements were typically charismatic leaders answering a personal call and, as such, they did not emerge from the priesthood whose claim to authority rested on knowledge of a sacred tradition. Many of the followers were recruited from the middle and lower castes, for whom the organization of the sect offered opportunities for social mobility through purely ritual channels. Over time there usually developed a tendency for caste distinctions to be reemphasized and for fission within the sect to occur along caste lines with the result that movements whose initial appeal lay in their openness without regard to caste became in varying degrees subject to Brahmanical influence. Over time this oscillation between opposing systems forms an identifiable pattern[3] in which the tradition evolves by incorporating the deviant values of successful protest movements.[4]

India today contains two major traditions: the tradition of Hinduism (and also of non-Hindu cultures influenced by Hinduism in varying degrees) and a Western tradition supported by powerful technological forces which is in large measure the legacy of British rule. These traditions are patently in conflict and although many Western elements have indeed taken on an Indian colour (cf. the democratic process) and others are to be found masquerading in Indian dress (cf. the "reform" sects), their relationship, even within one and the same individual, is often one of alternation rather than genuine synthesis. The extent to which the new India can successfully relate to the Western intrusion while maintaining continuity with her past will be largely determined by the fluid movements of numerous collectivities and groups developing and manipulating ideas in the competitive struggle for power and the ineradicable desire for status.

[3]The oscillation in Hinduism between Brahmanical orthodoxy and *bhakti* recalls the pendulum swing of Islam discussed by Gellner (1968). The characteristics of his alternating syndromes are exactly paralleled except for the last in each case.

[4]Editor's note: See Boulton's paper, 231-266.

REFERENCES

Acton, H.B., 1952. "Tradition and some other forms of order," *Proceedings of the Aristotelian Society.*

Coleman, Samuel, 1968. "Is there reason in tradition?," *Politics and Experience* (ed. Preston King and B.C. Parekh), Cambridge.

Derrett, J. Duncan M., 1968. *Religion, Law and the State in India.*

Durkheim, Emile, 1954. *The Elementary Forms of the Religious Life.*

Gellner, E., 1968. "A pendulum swing theory of Islam," *Annales de Sociologie.*

Hoselitz, Bert F., 1961. "Tradition and economic growth," *Tradition, Values and Socio-Economic Development* (ed. Ralph Braibanti and Joseph J. Spengler), Cambridge.

Kothari, Rajni, 1968. "Tradition and modernity revisited," *Government and Opposition.*

Minogue, K.R., 1968. "Revolution, tradition and political continuity," *Politics and Experience* (ed. Preston King and B.C. Parekh), Cambridge.

Oakeshott, Michael, 1967. *Rationalism in Politics.*

Pocock, J.G.A., 1968. "Time, institutions and action: an essay on traditions and their understanding," *Politics and Experience* (ed. Preston King and B.C. Parekh), Cambridge.

Rudolph, Llyod I. and Susanne Hoeber Rudolph, 1967. *The Modernity of Tradition*, Chicago.

Shils, Edward, 1955. "Tradition and liberty: antinomy and interdependence," *Ethics.*

Weber, Max, 1957. *The Theory of Social and Economic Organization*, Glencoe, Illinois.

Addendum: Since the above was written a substantial body of information has come to hand concerning dispute-settlement of a traditional character which is strictly speaking outside law. The popularity of caste panchayats in Mysore, Madras and Andhra Pradesh, and the unquestioned authority of *Mathādhipatis* to give final answers in matters of *dharmaśāstra* and to supervise the activities of panchayats in matrimonial and ritual questions (including property matters which have developed a social aspect) is well demonstrated in K. Gnanambal, *Religious Institutions and Caste Panchayats in South India* (Calcutta, Indian Museum, 1973).

2. Beyond Modernity and Tradition—Theoretical and Ideological Aspects of Comparative Social Sciences

SUSANNE HOEBER RUDOLPH

This essay will reemphasize and press somewhat further the theoretical critique, which has now become quite general in the social sciences, of the modernity-tradition dichotomy, and indicate how one might move beyond the dichotomy. It will also examine the adventures of the critique itself during the last five years. The adventures have varied with the ideological tuning of the critique's audiences, and they represent an interesting commentary on the fact that theory takes its meaning as much from listeners and their dispositions as from formulators and their intentions.

I

The modernity-tradition dichotomy, and the lists of attributes associated with each side of the division, have functioned as a paradigm for social scientists. Like a scientific paradigm,[1] the dichotomy has provided social scientists with a generalized map of their world and

[1]While I have borrowed the idea of a paradigm from Thomas Kuhn, *The Structure of Scientific Revolutions* (Chicago, 1962), I use the word in ways the author would not sanction. Paradigms are scientific world views which command consensus in the scientific community. Kuhn believes the social sciences have not "yet" achieved such consensualism. I judge that they will not; that because science and social science are in certain essential ways different, a plurality of paradigms will continue to characterize social science. Because the observers are part of the observed, and are shaped by as well as shape it, and because so much of the data of social science is created by consciousness, by words and actions and their meaning and evaluation, social science formulations cannot gain the consensualism of natural science formulations validated by experiment, prediction and measurement.

invited them to refine and establish it by filling in the interstices. It has represented a world view of differences between types of societies, and, implicitly, of the manner of cultural and structural change. The social scientific consensus on the paradigm has weakened in recent years, especially among those who have noted that attributes assigned to one side of the dichotomy are found, in empirical reality, so frequently or in such important ways on the other side that the model misleads rather than aids perception.

Despite the weakening of consensus, the paradigm's role as a constraint on the empirical and normative imagination persists. It is a constraint on the empirical imagination in that it tends to sift out, as deviant or theoretically less important, the instances that do not correspond to the assumed ideal type congery of traits; it is a constraint on the normative imagination in that it suggests that immanent or objective historical forces dictate certain congeries of traits for those who can be identified as modern. The normative and empirical issues are closely linked. The dichotomy has functioned as a systematic deflector from empirical evidence and normative impulses that point toward cultural and structural mixes other than those dominant in American and continental modernity. Extant structural and cultural mixes within Western societies, which fly in the face of the congeries that are "expected" in "modern" societies are not taken as serious objects of study or meaningful alternatives to "mainstream" reality.

In consequence, the image of the modern becomes stereotyped, as though it had but a single expression, while evidently it is capable of several.

If one has a more processually oriented notion of social analysis, and avoids a historicist frame of mind, the deviant case is of interest because it may represent a lost historical option, a probability as well as a possibility lost by "chance" or accident rather than by "necessity." It may represent a continuing historical option that will establish itself as the dominant case, or at least as an alternative case. Let me take an example.

It is generally assumed that rural out-migration, consequent urbanization, and industrialization are usual and interlinked features of modernizing societies. If one views this as a natural congery of processes, one might suppose that in order to have industrialization one must encourage the other two (they are requisites), or accept them (they are consequences). Normatively, it means that the rest of the world must accept being as badly off as some portions of the urbanized world in order to enjoy the benefits of industrialization. The source of the model is predominantly the concatenation of events allegedly characterizing 19th century British history, but also the history of other conspicuous modern states. (Conspicuousness, especially that arising from great size or political and material prominence,seems strongly to affect the choice of instances for constructing ideal types.)[2] Actually, Britain is an unsatisfactory source because while industrialization and urbanization occurred there simultaneously it is not plain that either created the other. The 19th century growth in British urban populations was due not to a rise in rural migration (which was much older) but to a phenomenal growth of the population already in cities.[3] Nor is it clear that high levels of urbanization are required for industrialization. In India, at the moment, there is no correlation between the overall rate of urbanization and the overall rate of industrialization.[4] Industrialization rates correlate least with proportion

[2]This charge is not one of the several that can be brought against aggregate data approaches in development theory.

[3]Adna Ferrin Weber's evidence suggests that urbanization in the industrial societies during the 19th century has been greatly exaggerated, if indeed it was not mythical: "...the *manner* in which the modern growth of cities has taken place is rather a larger natural increase in the city populations themselves (lower death rate!) than an increase in immigration from the rural districts; the current of migration cityward has been observed for several centuries; but it is only in the 19th century that any considerable number of cities have had a regular surplus of births over deaths." *The Growth of Cities in the Nineteenth Century: A Study in Statistics*, Ithaca, N.Y., 1965.

Urbanization in 19th century Europe may be something of a cultural and social as well as a demographic myth. William L. Parrish, for example, has argued that "change in the forms of migration that weaken primary groups has been small." See his carefully researched and argued paper, "Migration, Primary Groups and Modernization" (forthcoming). I am indebted to him for introducing me to literature on the relationship of industrialization and urbanization.

[4]According to Deb Kumar Bose, "recent trends in the process of urbanization in India show...no association between the overall rate of urbanization, as defined by the proportions of total population living in urban areas, and the level of industrialization in the economy, as indicated by the proportion of the work-force engaged in mining and manufacturing industries, can be clearly established...A good measure of relationship between urbanization and industrialization can be found when the medium-sized towns with population between 20,000 and 50,000 are considered separately [correlation co-efficient at 5 per cent level, 0.7308]. The relationship is found to be weakest in respect of bigger towns and cities with populations of 100,000 and over [correlation co-efficient, 0.3736]." Correlation co-efficients for towns 50,000 and above, 20,000 and

of population in cities above 100,000, most with proportion of population in cities of the 20,000 to 50,000 range. Depending upon one's theoretical bias, one will interpret this evidence differently. If one regards the urbanization-industrialization connection as an immanent historical necessity, one might view the current Indian evidence as a transitional point along a slope which will lead to higher rates of urbanization("transition"), or as a shortfall pointing to delays in industrialization. If one takes an empirical rather than an immanentist view, regarding the association of urban and industrial, where it has existed, as due to specific concatenations of events which history may or may not reproduce, one might regard the Indian evidence as provisional data for several other hypotheses; for example, the hypothesis that a new urban-rural mix may emerge which can avoid the concentrations which appear increasingly as "mistakes" of Western history. Any of the possibilities might be favoured by those taking decisions that affect the process of change. The range of hypotheses generated and policy options considered is narrowed by the conventional assumption.

The cases of Sweden and Switzerland, typically unregarded by both political and social scientists, perhaps because of their imperial inconspicuousness, imply in fact a different "model." The industrial-urban association is greatly diluted, in that urban—rural distributions are more in favour of rural than those of, say, Britain or the U.S.A. As a writer on Switzerland, evidently in the grip of the prevailing paradigm, has written, "industrialization has spread rapidly while the process of urban concentration has *lagged behind*" (italics mine).[5] Sweden, like Switzerland, performs well on various indicators of social and economic well-being, without the rural sector

---

above, and 10,000 and above are 0.4818, 0.6094, and 0.6053 respectively. When 20,000 to 50,000 is taken separately, the highest correlation (0.7308) is achieved. "Urbanization, Industrialization and Planning for Regional Development," *Economic and Political Weekly*, Vol. IV, Nos. 28-30 (Special Number of July 1969), pp. 1169-1172.

For evidence concerning the low rate of urbanization in India —migration into and out of cities is relatively even—see Ashish Bose, *Patterns of Population Change in India, 1951-61*, New Delhi, 1967. As in 19th century Britain, urban population growth in India stems primarily from the population growth of urban populations already in existence rather than from high rates of urban migration.

[5]See Kurt B. Mayer, *The Population of Switzerland*, New York, 1952, particularly Chapter 11, "Urbanization & Industrialization," pp. 243-258.

being superseded.[6]

In brief, the conventional assumptions of what is styled "comparative" sociology take for granted that urbanization and rural outmigration are invariable concomitants of industrialization, and of development. Like the 19th century critics of "utopian" visions of decentralized societies, 20th century comparativists are often disposed to consider "ruralized" development as, at best, a transitional phenomenon. And yet there are extant cases diverging from the generality. There is no scientific reason (historical majoritarianism is not such a reason) why such cases may not be treated as alternative models rather than as exceptions to the model.

These preliminary observations suggest certain general considerations about the modernity-tradition dichotomy. It is by no means agreed, even among those who now question its usefulness, what should replace it. Some long-standing adherents of the model have responded to doubts being cast upon particular features of it by retreating to more abstract or general formulations. Where there were five or ten attributes distinguishing societies, there are now only two or three. But this does not meet two of the essential flaws in the original formulation: its evolutionary bias and its undiscriminating monolithic quality. Indeed, the second fault may be accentuated.

The evolutionary bias, splendidly discussed by Robert Nisbet[7] in terms of the "metaphor of growth," leads scholars to ask whether particular institutions have "yet" reached a certain evolutionary point teleologically or organically implicit within the original institutional acorn. Dealing with this flaw in the modernity-tradition dichotomy requires a much higher degree of agnosticism concerning the direction of human events than has been characteristic of the social sciences. Dealing with the monolithic quality of the formulation requires a shift to more pluralistic ways of visualizing both change and "endpoints." Comparative method generally posits two points, one earlier, one later, one less, one more evolved, and visualizes change as movement between them. The decay theories, too, only visualize stagnation or disintegration along "the way," not a variety of paths. Instead, one may have to have recourse to a multinodal "model"—imagine the model of the molecular structure of a

[6]Dorothy S. Thomas, *Social & Economic Aspects of Swedish Population Movements*, New York, 1941.

[7]Robert Nisbet, *Social Change and History: Aspects of the Western Theory of Development*, New York, 1969.

complicated element—which does not imply directionality, or at least not so clearly as does a line with a beginning and endpoint. Any point in the structure could be conceived of as representing a partial pattern of emulation for any other. The theory of process and change implied by such a model would be less regular and orderly than that implied by unidirectional models, forcing comparativists into actual empirical observation rather than encouraging an evolutionary faith. It would imply neither regular sequences nor presumed stages. Normatively, one is tempted to designate it as a more existential social science.

The very agnosticism and unpatterned quality of such a substitute highlights the remarkably metaphysical quality of the extant formulations, developed though they are by scholars whose commitment to methodological empiricism is much stronger than it was among the 19th century sociologists who set the parameters of the comparative method. It is evident too that such a pluralism of models arranged on no obvious line or pattern would render the task of generalization more complex. It would also, perhaps, make it more faithful to less patterned realities where they exist.

These remarks are not an invitation to suspend theorizing or the process of formulating generalizations about change. Replacing the dominant theoretical style in comparative social sciences involves substituting a plurality of models for a single model and its variants, and a plurality of views of process and change. It requires a more discriminating view of the permutations and combinations that are possible, and the costs and benefits of each. Comparative politics since Aristotle has always tended to work with such multiple model conceptualizations except when overtaken by the sociological monism of modernization studies. Comparative social sciences generally could now be sharpened by such an approach. To avoid the deterministic flaws of the existing view, however, plural models would have to be held with great tentativeness, as abstractions from reality made to identify and relate variables and facilitate comparison, rather than as standards to which existing reality is commanded to repair on pain of being declared exceptional or transitional.

It is already becoming evident, for example, that while Japanese modernization has much in common with the experience of several Western nations, its emphasis on collective patterns of organizing modern enterprise is likely to distinguish a substantial part, though not all, of its industrial sector. Similarly, in India, a sort of joint family socialism, in which employees—of the private and the public sector—expect and get welfare benefits from the patron firm, is not regarded by trade unions as paternalism inimical to workers' freedom, but what workers (and executives) have a right to expect. Combining these competitive polity instances with like instances and patterns drawn from the non-competitive polities, we may find patterns of modernization which diverge fundamentally from modernization in the Atlantic community. The differences between a communitarian or collectivist model and a more atomistic and individualistic one may prove much more striking than the common features which distinguish both from "traditional" societies. It would be difficult to assign each to "higher" and "lower" stages. There may be other "models" which picture structural or cultural patterns more lucidly by cutting across the tradition-modernity continuum. In any case, reality would be less constrained, and historical alternatives more clarified, if multiplicity were to replace the singularity of the modernity-tradition dichotomy.

II

Offering a critique of the modernity-tradition dichotomy has quite different meanings and implications, depending on one's audience and its situation. It has remarkably different implications in each of three milieux: (1) that of the Weberian-Parsonian social scientists, notably in North America; (2) that of students whom one teaches; and (3) that of Indian colleagues, whose reactions have differed with their outlook, whether primarily Marxist or nationalist. In each case, a somewhat different ideological orientation accounts for variations in the fate of the critique.

The critique was formulated with an eye on one particular reference group, the American social scientists espousing what was considered the comparative method in the late 1950s and early 1960s. Their approach was heavily influenced by Talcott Parsons' systematization and reformulation of European, especially German, sociology.[8] Some aspects of that critique have been referred to above.

[8]One version of the critique is Lloyd I. Rudolph and Susanne Hoeber Rudolph, *The Modernity of Tradition: Political Development in India*, Chicago, 1967.

Here I want merely to mention, in telescopic form, the items which have had a curious and differential history as they encountered different audiences.

(1) The critique of the assumption that individualist forms of organization typically replace (must replace?) collective, communitarian ones in modern society.

(2) The critique of the assumption that calculating contractualism typically replaces ascriptive and affective relations.

(3) The critique of the idea that primary bonds expressed through caste and community and religion typically give way to voluntary ties of class and interest.

(4) The critique (elaborated above) of the idea that high levels of urbanization are typically associated with industrialization and development.

(5) The critique of the idea that certain traits, thought to be essential for development, were absent in "traditional" societies, for example an achievement ethos, or a propensity to be "world-mastering" (as opposed to fatalistic).

(6) The critique of the idea that traditional values and structures were *ipso facto* and necessarily useless and inimical to modernization.

(7) The critique of the concepts themselves, as excessively culture-bound and even ethnocentric, representing an "imperialism of categories" in the social sciences.

These are instances relevant for examining the fate of the critique in various contexts, not a comprehensive statement. The general burden of the critique, in addition to what has been said above, was that if many items of a congery of traits allegedly associated with either "modern" or "traditional" societies could be shown to occur frequently on the "wrong" side of the dichotomy, then the models of modernity and tradition were themselves in doubt.

There is nothing very surprising about the adventures of the critique among the North American social scientists. More sensitive research among new nations has led to revisions of theory; evolutionism has experienced not only intellectual attacks but also the sobering effects of the pessimistic American spirit in the late sixties. There is some retreat from the grand theorizing of the fifties. The mills against which the critique tilted have shown some resistance and some responsiveness to the attack.

The adventures of the critique in its second milieu, the students, have been more surprising. Since academic writers are usually teachers as well, they place their ideas before their students. If one had formulated a critique of the modernity-tradition dichotomy with the first milieu in mind, one was apt to have disorienting experiences in the second. A lecture designed to disillusion believers in the dichotomy not only encountered none of the expected resistance, but its meaning was altered radically in the process of reception. If one declared, for example, that modern Europe and America did not exhaust the possible futures of mankind there was enthusiastic agreement. Students required no persuasion that the world was not inexorably moving toward the conventional attributes of the modern as they were abstracted from the Eisenhower era in America. They were not interested in the empirical evidence one might develop to challenge the conventional developmental assumption; only in the normative arguments why that alleged inevitability had to be deterred. If one told them that new nations had an achievement ethos—which some of one's colleagues found hard to believe but which they considered grounds for hope—one's students mourned, because they were organizing the revolt against the achievement ethic, and liked to think they had allies. In fact, they had been planning to go to allegedly non-achieving India next summer, where they would no doubt encounter the indignant consternation of the achieving Indian middle classes who feel as uneasy about hippies as do "square" Americans. For those who organized collectives as a protest against individualism, traditional communitarian principles of social organization, their constraining features suppressed, exercised a considerable appeal. And if one said that high levels of urbanization need not, perhaps, be requisites for development, they said they certainly hoped so.

Indeed, many students showed a propensity to convert a scholarly critique of the dichotomy into an ideological stick with which to beat an establishment that was thought to value all the deplorable variables on the modern side of the dichotomy: achievement, cities, industry, individualism, differentiation. Only universalism was acceptable and it was too abstract and monochrome: do your own thing—be different—but be equal.

Shaken by this experience of having one's ideas taken rather more literally than one had intended, one then travelled back to

India. It seemed that there the intellectual action revolved especially around items six and seven of the above list, the critique of the irrelevance for change of traditional values and structures, and the critique of the comparative method as representing an "imperialism of categories."[9] (One should have known that word would not be taken as a harmless metaphor.)

In some of our work, my husband and I had analyzed the transformation of caste and its use for political purposes. Contrary to the belief which had prevailed among most intellectuals and civil servants some ten years earlier, we had argued that a transformed version of this "traditional" structure had become a vehicle for representative and parliamentary democracy and was functioning as a democratizing force. Caste, we had argued, was anti-caste, in that the horizontal mobilization of large lower caste communities (Chamars, Ahirs in the north; Nadars, Ezhavas in the south) was gaining them power, status and wealth which allowed them to challenge and overturn the hierarchy of caste as ritual rank. Concepts from the ritual order, particularly *jati,* remained, though so greatly diluted and expanded that they had new meanings. In this sense, "traditional" structures and communities of sentiment, identity and action seemed to us by no means irrelevant even to competitive democratic politics and the realization of egalitarian values.

This proposition, and related ones among colleagues both Indian and non-Indian, experienced two very different fates.[10] Marxist and Marxist influenced social scientists have viewed dimly any such attempt to speak of the adaptive capacities of traditional institutions (though Marxist parties have been skilful in recognizing the political utility of mobilizing ascriptive loyalties for non-ascriptive partisan goals). We have had our writings viewed as a Jan Sangh defence of traditional values. Our observation that (transformed) ascriptive identities remain a potent aspect of American politics and society had been seen not as evidence that Americans may, very sensibly, prefer to avoid the sterility of universalism and impersonality by retaining and sometimes revitalizing their "traditonal" cultural heritages; or that some version of primary bonds may persist in industrial and post-industrial societies; but as evidence that America

[9]Rudolph and Rudolph, *The Modernity of Tradition*, p. 7.

[10]See Part I, "Traditional Structures and Modern Politics: Caste," in *The Modernity of Tradition;* Rajni Kothari (ed.), *Caste in Indian Politics*, New Delhi, 1969.

is as yet insufficiently evolved.

This reception is hardly surprising, for several reasons. First, Indian Marxists, like Marx himself, have much more in common with the conventional American social scientists of the 1960s than either would like to believe. They share the evolutionary model; they share the faith in "stages" of development; they believe in the historical trashheap, to which outmoded values and structures shall be relegated before a new society can live. Both are "immanentist," believing that objective forces are moving through history to realize themselves in some highest stage, which, however, not all may attain in practice. While American social scientists sometimes tended to be insensitive to varieties within traditional societies out of an ethnocentric faith that their society had reached the highest stage, some Indian Marxists shared this insensitivity because their internationalism freed them, relatively, from nationalism and chauvinism.

A second reason for the negative Marxist reception to the notion that traditional values and structures were adaptive may be lack of imagination. The idea that caste is anti-caste is no more reactionary than the Marxist idea that capitalism becomes, as it evolves, anticapitalist—it is the capitalist's factory, developed to ever expanding size, that unites the working people under its roof into a common class, with common consciousness and organization. That an old form, caste, can assume entirely new meanings, even as it changes its ideological and structural outlines, is quite compatible with Marxist analysis.

But the most important reason for the negative reception is the meaning this interpretation is apt to assume in the Indian political spectrum. That caste is adaptive fits with Indian traditionalism as a political and social ideology. In Indian academia, schools persist which argue that only *Śāstric* institutions are suitable to India. In Indian public life, the empirical assertion that traditional institutions and values have functioned as modernizing vehicles becomes the normative proposition that traditional institutions and values must serve as the vehicles of modernization. When that proposition, in turn, shows up rather systematically among Jan Sangh spokesmen, it becomes suspect as an item of traditionalist, or possibly even Hindu, ideology. If Rajni Kothari, a reasonably non-political, nationalist social scientist quotes Gandhi:

I do not want my house to be walled on all sides and my windows

> stuffed. I want the cultures of all the lands to be blown about my house as freely as possible. But I refuse to be blown off my feet by any.[11]

that means one thing, but if M.L. Sondhi, Jan Sangh M.P., says the same, it takes on a different implication. Indianization, says Sondhi, means "following of traditional values. We need Indianization because we need a sense of commitment and tradition as a source of commitment...Indianization is not static...it is a dynamic concept meant to steer us toward modernizing goals."[12]

A critique that found an excessively enthusiastic reception among American radical students because of its apparently radical and counter-establishment meaning, among Indian traditionalists is received as a defence of traditional values and structures.

While there are left-right differences in India with respect to the proposition that traditional values and structures are apt to persist, there is more agreement that Western social science represents an "imperialism of categories." There has been a general call for the Indianization of concepts. This call, however, is subject to widely different interpretations. At one extreme, there are interpretations which imply one should opt out of international social science altogether, because it is politically contaminating, because it implies attentiveness to foreign reference groups, and because it means subjection to intellectual colonialism.[13] The solution lies in the direction

[11]Rajni Kothari, *Politics in India*, 1970, p. xv.

[12]*Statesman*, 3 January 1971. The idea of adaptive traditional identities has also been used in connection with Muslim identities: "Sometimes it is suggested that the democratic reincarnation of caste or sectarian groups is one thing and the use of religious solidarity by the Muslims quite another.... [This ignores the fact that] if the use of a religious solidarity proved disruptive earlier there is no reason that it must do so again." Imtiaz Ahmed, "Reader's Views," *Times of India*, Delhi, 25 August 1970.

[13]A series of articles on this subject may be found in "Academic Colonialism: A Symposium on the Influences which Destroy Intellectual Independence," *Seminar*, No. 112, December 1968.

Satish Sabervallah has summed up at length that critique of defence-related social science research in North America which has, in recent times, been offered in American professional associations. While such research may harm the quality of American social science production, and be inimical to the interests of some new nations, it does not account for the skew of Western social science. The ethnocentric aspects of the works of Marx and Weber preceded defence department subsidies. "International Social Science: Some Political Aspects,"

of high intellectual tariff barriers. Other versions suggest that the task is to use interpretive and empirical work with respect to Indian values and institutions as a vehicle for criticizing, infiltrating, and revising available formulations. The second path is obviously much less protectionist and timid; it assumes that Indian intellectual commodities can compete well with foreign on the domestic market, and will penetrate foreign markets.

The task of constructing an "Indian" social science will be a step forward if it means seeing what Indian data, and conceptualizations based on them, will do to general theory developed in other contexts. There are too many procrustean books, written by both Indians and foreigners, which act as though certain generalizations of "universal" social science can be fitted into the Indian context without adaptation or re-examination. An Indian social science will also be a step forward if it means replacing or supplementing high quality foreign reference groups by high quality indigenous ones.[14] This step has already been taken in some disciplines; history, economics and anthropology come to mind. But the most interesting task will be to see just what it means to ground theory in, or develop concepts from, the Indian experience. Some philosophers of the social sciences have recently argued that science falsifies when it is founded on conceptualizations remote from the ordinary language or "common sense" meanings by which men grasp their world. But it is peculiarly difficult to identify common sense meanings in a society whose own world view is in flux, and in which sense is not "common" but varies with cultural or historical orientation, class situation, and other variables.

There are several specific constituencies whose "ordinary language" could provide the point of departure for an Indian social science: (1) traditional Indian high culture, which is, to be sure, itself most diverse: shall one use the hierarchical or purity oriented formulations of the *Dharma Śāstras*, or the universalistic and egalitarian implications of the *bhakti* cults? (2) the frame of mind of men imbued with the fall-out of 18th and 19th century liberal and socialist thought; (3) the point of view of peasants and workers—which is presumably similar to (2), only under more democratic and socialist titles. There are some real choices to be made.

Economic and Political Weekly, 4 July 1970. See also Ward Morehouse's excellent "Comment" on this piece, *ibid.*, 7 November 1970.

[14]See I. P. Desai, "The New Elite," T.K.N. Unnithan *et al.*, *Towards a Sociology of Culture in India*. New Delhi, 1965, pp. 150-156.

Conceiving of and ordering most of the Indian experience in terms of the purity—pollution continuum, as Dumont has done, surely represents an attempt to use indigenous world views for theoretical purposes.[15] But it raises the question whether this is the dominant world view for most classes (and castes); whether it in fact ever dominated all aspects of life (or was crosscut by competing categories); whether it can serve as a satisfactory ordering for dominant intellectual classes who mean to opt out of an old Hindu world view; and whether it would provide an adequate base for a "Muslim social science" (or a tribal or Christian one) in India.

Those who take seriously either the socialist or liberal world views of 18th and 19th century European thought have the possibility of nationalizing the conceptions developed by that thought, and thus, by re-export, making it as universal as it now claims to be.[16] But, whether Marxist or non-Marxist, it is unlikely that they can remain social scientists without living to some extent in a common intellectual framework with Western social science. This cannot be a path to full-fledged Indianization.

Those who share the notion that thought can be founded on the interest and consciousness of peasants and workers, and that old (Western) concepts will be toppled by the new consciousness arising out of revolutionary change, may encounter difficulties. While there are Marxist and non-Marxist versions of developmental theory, and the Marxist versions are indeed more revolutionary in their implications for action, they are by no means revolutionary with respect to the dominance of Western conceptualization. Marxian thought is not a sport in the West; it is one logical consequence of developmental theory. To embrace it does not mean attacking Western conceptualization; it may mean attacking the interests of many Western countries. It solves a problem for Indian nationalists or revolutionaries, not for Indian scholars.

The cry for a radical Indian social science shares certain features

[15] Louis Dumont, *Homo Hierarchicus*, Paris, 1966.

[16] A thoughtful discussion from this point of view is Indra Deva, "Possibility of an 'Indian Sociology'," in T.K.N. Unnithan *et al.*, *Sociology for India*, Jaipur, 1967, pp. 71-83. He concludes that "social facts in India do not yield properly to the existing tools of sociology not so much because they are Indian but because they are pre-modern, chiefly peasant" (p. 83). This conclusion takes the extent stage-oriented developmental theory more seriously than it warrants. But elsewhere, the author emphasizes that Indian sociology well elaborated can contribute to social science generally (p. 82).

of the cry for a radical social science in North America. The insight that all social science has an ideological implication—related to the historical, cultural, or class situation of the formulator—tends to be converted into the assertion that social science is nothing but ideology; hence, to replace theoretical frameworks, one needs but to take a contrary ideological position. Taking up an ideological position can in fact be a fruitful beginning for serious conceptualization. But it is not the same. The DMK spokesmen who questioned "northern Brahminical" versions of southern history have obliged serious historians of south India to look to their biases. But the ideological cry by itself cannot establish new paradigms of Indian history without much more probing into the theoretical and empirical work. Those who come after us will see the ideological component in our work only too clearly. Those conceptualizations are likely to have a future which, while shaped by today's historical context or ideological impulse, come to a wider, less time and value bound perspective, and establish themselves by reference to empirical and logical materials that will bear the inspection of tomorrow's scholar. Scholars as intellectuals participate and have a role in the revolutions of their time. But if they mean to be academic scholars, their reference group is not merely their countrymen or ideological colleagues of today, but also someone of equivalent scholarly rigour who is not held by the same cultural and historical and class constraints as he. Scholars cannot help living in history. But they must attempt, at least, to transcend it.

3 Tradition and Law in India

J. DUNCAN M. DERRETT

1. TRADITION DEFINED

For the purposes of this paper, "tradition" is that element in the present which represents (and re-presents) the past. Whether or not people are conscious of it, whether or not they accept it, a people's past, when represented in their present, is their tradition. An institution is traditional if the present society conformed to it in the past. An outlook is traditional if previous generations approached the same matters in the same way.

"Tradition" is a living phenomenon, but there are two kinds of tradition, as there are two ways of self-consciously employing it. One form of tradition is "fossilization," as when a ceremony is retained when its function has ceased. There is a psychological value in such traditions, since they give the comforting sense of continuity, and contact with roots. Another form of tradition, with which this paper is concerned, is the opposite of fossilization: the old is continued functionally in the current, and thus grows and moves in keeping with the needs and general growth of the society. This tradition has a furtive and slightly fraudulent air: it masquerades as the same, and yet it is constantly subject to change. The society believes in its continuity, and seeks for reassurance that it conforms to the standards of earlier generations (or at least to the ideals which they professed), yet that which it believes to be traditional is not seldom subtly different. Thus all discussions of tradition must start with the expectation that what is traditional is not the past unchanged, but the past represented by a lineally derivative representative. Continuity subsumes, if it does not always presume, change.

Teachers, and those whose function would be impossible without the tradition which enables them to evoke predictable responses from their audiences, use tradition in one of two ways. These are well known, but the appropriate names for them are not so well known. The two methods are *paradotic* and *syndialeptic*. A *paradotic* method of utilization of tradition represents to the audience that that which was believed or codified in the past is literally and specifically true for the present, and may not be departed from without peril. Continuity, in this view, represents the reproduction, faithfully *and* literally, of the past. Conservative forces tend to be rationalized in *paradotic* ways. The *paradotic* method is faithful to the letter sometimes at the cost of the spirit. It contends that the letter handed down from the past fully satisfies the needs of the present; which, in a time of social development, is *prima facie* unlikely. The *paradotics* or conservatives answer this objection by saying that society has not changed, it is only threatened by subversive elements.

The *syndialeptic* method is the harder, and greater intelligence is needed in its exponents. Nevertheless an element of deception, and possibly even fraud, is inherent in the process. This method requires that present-day society should be exhorted to believe that norms which are appropriate for the present were foreseen in, and are justified by, the authority of antiquity. Propositions, maxims, statutes, laws, and teachings hallowed by continuous reverence, even if this has decayed into lip-service, are supposed to be still alive and valid in the present, *provided they are properly understood.* Great teachers of scripture tend to be *syndialeptics*, and apparently the future of scripture can lie only with them. They are the commentators, who derive from their texts meanings which might perhaps astonish the texts' original authors, and, in so far as the former persuade their contemporaries that the authorities really foresaw the needs of the present, they can be cheats. Conscience can be salved by the almost certainly correct perception that the authors of scripture were engaged in exactly the same task—for an *original* scripture has never been found.

In modern India during the last thirty years the *paradotics* have become progressively less vocal; but the *syndialeptic* approach continually struggles to be noticed, and ought not to be ignored. Tradition in the *paradotic* sense survives in several contexts which are socially relevant, for example in marriage ceremonies, initiation ceremonies, and *śrāddhas*. The intellectual affronts which the pre-Independence social and intellectual balance received at or shortly after Independence are already being recovered from; and they have generated a keener interest in India's traditional values, for it is only when these have been identified objectively (and without humbug) that peace of mind can be reached. Hence a *syndialeptic* treatment of tradition is opportune and necessary: and an audience for it is ready and waiting.

2. THE OBJECT OF THIS PAPER

The object of this paper is to explore the actual extent of tradition in the current make-up of an aspect of Indian life. The time for this has come, because two traditions, the tradition induced in India by foreign rule, and the indigenous tradition of Hinduism (and to a very minor extent of non-Hindu cultures, which were themselves greatly influenced by the social and intellectual background of their Hindu ancestors) are everywhere patently in conflict, which is giving Indians widespread discomfort.[1]

It was supposed, and the author of this paper used to suppose along with his elders and betters, that Indians had learnt English ways and values as they had learnt the English language, and that, as a race of would-be parrots they "have done remarkably well, considering." One perceived with pained surprise the conflict between profession and performance. Indians trained almost exclusively in Western arts and sciences reacted as irredeemable orientals in any crisis. They reinforced this feeling again and again by their lack of confidence when faced with a new problem, their pathetic desire for foreign advice (which they would shelve when they had paid for it), and their "going through the motions" like a tight-rope walker who walks his rope for the sake of walking it, or like a somnambulist, avoiding desperate accidents but unable to say why.

The attitude of the British to India has been moulded in large part by these considerations. At home the Indian is a real person, a real member of a living culture: in the office he is a passable imitation of someone, or something, quite different. This seldom leads to the respect which many feel such heroic efforts at imitation and adaptation ought to deserve.

Very late in the day the present writer woke up to what he believes to be the fact, namely that Indian tradition has been "in charge" throughout, and that English ideas and English ways, like the English language, have been used for Indian purposes. That, in fact,

[1] A.B. Creel, *Dharma in Hindu Ethics*, Calcutta, KLM, 1977.

it is the British who were manipulated, the British who were the silly somnambulists. My Indian brother is not a brown Englishman, he is an Indian who has learned to move around in my drawing-room, and will move around in it so long as it suits him for his own purposes. And when he adopts my ideas he does so to suit himself, and retains them so far and as long as it suits him.

3. Law as a Field of Enquiry

One might wonder whether law is a propitious field for investigating the truth of this. Law is written in English, and the art of administering it was learnt entirely from the English. Legal administration as known to every single lawyer in India is a foreign import in its totality. It would seem at first sight that law would be the last field in which one would seek for confirmation that tradition in India rules, as it has ruled.

Literature would seem a most likely field to support the thesis that India is still oriental, and only superficially westernized. Politics in its earthy, smelly way would be even better. There the lust for money and prestige is not even covered with a cloak. Sociology would turn up evidence that factors which characterized India long ago are vital still, and anthropology confirms the sad reflection that enough of the ancient past survives here and there for the occasional *sati* and human sacrifice to be not so much an aberration as a proof of continuity. Law would not seem to have a chance of competing with these realms of study.

Moreover the lawyer is always a "mere lawyer." His interest in detail, and concern for precision, his pedantry and pomposity, preclude his appearing to offer, and dissuade his more "humane" colleagues from taking, light which could be more substantial than theirs. The lawyer is assumed to be narrow—for his art prevents his making the generalizations through which his colleagues in other faculties acquire renown. For *his* mistakes someone may have to pay dearly: for *theirs* they themselves may perhaps be decorated, or more substantially rewarded.

Yet one cannot get away from the fact that in India law speaks the truth, as nothing else does. With every decision liberty is lost (and sometimes life itself), or money passes, or both. The final decree or sentence is a real event; and what is able to touch the bottom of the purse is never far from the heart. The one, and great, caveat is that many disputes do not come before the courts, and that many that *do* come are for other reasons than are disclosed to the judge, and are settled upon issues which are only partially relevant to the true dispute. To some observers this may seem a fatal flaw in law's capacity to instruct us. But *so far as law goes* she remains an objective test of what India suffers, and suffers willingly, desires, or acquiesces in: and thus it is an indicator, uncontaminated by the humbug of those who are subject to it.

4. Subdivisions of the Material

Indian legal material is so vast, and accumulates at such a pace, that a room full of books would not contain it. No individual is up-to-date with it, and indeed judges have to find it out from the researches of advocates. A complete survey of Indian law would be impossible except by a team, and no one is going to finance such an undertaking. A survey merely of *English* statutes applicable to India was a task which took the Indian Law Commission a considerable time and much effort, and that was a marginal investigation of limited significance. The first task before us now is to settle criteria of relevance.

To detect whether tradition exists in Indian law, and what weight it carries there, one must sift through the material and classify it roughly into categories. These can then be weighed up and compared, and the significance of the results can be determined and expressed by way of our conclusion. But what categories are appropriate? As tradition is a living thing it seldom expresses itself with some kind of "signature." No marginal notes say "Hallo! This bit is traditional!" A thoroughly Hindu thing may masquerade in English dress. Princes of north-western India chattered away glibly in Greek to Western visitors after Alexander's time. They will have quoted Euripides until their guests were bored stiff, and their collections of Hellenic sculpture will have rivalled for taste and multitude the comparable collections of princes of the Deccan in our own day. But no one will have mistaken the Indian for a Greek, and his philhellenic attitudes will have impressed only his subjects (which was what was intended). When the Indian spoke of *eusebeia* ("piety") he meant *dharma* ("righteousness"), and a Greek who did not pick up the distinction might be gravely misled. "Democracy" is another of these cant phrases which can have very different meanings, as everyone knows; and "socialism" in the mouth of a Nehru hardly meant the same thing as it meant to British labour leaders. That he may conceivably have thought that it did, complicates the question, but from the way India's laws have been framed, enacted, *and administered* we find out what was really at the back of people's minds—and that is what counts.

Thus there are Indian laws which are purely traditional, in substance and in form; there are those which, though traditional in form are in fact non-traditional in substance; there are those which are traditional in substance, though not in form (and these are very numerous); and there remains a residue of Indian law which is irrelevant to tradition, while there is some which is, at least in form, hostile to it.

It is difficult to make a distinction between that which is non-traditional in substance but traditional in form, on the one hand, and, on the other, that which is hostile to tradition. It is difficult because public resistance to both is about equal. But the resistance is not based on the same causes. In the case of laws which are non-traditional in substance, but traditional in form, the resistance would have been the same had the law been framed in a traditional way and enforced through traditional means—for the laws in question are norms, and the whole point about a norm is that it offers a goal for behaviour, and between the two there must remain a tension. Resistance, however, to a law which is hostile to a tradition is based on a spirit of non-belief, non-cooperation: the law is alien and meaningless, and the public cannot be persuaded to work it.

It goes without saying that these elements may be found mixed in various laws: one aspect of a law may be traditional and successful, another non-traditional and a failure.

And in our search we must be aware that the humbug of past generations may attempt to deceive us as to the traditionality of Indian ideas and ways.

In this paper no account is taken of the fashionable distinction between the so-called "great tradition" and "little traditions." It is a feature of any tradition, whether or not little, that it must have what is called a "great tradition" as its theoretical component. Hence there is no tradition which does not presuppose some degree of acceptance of the pervasive Hindu civilization. Primitive peoples which have totally resisted this civilization are not Indian for the purposes of this paper, and are ignored in it, even if Indian law to some extent applies to them. It is notable, however, that the more prominent of the scheduled tribes do not in fact have all Indian law applied to them, and from much otherwise general law they are exempt.

Tradition in India includes traditions formed in the early British period and continued, and developed, during that period and after. But the formation of such a tradition implies compatibility with pre-British standards and ideals. Thus the Indian lived on in the British Indian, and an Anglo-Indian and subsequently a purely Indian tradition has deeper Indian roots than it has Anglo-Indian roots. To disentangle the indigenous Indian from Anglo-Indian elements will be a mammoth undertaking, but probably worth attempting. In this paper some clues may be offered as to what may possibly be discovered, and a tentative conclusion will be offered with the intention of inspiring others to broach that project in right earnest.

In turning out the dustbin that is the Indian law one can do a good job of analysis without much effort, namely one can put the empty tins to one side and the boiler-ash on another; it is no hardship to do this and to come to the conclusion that the dustbin contains diverse items, namely exhausted cans and the spoil of boilers, etc. A Sherlock Holmes would be able to conclude from the contents of the dustbin the number of members in the household, their diet, their way of life, the occupations of the inmates, and many other fascinating products of the art of detection. But I doubt whether even he could determine from the Indian law, that amalgam of imperfectly digested nostrums for an infinity of ailments, what degree of disease in the Indian body politic is to be attributed to heredity and what to environment, what to the patient's defective constitution and what again to his insouciance or limited intelligence. But the recognition that the element of heredity must be taken into account, like the discovery that the house is not warmed by an oil-fired furnace, is a discovery of importance, and is worth making.

5. Elements of Indian Law which are Purely Traditional in Form and Substance

Elements of Indian law which are purely traditional, in form and substance, amount to a very small proportion of the whole. As in later sections of this paper, so in this one the air of meaningless miscellaneity obtains. The system was never directed by a single logical mind; it grew up out of many people's wishes and negligences. No one decided that the traditional should be protected in any particular area to any particular degree, and where traditional ideas have been deliberately protected they have not been exempt from interference. One thinks at once of the religious, or rather so-called religious laws. The personal law system is surely a traditional feature, one which distinguishes South Asia and areas of the world to which South Asians migrated before colonial expansion began. The religious laws of the Hindus, Muslims, Christians, Parsis, and Jews are nominally part and parcel of the law of the land. We shall take notice of the fact that not one of them is in force in the sense that orthodox specialists in the systems would regard it as law. Yet occasional elements are faithful representatives of the past. The freedom of religion which is guaranteed in the constitution is very far from being what any expert in any religion would regard as freedom. Yet it is a fact that Article 26 has protected the right of a religious community to excommunicate a member for breach of a rule of a religious character: and this position, deplored by almost all Indian observers (who can hardly believe that the right to excommunicate can be exercised incorruptly), faithfully continues the ancient situation, so far as it goes. Leaving the personal laws aside for the moment, one finds a miscellaneous collection of rules which are traditional and of great antiquity.

A strikingly traditional feature is the ubiquity of rules of law which ignore the demand for a fail-safe method of passing title to land: purchasers from guardians and limited owners still do so entirely at their own risk. Religious endowments have a strongly traditional air, and the personal laws protect them, their weaknesses and corruptions included. In Muhammadan law the institution of the *wakf* (which developed in India in order to accommodate the strict Islamic law to the social needs of ex-Hindu converts, and has remained an abuse ever since) still allows quantities of property to be enjoyed by idle descendants of the founder under the excuse that the capital is dedicated to God. So powerful was the demand for such a device that when the Privy Council in London quite rightly held illusory gifts to the poor to be void the Indian legislature altered the law by statute with the intention of restoring a Muslim's right to make such colourable dispositions, to the joy of Islamic scholars ever since. This alliance between money and religion, between hypocrisy and fraud, is surely essentially traditional. Another unpleasant institution, namely pre-emption, has survived notwithstanding attempts to prevent it even by orthodox Muslims. Pre-emption, developed in India more than anywhere, serves to protect landowners from undesirable neighbours if they are able to buy the property at the price the undesirables could have afforded. The constitution has dealt pre-emption a mighty blow, and courts have ruled that a right of pre-emption based solely upon vicinage is void: but it flourishes in other contexts and is enshrined in numerous state statutes. It is the charter of the "ghetto," and is nothing if not traditional.

A device whereby debts freely incurred by people anxious to obtain loans, and agreeing to pay a rate of interest proposed by the lender, should be able to evade their obligations and have the debts scaled down in their favour, is ancient, passing under the name of *damdupat*. A great many Indian statutes provide for the compulsory scaling down of debts, particularly those incurred by agriculturalists. It is a traditional notion that one should not starve the cow to the point where it ceases to give milk, and naturally the money-lenders have an interest in the survival of the people upon whom they are parasitic. Rajasthan of all places has held that *damdupat* is no longer valid, that is, a Hindu must pay as much interest as he would have to pay were he a Muslim—but the notion has not attracted wide attention, and there is no sign of *damdupat* being abolished specifically by legislation.

Numerous ancient institutions survive in the Indian legal set-up. Native letters of credit and bills of exchange survive and flourish irrespective of the statute law on Negotiable Instruments. Native agencies with customary incidents survive likewise, irrespective of the Contract Act. Gambling in futures seems to be allowed, though the terms of the contracts would be novel outside India. The ancient type of suretyship or assignment known as *havālā* goes on in a kind of legal underground.[2] There are traditional kinds of mortgages which the Transfer of Property Act acknowledges or at least allows for: the so-called "English" mortgage strongly resembles the ancient possessory mortgage, and there are anomalous mortgages which in many cases are clearly customary and traditional. *Benami* transactions are the traditional feature *par excellence*. An institution intended from the first to deceive third parties into believing that

[2]M.S. Vaidya at (1969) 71 Bom. L.R., J., pp. 7-10.

property belonged to X when it really belonged to Y, this is well recognized in Indian law and is employed by Hindus and Muslims constantly, often in the hope of frustrating statute law relating to the holding or acquisition of property or other advantages.

Some traditional features are clogs on progress. Gifts to unborn persons are limited in Hindu law, and in Muslim law the creating of limited and conditional tenures and the transfer of individual shares are subject to restraint, which represents nothing but the fetter of antiquity upon the demands of the present age. The Hindu law is a field to which more than enough attention has been drawn. Here the traditional and the modern come into constant clash. The law of minority and guardianship would be entirely traditional, were it not for recent legislation indirectly requiring the court's consent to transactions which used to stand upon another footing. Adoption has been rescued from its limited and traditional condition by a statute of 1956, and the adoption of girls, there introduced for the benefit of all classes, is irrelevant to tradition, likewise the obviously beneficial novelty, namely the adoption of orphans. However the strength of tradition has appeared in the recent case of *Sawan Ram*[3] in which the Supreme Court embarrassingly declared that notwithstanding the tenor of the statute all adoptions would relate the adopted child to the lineage of the adopting female's husband (past, present, or future).

The Hindu law of marriage and divorce has all the appearance of being non-traditional, and has aroused alarm on that account. Indeed the abolition of plural unions is an element hostile to tradition. But the absence (until 1976) of cruelty or desertion as grounds for divorce, when read against the background of the undoubted prevalence of very much freer manners in custom than were tolerated in the classical book-law, indicates substantial regard for orthodox tradition. The new measures enabling wives to become free from their husbands on good terms are contrary to tradition in the higher castes, but there is something to be said for their being interpreted as appertaining to a new phase of tradition (on which see below) rather than their being manifestations of the importation of a cultural anomaly.

In the law of the joint family and partition the element of tradition is somewhat controversial. Joint ownership is the traditional mode. True, the British introduced a form whereby undivided interests could be alienated in south India, but this agreed with the public's

[3]Criticized by C.K. Dabke at (1968) 70 Bom. L.R., J., pp. 143-148.

needs and tended to preserve the family as a psychological entity rather than to break it. The great question whether property a man earns belongs to his family when the family have given him a leg up to the spot where he could earn it has long agitated the courts, as it has worried the public. In the recent case of *Dhanwatey* the Supreme Court, by a majority, held in favour of retaining the old conception of the family's rights, while the minority judgement asserted that ancient texts should be reinterpreted in the light of modern needs. The minority judgement eventually became law, but it will be interpreted to strengthen the family's position *vis-a-vis* the revenue. The law of intestate succession has many novel features and the departures from the classical book-law as interpreted by the Privy Council and the Indian High Courts are notable: the limited estate formerly held by females has been abolished with consequent confusion and litigation; husbands compete with a woman's issue in succession to her property and the mother competes with both the widow and the issue in succession to her son's property; in particular the undivided interest in joint family property almost always passes by succession as if it were divided by partition at the decedent's death. But it remains the case that agnatic preference over cognates appears from time to time in the scheme, the source of a woman's property is taken into account when deciding where it should go on her death intestate, and there remain the residual cases where the old law will apply. The general set-up of the joint family was left intact even after these tremendous reforms in 1956. Testamentary succession was not interfered with greatly. There is no doubt but that testaments became acclimatized very rapidly; Hindus had perpetuated endowments similarly before 1772, and the device spread. The Indian rule that probate is not required before the estate vests in the executor has not been modified in spite of many modifications introduced lately in favour of judicial interference in family affairs.

Some Indian traditional features hardly deserve more than passing mention. The Coinage Act (1906), and the protection of the coinage afforded in the Penal Code, continue the indigenous rule that the sovereign alone has the right of providing legal tender. Under the Easements Act (1882), the easements of air and privacy are regularized: they were Indian customary features not known in England. The Oaths Act (1873), even as replaced by certain state statutes, continues in legal form the custom to propose and to take an ordeal, and thereby determine an issue in litigation.

It can be said in conclusion that miscellaneous items retain their traditional content and function largely because they are either inevitable or have not accumulated sufficient weight of opposition to submit to abolition. Purely traditional elements can hardly be claimed to be characteristic of Indian law, if the latter is taken as a whole. But the non-traditionality of the great bulk of that law is deceptive.

6. Elements Traditional in Form but not in Substance

In contrast to the Hindu law, which has undergone a process somewhat misleadingly called "codification," the Muhammadan law has remained virtually immune from reform. No one knows how long this will continue. The possibility of a Muslim entering into plural marriages, and of divorcing his wife or wives by merely pronouncing the word *talaq* is still a feature of Indian law, and indeed of Indian practice. The Muhammadan law of succession, greatly modified by custom where the long arm of that extraordinarily recessive statute, the Shariat Act of 1937, cannot reach, continues in vigour. To make matters worse various varieties of Muhammadan law are in force, and there are unknown extents to which custom may apply amongst the anomalous Muslim communities whose laws retain some flavour of the groups' non-Muslim origins. Muhammadan law could be proposed as an excellent example of the traditional, over-ripe for the knife of the parliamentary surgeon—or so it is commonly said in India. India's refusal to follow Pakistan's lead in certain well-merited reforms is traditional, in that the indecision and lack of confidence of the majority community holds the latter back from giving an overdue relief to the minority. But while all this is true, the Muhammadan law, better than the Hindu law, demonstrates the peculiar quality of the Indian legal system, namely the interpenetration of foreign ideas into the inherited framework, so that the result whilst appearing to be traditional is in fact a blend of the traditional and the novel.[4]

Muhammadan law as known in India abhors "tricks" (see 7 All.

[4]An exceptionally good example of this interpenetration is *I.N.S.J. Tiruvenkatachariar* v. *Andalamma* (1969) 1 An. W.R. 142 F.B. where traditional rights are denied legal effect.

775FB), whilst the Islamic law finds them necessary. Fyzee, who has studied the topic intensively, finds that Muhammadan law in India underwent considerable modification, whilst remaining nominally intact. He finds cases where the Muhammadan law is the same as English law, but English terms, phraseology and doctrines are employed; cases where it is modified by doctrines of the common law or of equity; cases where Muhammadan law is varied by custom (contrary to the tenor of Islamic law but consistently with Indian custom), and cases where it is abolished or modified by statutory law. One may consult his *Cases in the Muhammadan Law of India and Pakistan*, pp. xxi-xxxiv, for details. In many cases the known Islamic rules were simply set aside judicially. In others they were ignorantly overlooked, but the omission has not been rectified. The whole concept of the "anomalous Muslim," that is, Muslims governed by laws, as customs, which do not coincide with the Islamic law, is foreign to Islamic tradition, though it agrees with Indian usage. The Dissolution of Muslim Marriages Act (1939), introduced, *sub modo*, rules from a non-Indian school of Islamic law into India for the relief of Indian Muslims whose own dominant school could not have afforded this relief. The statute, along with many Indian statutes of a general character and those applicable to Hindus, illustrates the Indian practice of dealing with matters which are nominally the preserve of religion, as if the religious aspect could be ignored and the secular aspects were entirely fit for legislative interference. Thus marriages can be dissolved by statute while remaining in full force and effect from the point of view of the religion of the spouses. It has become Indian tradition to do this. This tradition is of Anglo-Indian origin. But it could not have started but for the Indian belief that the king can validly provide by regulation for the "seen" (i.e. secular) aspects of behaviour, whereas he cannot interfere with matters of an "unseen" (i.e. supersensory or superstitious) character. This is the famous Indian "schizophrenia."

Other features of Indian law seem to be traditional while they are not. The panchayat system regularized by statute is not that of the panchayat of pre-British times. The Income Tax Act (1922), and the Central Sales Tax Act (1956), apart from other types of indirect taxation, appear to continue the simple traditional rule that all classes must contribute according to their wealth to the cost of government. It can be argued that there is nothing untraditional in this. But since the traditional concept of taxation did not provide for the ruler to put the subject to examination as to his annual income outside the scope of the land revenue, and since the raising of revenue from other sources was in ancient times largely a matter of irregular and *ad hoc* levies from wealthy classes upon the basis of bargains between their representatives and the ruler, whereas local taxation was a matter of voluntary self-taxation by villagers, it can equally well be argued that a disposition to evade the revenue laws where possible can be traced to a widespread disbelief in the state's right to participate forcibly (as opposed to ideally) in each individual's prosperity. The tension between ruler and ruled in the pre-British periods seems to persist into our own days. Certainly a persistent refusal to pay more than a proportion of the tax due has led to many devices in India, including that dubious and much discussed device of refusing to produce accounts in the course of litigation dealing with totally different matters, quite apart from the production of false accounts for tax purposes.

But the most notorious failure of form to agree with substance is the legal system itself.[5] The concept of law and litigation does not agree with that prevailing before the British period. That the ruler was the fountain of "justice" is certain, but the "justice" of the British is not that of the native arbitrator. Legal administration, with its artificialities and technicalities, the limitation of actions, the rule that plaintiffs must pay court fees, and finally the law of evidence, affront the traditional notions of obtaining justice. It could be argued that British justice, and its Indian successor which is like it in every way, are a foreign import, not very efficient, and often put to perverse uses. In form the legal system achieves the same end as the previous system, but in substance it fails to achieve all that, and achieves, as by-products, much that is different. On the other hand it could be argued that the Indian legal system of today would not have proved so popular had it not served an Indian need. This is true, but its implications should be reserved until we assess how far, under the umbrella of the foreign and novel, the Indian achieves purposes which are atavistic and regressive.

7. Elements Traditional in Substance but not in Form

The desire to believe that the Indian legal system is traditional is

[5]Derrett 'Emergency and preventive detention in India', in P. Robb and D. Taylor, edd., *Rule, Protest, Identity*, London, Curzon Press, 1978, pp. 83-119.

very strong. A seminar at Madras seriously considered a long thesis which claimed that the constitution itself was based on Hindu principles.[6] The speaker was perhaps more nearly right than he knew. The authors of the constitution had nothing further from their minds than Hindu culture: but in so far as the majority of them were Hindus, Hindu notions percolated through their Anglo-Indian thinking, and made for much of the strength as well as the weaknesses of the remarkable document they adopted as the ground-plan of the country's laws. The desire to bring the Indian legal system into touch with the pre-British principles has given birth to a project to which was devoted a conference in Patna in March 1969. Lip-service,if not more, is given to Hindu ideas in many places where they have no direct claim to attention. Manu has been quoted by a Sessions Judge in a sensational murder case. Hindu philanthropic ideas have triumphed over English principles more than once (e.g. the case of *Sri Ram* in the Supreme Court in 1976). Justice V.R. Krishna Iyer has demanded the revival of a genuine Indian jurisprudence.[7]

We must not lose sight of the fact that, whatever the form of the law, the Hindu is happy if he can see a thread joining it with his ancient past. In *Saminatha* v. *Vageesan* [1940] Mad. at p. 108 Mr Justice Patanjali Sastri, who subsequently became a justice of the Supreme Court, distinguished for his pioneering work in constitutional law, spoke as follows:

> It is a matter of satisfaction that our conclusion, which is in consonance with modern ideas which tend more and more to favour the disentanglement of civil rights and obligations from the meshes of Hindu ceremonial law, could be supported on the authority of an ancient text.

In that case a spurious text of Yama which had obtained respectability through judicial decisions relying upon it, authorized a Brahmin to adopt his daughter's son without performing the ritual of a sacrifice in fire (which would effect a transfer from one *gotra* to another in a supersensory fashion). The current law (post-1956) on the subject states that the sacrifice is never required. A continuity with the past is claimed, though in fact that rule does not agree with

[6] *Bull. Inst. Trad. Culture* (Madras), 2 (1964), pp. 195-234.

[7] *Rattan Lal* v. *Vardesh* (1976) 2 S.C.C. 103: (1976) 2 S.C.C., Journal, pp. 1-16.

the spirit of the ancient civilization, which required that the ceremony should be performed. Though this citation is from a judgment delivered in 1939, the spirit of the attitude it evinces remains alive. Textual support for even radical changes is eagerly sought, and Dr S. Radhakrishnan in commending modern reforms not seldom utilized the possibilities of this approach.

Hindu ideas are consulted even outside the personal law: on the subject of gambling, on wagering contracts, caste membership for the purpose of elections, and the protection of cows; likewise on the question whether a sect was "Hindu" for the purposes of the Temple Entry laws. In a case with no Hindu connection a judge has cited the text of Brihaspati on the need for equity. The *Arthaśāstra* has been cited by another in a context requiring no such reference. In cases on customary laws the personal law is nominally excluded, yet references to Hindu principles are frequent.

Hindu ideas tentatively push themselves forward in unlikely contexts. That a wife cannot enter into a separation agreement when she marries, that an unchaste wife can never obtain alimony, that a marriage can be annulled for fraud even though no representations were made actually to the intended spouse, and that the doctrine of approbation has no place in the Hindu law of nullity for impotence—these are ideas which may not ultimately be found to be valid but which claim to be genuine non-imported, indigenous Indian concepts within the Indian law and living alongside rules of purely foreign origin.

Though the Indian law makes little direct reference to it, the canon law of marriage still has its place in the law of marriage for Christians. Some traditional rules for the matrimonial regimes of Christians in Kerala remain notwithstanding the extension to Kerala of the central statutes on the subjects. In the Penal Code the treatment of adultery as a crime is a traditional feature. The whole subject of land revenue, with what is called Agricultural Income Tax, is thoroughly traditional in substance, whatever the form. The much agitated subject of the national language or languages reveals Indian traditions triumphing over chauvinism and sectional interests: and the reprehensible stages through which the deplorable business has passed make sense against the background of the uninhibited jostling to obtain the ruler's favour which is the uninterrupted story of caste progress in pre-British and British periods.

A vast area of Indian law is taken up with industrial disputes legislation and matters appertaining to the protection of the workman; with welfare legislation intended to mitigate the rigours of overpopulation and underemployment and employers' lack of sympathy with their work-force; with legislation intended to control the availability of scarce supplies. It could be argued that this has little contact with law and society prior to the British period; but in my view this would not be a correct analysis.

Nothing is more certain than that the Indian worker regarded his employer as personally concerned (nay, liable) for his welfare and the welfare of his family, and it can be argued that legislation tending to prevent exploitation and to ensure that the employer performs his humanitarian duty is not foreign in substance, however foreign it may be in form. Thus the large group of statutes dealing with safety and welfare can be regarded as harmonious with tradition: it includes the following Acts of the central legislature: Fatal Accidents (1855), Workmen's Compensation (1923), Mines (1923, 1941), Children (Pledging of Labour) (1933), Dock Labourers (1934), Employers' Liability (1938), Employment of Children (1938), Payment of Wages (1936), Weekly Holidays (1942), Mica Mines Labour Welfare Fund (1946), Coal Mines Labour Welfare Fund (1947), Dock Workers (Regulation of Employment) (1948), Minimum Wages (1948), Employees' State Insurance (1948), Coal Mines Provident Fund (1948), Factories (1948), Plantation Labour (1951), Employees' Provident Fund (1952), Working Journalists (1955, 1958), and Personal Injuries (Compensation Insurance) (1963).

It might be argued that legislation facilitating trade union activity and regulating the resolution of trade disputes was thoroughly foreign. That workers should band together and threaten or coerce their employers seems an altogether modern development. However, notwithstanding the paternalistic tradition of Indian labour it is clear that trade unions rapidly grasped the power available to them, and it can as well be argued that the concept of the strike, and non-cooperation, in fact mass action to enforce real or supposed claims has always been at the very bottom of Indian social organization, and that what the past lacked was organization in the mechanical sense, namely the assurance that a caste or sectional decision would be totally implemented. Thus the Trade Unions Act (1926), the Trade Disputes Act (1929), the Industrial Employment (Standing Orders) Act (1946), the Industrial Disputes Act (1947), and the Payment of Bonus Act (1965), which have all introduced voluminous quantities of law into Indian reports, rapidly and successfully naturalized there, can be claimed, with a fair measure of verisimilitude, to be articulations of latent traditional features. Meanwhile the *gherao* is a form of intimidation similar to the pre-British *dhārnā*.

Numerous quite different topics merit a similar approach. It would appear at first sight that the Essential Commodities Act (1955) which gives the government wide powers to procure and distribute essential commodities at fixed prices, is a novelty. However, the ruler in pre-British times had the power to create monopolies and to fix prices, to prohibit exports and to monopolize certain imports—in fact the state's attempted control over commerce was considerable. The only difference would seem to be the efficiency of the system—but here again the difference may be more apparent than real.

The Cooperative Societies Act (1912), the Companies Acts (1913, 1965), and the Partnership Act (1932) would seem to be either novel or superfluous. The machinery envisaged in all these was certainly new when it was introduced. But the complex systems of raising and employing capital in use before the British period were adequate for very extended and successful commerce in South Asia and beyond: what the statutes have done is mainly to enable Europeans to deal upon terms of roughly equal chances of honesty with Indian merchants, and to participate to mutual advantage along with Indians in Indian and foreign commerce. The cooperative societies, which have been successful, and are an established feature of the Indian scene, without ousting the traditional money-lender, are in a sense descendants of the ancient sources of capital for the relief of rural distress and the development of rural amenities—principally temples and other religious institutions, the great communal money-lenders of the past.

Two central statutes seem at first sight utterly untraditional, namely the All India Services Acts (1951, 1963) and the rules made thereunder, and the Prevention of Corruption Act (1947). The latter would seem extremely foreign in purpose as well as style. However, the status of the public servant of pre-British times was always hedged around with risks and limitations balancing his special prestige and power, and the ruler's jealousy of his subordinates' corruptions was a permanent feature of political life. The theory that one can take bribes, but not too much, and not from the wrong people, was a distinct limitation upon an official's cupidity—and I may not be wrong in guessing that this is exactly how the Prevention of Corruption Act works in practice. The notion of trapping officials, which prevails under that Act, reproduces in a remarkable way the outlook, if not the very words, of the *Arthaśāstra*.

The state's acquisition and control of major sources of wealth could be put down to "socialism," and could be ascribed to the new age of enlightenment. However, the Coal Bearing Areas (Acquisition and Development) Act (1957), like the Oilfields (Regulation and Development) Act (1948), corresponds to the undoubted monopoly of the soil and its produce which ancient texts assert with such persistence.

The Preventive Detention Act (1950), of which many Indians are, reasonably, ashamed, and which, along with the Unlawful Activities (Prevention) Act (1967), curbs freedom in ways not originally contemplated by the architects of Indian Independence, is a fair test of whether Indian law is or is not traditional. Nothing in the conception of the statutes or the occasions for their use refers explicitly or even by inference to the pre-British period. However, the tradition in force in the British period, especially the concept of sedition which obtained then, was accepted for a long time because it corresponded to the powers which the pre-British ruler automatically held by virtue of his office. It is not fashionable in these days to speak of pre-British rulers as despots, and a great deal of effort has been spent making out that Indians were basically self-governing people, whose kings were also subject to law. Yet the *Dharmaśāstra* insists upon the special divinity of rulers, urges them not to abuse their otherwise unlimited authority, and lays down that it is sinful to criticize or denigrate one's own ruler (Kullūka on Manu XII. 6). Determined agitation against the ruler, plotting to overthrow the dynasty, insurrections and intrigues, were a permanent feature of Indian political life before the British period and seem by no means to have been deprecated, no matter how severe their effects. That the people in power had the right to imprison, or punish, or otherwise inhibit their "enemies" or potential enemies is beyond question, and the early British period reveals this going on on a grand scale. What is so striking is the bold and irrepressible way in which elements made repeated bids for power, and suspicion was endemic that one's most intimate acquaintance would be the most likely nucleus for an intrigue against one. The uncontrolled verbosity and foolish enterprise of the "patriots" during the British period could be seen most naturally as a continuation of the undisciplined, but normal, competitive life of earlier times, and the "indiscipline" and "selfishness" of which Indian leaders complain today is surely a continuation of something which was traditional and which never obtained an effective alternative during the brief episode of the English. I shall come back to this point in my Conclusion.

An unexpected item which links modern legal India with tradition is the notion that, now she is free, India will play an historic role in international affairs. The interest in India has not abated due to her own lapses in international relations, and recently K.R.R. Sastry gave lectures on Internationl Law and Indian contributions thereto, a survey of Hinduism and Hindu principles in action in the international scene, which, while it probably convinced no one, shows that there is an aroma of plausibility about the idea which has captivated some minds—and that can hardly be totally baseless.

8. Elements Irrelevant to Tradition

A very great deal of Indian law seems to have no contact with tradition at all. The Contract Act (1872), the Majority Act(1875), the Specific Relief Act (1877), the two Insolvency Acts (1909, 1920), and the Insurance Act (1912) add to what was in use before, but appear not to touch upon tradition. The Army and the Air Force Acts (1950) can hardly be relevant to our enquiry. Very many more Acts add, without touching existing institutions: Electricity (1910), Railways (1890), Aircraft (1934), Patents and Designs (1911), Post Office (1898), Universities (1904-) (a topic to which we must return), Institutes of Technology (1961), Copyright (1914), Motor Vehicles (1914-39), Carriage of Goods by Sea (1925), and so forth.

A curious area which appears to touch tradition, but seems to have remained irrelevant to it, consists of the legislation in family matters, for example, the Divorce Act, (1869), the Special Marriage Acts (1872 and 1954), the Succession Act (1925), and even the Hindu Widows Remarriage Act (1865), which remains obstinately unused by the majority of those for whom it was designed, and the Hindu Wills Act (1870).

One could argue that the following statutes are hostile to Indian tradition, and not merely irrelevant to it: the Bombay Homeopathic and Biochemic Practitioners Act (1959), the Maharashtra Medical

Practitioners Act (1961), the Dentists Act (1948), and the Pharmacy Act (1948). In the catch-as-catch-can life of India in which every charlatan has his day, it seems cruel to thieves and cheats that their activities should be limited in any manner by legislation. It would be nearer the truth, perhaps, to see these statutes as attempts to create a situation unknown to tradition, without any real hope of interfering with tradition. The same could be said with justice of the interesting Suppression of Immoral Traffic in Women and Girls Act (1956). This statute attempts to prevent the exploitation of women for prostitution and makes the keeping of a brothel and the living upon immoral earnings criminal offences: it also empowers magistrates to move prostitutes from one area to another and even out of town. One would have thought that this interference with the oldest profession was tampering with tradition in a big way. One would also be tempted to say that the "high moral tone" which prevails in many quarters (the Victorianism of the 20th century Indian) has had its way for the while, and that one tradition is getting across another. The truth may be, rather, that window-dressing accounts for a good deal of legislation, and that this Act is a specimen. It has no great impact on prostitution, though it may beneficially affect the incomes of the police. The prevalent Hindu sympathy with all sorts and conditions of people would never permit the oppressive removal of prostitutes from Indian life: their function is a marginal one, having sharply decreased during the British period, and this statute is likewise marginal to Indian tradition.

The unhappy legislation tending to enforce prohibition of consumption of alcohol has had its effects on state revenues and the incomes of the police: it could be argued that it is hostile to tradition in that it oppressively affects the livelihoods of toddy-tappers and others. There is some truth in this, and indeed prohibition is not near the hearts of any except bigots, and those few in a position to see positive benefits (e.g. fall in the murder rate in some areas). It is, as a phenomenon, not so much a specimen of "high moral tone" as an example of missionary endeavour. The Hindu attitude towards missionary activity has always been ambivalent, but more permissive than sceptical. Tradition did not forbid alcohol to any but Brahmins, and yet many proponents of prohibition are non-Brahmins. It could be that this belated faith in Brahmin ethics has a social and even a political validity of which I am unaware. Anyhow prohibition is something which lies upon theborders of irrelevance to tradition and hostility to tradition. The Child Marriage Restraint Acts would seem to be in exactly the same ambiguous position.

9. Elements Hostile to Tradition

Accounts of how the British abolished, or encouraged Indians to abolish, customs of which they disapproved are in everyone's hands, and there is no need to dilate on the abolition of *sati*, *dhārnā*, the sacrificing of children and so forth. Only slightly less well known are the abolitions of disqualification arising from change of religion or loss of caste, the abolition of the disqualifications from inheriting or adopting in Hindu law, the dramatic changes in the property rights of women. The Dowry Prohibition Act (1961) is a recent attempt to abolish an institution deeply rooted in many castes (it does not apply to Muslims and perhaps not to Christians). The public are paying little attention to it, though attempts to get rid of the institution have gone on through the ages. The statute is traditional in that it is a repetition of age-old attempts, and traditional in its lack of success. But overtly it constitutes a blow to traditional practices. The Untouchability (Offences) Act is certainly a direct affront to tradition (though the institution was gradually becoming abhorrent to the public and so ripe for abolition even from the *Dharmaśāstra* point of view), so too the prevention of dedication of *devadāsīs*. The Madras, Andhra, and now Kerala statutes prohibiting sacrifices of animals or birds in or near temples are also opposed to tradition. The state's dissociating itself, long ago, from responsibility for temples, etc., was a breach with tradition: yet, curiously, the court can determine many matters of interest to temples, for example, what ceremonies may or may not be used therein (the *Tirupati case* is the best example), and the state's superintendance of the expenditure of temple properties has come back again by the back door in the Public Trusts Acts of the various states. The law's indifference to ceremonies (with the possible exception of the marriage ceremony)[8] is very interesting, and is a breach with tradition. Custom has throughout been treated in a very cavalier manner. Where customs can be proved strictly they are allowed, but many Indian customs of notoriety and antiquity have been held invalid for want of reasonable-

[8]Indian law (subject to a Madras statute of 1967) continues to insist that no new marriage ceremonies may ever be invented, except by statute.

ness. The courts feel themselves to be vastly superior to all actual practices as such. This goes well beyond the king's traditional right to ignore or deprecate anomalous or abhorrent customs under the indigenous jurisprudence.

The Bombay Hindu Ceremonial Emoluments Act (1926) did away with the ancient right of a *purohit* to fees from his "client" whether or not the traditional ceremonies were performed by him or by another. The exclusive right to perform religious ceremonies, and any custom that religious ceremonies shall be performed exclusively by particular persons, is liable to be struck down as violating the fundamental rights of freedom to practise religion (Article 25) and freedom to practise one's profession (Article 19 (1) (g)), guaranteed by the constitution.[9]

Land reforms, the abolition of zamindaris and impartible estates, the enforcement of "ceilings," and semi-enforced cooperative farming: all are prominently and unquestionably hostile to Indian tradition. No resort to pre-British history can justify these covert attempts at expropriation, which, characteristically, the Supreme Court has attempted to restrain by strict literal interpretation of the constitution, but which parliament has again and again supported by constitutional amendment.[10]

All the movements to abolish caste and its manifestations, and the abolition of the right of superiors to the labour of their inferiors (Article 23) are opposed to tradition, hastening the movement from status to contract which, while under way, was not yet fully advanced. The concept of adult franchise, and the provisions of the Representation of the People Act (1951) are totally foreign to Indian tradition. It is not surprising that this innovation has led to widespread despondency. It is difficult, however, to envisage an alternative.

Another element foreign to tradition, and unquestionably hostile to it, is the vast interference of government by way of management and finally ownership in the public sector of the economy and the mixed sector: the right to take over or virtually to take over concerns which are wholly privately owned is something new to India. That government should tax, and should have its own monopolies would not have been new: but that government should compete with private enterprise or absorb it was something untried and repugnant.

[9]And see the case referred to at p 42, n 3, above.

[10]See the works of S.P. Sathe and H.M. Jain reviewed by the present author at (1969) 18 Int. Comp. L.Q., pp. 511-512; also works of Rajeev Dhavan.

The traditional concept of government is that it shall hold the balance between competing forces, not that it should enter the arena itself. The concept of the following statutes is therefore alien: Air Corporations (1953), Industrial Finance Corporation (1948), Road Transport Corporation (1950), Industries (Development and Regulation) (1951), Banking Companies (1949), Rice Milling Industry (Regulation) (1958) and Banking Laws (Misc. Prov.) (1963).

We may end with a doubtful case. It could be argued of the Prevention of Food Adulteration Act (1954), that it was like the statutes regulating medical and dental practice and pharmacy—that it was in no way different from other laws attempting to protect the public from its own ignorance or negligence, that it was a piece of "welfare," and that welfare has been, after all, the duty of the state from pre-British times. However, it is as a fact traditional in India that rogues and cheats should have as much freedom as honest people, and the milkman may be said to have an ancient and inalienable right to water the milk. Interference with this, even in the interests of the general public, is as bold an attack upon tradition as any. It may be argued, indeed, that ancient Hindu texts prescribe in detail how artisans and craftsmen and tradesmen are to go about their work, and authorize the ruler to penalize those that cheat the public. The *Dharmaśāstra* and the *Arthaśāstra* fulminate against fraud and untruth, and authorize the ruler to set aside contracts vitiated by these factors. But the India we know, the Old India, is tolerant of deception of all kinds, given that the deceived, if he wakes up soon enough, can have his remedy if he can muster enough power to enforce it. India loves the honest man no better than the cheat[11]—and to suggest that the detailed provisions of the Penal Code, or any other law, to punish or inhibit cheating have started a new tradition favourable to honesty is to indulge in humbug.

Conclusion

I have already intimated that to summarize Indian law would be like summarizing the contents of a dustbin. Indian law, as printed on paper, gives a very one-sided impression of India's nature or her

[11]It is one of the features of the *Dharmaśāstra* that it regulates partnerships between thieves, and enjoins the king to recognize and enforce by-laws passed by thieving fraternities or covens.

life—still more inadequately does it represent her tradition. Traditional elements are found side by side with novel elements, and elements which can be read in different ways. There would be no point in trying to assess the presence of tradition in Indian law were it not for a presupposition which I fully accept for the purposes of this endeavour, namely that elements in Indian law which are traditional have in a sense stood the test of time and are likely to work, either as they were intended to do, or in some other more or less predictable way. Elements which are not traditional will either be distorted to perform functions for which they were not intended, or will be failures.

The very basis of law is open to discussion on this footing. The idea of a promise or a contract, and the idea of subordination to an overall scheme; also the notion of the personality, and the place of the individual and the question why, and to what extent, an individual, as an individual, should be subject to law at all—these have to be investigated.[12] I feel that Indian family life, the sub-caste, as the unit which contributes most to the individual's security and to which he is therefore willing to give most, and above this the competing factions and units, village, district, linguistic area, state, and so on, are the real basis of the individual's notion of *obligation*, and his psychology is framed within those concentric horizons. Indians brought up in East Africa, Fiji, Guyana, or Britain would soon show us the difference. Indians by race who are thorough citizens of Camden will soon be on our own doorsteps as students. Their idea of their place in society is bound to be very different from that of their cousins in India brought up under the scorching sun, victims of family, caste, village, district, party, and other pressures.

Competition is the key to it all, and in competition the stock factors are (1) favour, (2) promise of adherence (irrespective of merit), (3) distribution of rewards, (4) attempted monopoly of resources, and (5) the constantly presupposed arbiter, who will balance all demands and relate all claims within an ideal harmony. Thus obedience without reciprocal support from the leader is unthinkable; adjudication on mere merits useless; honesty is meaningful only in so far as it ensures favour; and the person is meaningless except in so far as he belongs to a mutual-support agglomeration or agglome-

[12]Cf. the unequivocal answer relative to Japan by T.B. Stephens, "Japanese traditional attitudes to law," *World Review* (St. Lucia, Queensland) 16/1 (1977), pp. 27-36.

rations, interlocking and sometimes incompatible. The child's stereotyped behaviour towards numerous mutually incompatible relations is the foundation of his attitude to life, and conditions his whole attitude to authority and to law. Courts are a means of obtaining an advantage over an opponent, not a fountain of "justice": indeed "justice" as known in the West is meaningless in India except in the form of "social justice," that is, the dispensations of the central and ultimate authority, the ruler. Catch-as-catch-can is the rule of Indian life, and its only mitigation is religion. Since it presses so hard on the individual it is not surprising that religion has developed more richly in India than anywhere else. Religion is not the opiate of the masses in India, but the counterpart and necessary concomitant of family and public life.[13]

It may be argued in reply that India is passing from her traditional ways as urban society becomes more individualistic. Individualism is pressing hard upon the personal law, the most traditional and conservative portion of the Indian law. This is unquestionably true, especially of mobile earners. This would have developed even if all foreign influence had been external, and had there been no element of colonialism in India's development. It may be argued that as the family becomes smaller, the pressures upon youth are less. One can indeed detect in the only child of the nuclear family and in the children of cross-caste unions a tone more akin to ours: the statement that India is a country of actual or potential rascals does not so much amuse (as it would amuse most Indians) as surprise them. But I am not prepared to abdicate my approach merely because of this development. I contend that the ills of Indian society, especially at their most deplorable, derive from the fact that the spirit and tradition of caste competition has continued in the ambitions of smaller units, and that the pervasive presuppositions of Indian life affect now different elements, differently constituted, while the morals remain the same. Thus the wholesale reform of Hindu law was really intended to produce a super-caste, caste not in name but in potential, in mutual-support capacity.[14] The instinct

[13]"Divorced and separated wives in the lower elite classes take to religion," Rama Mehta, *Divorced Hindu Woman* (New Delhi, 1975).

[14]The question has been asked (Marc Galanter, *Asian Review*, 2 (1969), p. 337) whether a high rate of intercaste marriage exists amongst the "haves." No surveys have been made, but the novels of Delhi-dwelling Mrs Jhabvala and my noting of "special marriages" that have broken down support my analysis *prima facie*. C.G. Deshpande, *On Intercaste Marriage*, Poona, 1972.

is to achieve the old end. Caste never was a supine, restful, Utopian satisfaction with life as it was: it was always a thrusting, selfish, undisciplined competition for scarce resources, and it presupposed a king who could hold down the stopper. Now that the king is a mobile collection of manipulators and fixers tradition has not ceased to look to them for that function—with the results we see.

I shall end with an example which should be vivid for all of us. Indian universities contain the best educated, deepest thinking, most highly developed and altruistic individuals that can be found anywhere in the country. Yet almost every university is governed, if not by a charter, then by a special act of parliament or of the state legislature. These statutes are continually being amended and modified. The vice-chancellors are continually in litigation with members of the university, from students to professors. Litigation on every topic, especially examinations and posts, goes on continually and bitterly. Universities are hampered by intrigue which centres upon appointments. How is this curious phenomenon to be explained? Most of the litigation, as indeed a vast and disgusting proportion of Indian litigation,[15] is over trifles of procedure and technicalities. The universities are not entirely non-traditional institutions. Their methods may be distinctly non-traditional, but their aims are not inherently foreign to education as known in India in her prime. Many men can be found in them whose intellectual and spiritual objects would conform to the best traditions of the days when teachers were supported by endowments and taught their students for nothing—and were proud to do so. How do we explain the phenomena of university intrigues and litigation?

First, the university is a source of prestige, and a source of a settled income not dependent in itself upon continuing favour—hence doubly prestige-worthy. Authority in a university confers power over students (therefore over many families of many castes) and the conferment of a qualification confers a favour which is worth money. Irrespective of a man's personal achievement and merit, his position in the university enables him to manipulate people, and he is a channel through which prestige flows to people and through which they obtain the two things needful for their families' happiness, namely prestige and wealth. If particular castes can obtain an ascendancy in any department it follows automatically that other

[15] For a recent expression of disgust see the Supreme Courts' restrained observations in *Amritsagar* v. *Sudesh* (1969) 1 S.C.W.R. p. 776.

castes (irrespective of their individuals' merits) will be at a disadvantage (or will be thought to be), and therefore care has to be exercised at the top to see that a balance of castes is maintained irrespective of the merits of appointees. The jostling for power in and across departments can be aided by infusions of prestige from outside. That is where you and I come in. And in a competition between equally "qualified" foreign-trained candidates another "independent" source may keep the balance, namely the courts! Hence litigation is not a luxury but a necessity. This is the background, *mutatis mutandis,* to all Indian litigation. No wonder it is popular.

4 Power and Authority in Indian Tradition

J.C. HEESTERMAN

The first and the last hurdle we encounter in dealing with the theme of power and authority is the obstinate problem of tradition. For tradition regulates the exercise of both power and authority even when it seems breached beyond repair. It is therefore appropriate to consider the nature of tradition at the outset.

The battle royal between tradition and modernity seems to have reached an uneasy armistice. Notwithstanding modernity's success in securing world-wide acceptance as an ideology, tradition appears to live on no less comfortably. Scrutiny of traditional institutions such as caste, world renunciation and Brahminical law has revealed their adaptive and indeed innovative potentialities.[1] Students of society and politics have been compelled to concede "the modernity of tradition."

It is obvious that anything can be modern only once, and that thereafter it becomes tradition, at best a "tradition of modernity." But this proposition is not altogether satisfactory, for it is based on a narrowly and exclusively diachronic view. We may equally well look at tradition and modernity as ideal types. This is useful in analyzing actual institutions and situations in the after all not so modern West or the perhaps not so traditional East (or South, as the case may be), but it has the disadvantage of abstracting the terms from the particular contexts that they describe.

Modernity, once it is dissociated from the realities of the "modern West," can with relative ease be defined as a Weberian ideal type, for instance as rationality. But we cannot safely disconnect tradition from its context. Or, if we do, this will not help us in understanding the incoherent mass of actual traditions, whether "traditions of modernity" or otherwise. In other words, whereas modernity, if it is not to be confused with the tradition-bound rea-

[1] Cf. L.I. and S.H. Rudolph, *The Modernity of Tradition*, Chicago, 1967.

lities of the "modern West," can only hold its own as a fiction, the field of reality is left to tradition in its manifold manifestations.[2]

Limiting ourselves to Indian tradition—but the same would seem to be true of other civilizations as well—the first thing that strikes us is the fluidity of tradition, defying definition and even compilation. Though irritating, this is not a surprising circumstance. It is not India's undoubted vastness and long history that account for variation and fluidity. Even within the local community—and especially there—tradition is seen to be manifold and fluid. In Professor Derrett's lucid formula: "tradition represents (and re-presents) the past";[3] it is not so much the unchangeable past that counts, but the present, the local situation, that models and remodels the view of the past. Tradition is part and parcel of the present with its continually shifting relationships and points of view. It cannot be immutable and uniform.

This can clearly be seen in customary law, which is notoriously refractory to codification. In fact the worst thing that can happen to it is codification, which deprives custom of its precious capacity to keep track of the ever-changing present. In the matter of religious tradition we may find greatly differing explanations given by participants in the same festival.[4] Or, to take another example: the vexed question of the size of the *bīghā,* which may vary even within the same village. This is not a matter of simple confusion but, as Neale argues, depends on the status of the tenure holder: "A *bīghā* was. . . a piece of land which satisfied the requirement that the tenure holder be able to farm some piece of land whose productivity accorded with his status rights."[5] I would add that here status is not to be taken in an absolute sense, but as dependent on the network of relationships of the participants and therefore as equally open to shifts and realignments.

If we view tradition as situational, as bound up with and expres-

[2]This does not mean that the tradition-modernity debate is meaningless. In fact it is reopened by S.H. Eisenstadt, who attempts "a redefinition of the nature of the distinction between traditional and modern socio-political and cultural orders", "Reflections on a Theory of Modernization," in A. Rivkin, (ed.), *Nations by Design*, New York. 1968.

[3]See above, p. 32.

[4]Cf. M. Marriott, "Little Communities in an Indigenous Civilization," in M. Marriott, *Village India*, Chicago, 1955, p. 194.

[5]Cf. W.C. Neale, in R. Frykenberg, (ed.), *Land Control and Social Structure in Indian History*, Madison-Milwaukee, 1969. p. 5.

sive of shifting relationships, its fluidity and flexibility do not cause surprise. The resultant vagueness may be its greatest strength. But this comes dangerously near to viewing tradition as a free-for-all, all-season fishing pond, abounding in red herrings that eagerly offer themselves for scholarly taxidermy. Still, tradition, for all its flexibility and inconsistency, is not irrelevant. It has a definite function to fulfill. It is there not only to provide an idiom for expressing and making understandable actual relationships and conduct in the present; the main point is that it provides legitimation. It fulfills its legitimizing function by referring to the past, which is by definition final and immutable, and therefore seems to offer a fixed yardstick to the shifting present. However, as implied in Professor Derrett's definition, while the past itself may be unchangeable, its representation in the present will greatly vary with the circumstances. Here we have a vicious circle.

II

The central problem of tradition is that in order to fufill its legitimizing function it should reconcile the irreconcilable. On the one hand it is bound up with the present, on the other hand it should stand above and be unimpaired by the present, so as to provide an immutable standard. It should be immanent and transcendent at the same time.

I think this is clearly demonstrated by the concept of *dharma*. *Dharma* has a transcendent authority that is not man-made. For it is based on supra-human revelation, on the Veda, the *śruti*. The transcendence of the Veda is guaranteed by putting it rigorously apart from society, out of reach of common man, who is not even supposed to know it. And if he knew it, his knowledge would not help him since the contents of the Veda provide very few, if any, rules for actual conduct. It is safely insulated from the relativizing impact of social practice. In fact there is no direct link between the contents of *śruti* and *dharma*, and the supposition that the whole of *dharma* derives from transcendent *śruti* can only be a fictitious, though necessary, construction. On the other hand *dharma* must legitimize and lend its transcendent authority to diverging actual custom. The tenuous linkage has to be provided by the exemplary conduct of the well-instructed, the *śiṣṭa,* who know the Veda and therefore can not go wrong, although they will hardly obtain any guidance from it.

Here, I think, we may find the key to the fundamental inconsistency of tradition. It is caught between the devil of everyday life and the deep blue sea of transcendence. At least this seems to be the lesson of India, where the problem is presented in particularly sharp contours.

One might be tempted to formulate the two aspects of tradition—transcendent and immanent—simply as textual fixity as against popular fluidity. But this would miss the point. For the fundamental inconsistency is carried over into the texts. For instance, Manu brands the eater of meat as the worst of sinners but at the same time he has to concede that after all there is nothing wrong with eating meat, because it is the natural way of acting (*pravritti*).[6] That is to say, for all his marked preference for vegetarianism, Manu still has to acknowledge the claims of normal life. The clue to understanding the dichotomy is revealed by Manu when he states, after conceding the naturalness of eating meat:"but abstention brings great reward," even more than the greatest of animal sacrifices. Abstention overcomes the natural way of acting; it is a transcendent value.

The example of vegetarianism can perhaps teach us still more about the uneasy relationship between the "normal" and the transcendent aspects of tradition. Normal social life is not simply characterized by licence for those who must have their meat. Though somewhat blurred by the overriding concern for the transcendent value of abstention, the rules about the use of meat seem to derive from a basic pattern of interdependence and interaction: briefly, the interdependence of two parties, of host and guest. The guest has to give the order for killing the animal and for preparing the meat, thus taking upon himself the onus of death. The host abstains till the guest has eaten and thereby made the food safe for his host. The same situation can be observed in the sacrifice, where the sacrificer has to abstain from the meat till the priest, whom Manu threatens with dire consequences in case his vegetarian punctilio would cause him to refuse, has eaten. Equally the mourner has to abstain, but must also offer a rich meal of meat to his guests at the funeral feast.

These rules, it would seem, exemplify the necessary interdepen-

[6]Cf. L. Alsdorf, *Beiträge...Vegetarismus and Rinderverehrung*, Wiesbaden, 1961, pp. 17-21 (on Manu): Review in *Indo-Ir. Journ.*, 9, (1966), pp. 147-149.

dence and interaction on which social life must be based. They may also go a long way to explain the well known coexistence of vegetarian and non-vegetarian cults, which so often bewilders the observer, not as the fortuitous result of a long and garbled history but as a structural feature.[7] It is this interdependence and interaction which continually threaten to overthrow fixed positions and to reverse relationships—as between host and guest—that transcendence has to overcome. Instead of the interdependence of high and low, pure and impure, life and death, it exclusively emphasizes purity and life. Though incapable of full realization, it is acknowledged as the superior norm, the magnetic north that rules the course in the troubled waters of interdependence. This is the background to what Professor Srinivas has called "sanskritization." Sanskritization then is not to be understood primarily as a historical process of change by which one culture is superseded by a different, sanskritic one—its utter slowness over 2,000 years or more already warns against this notion—but as a structural necessity; that is, the necessity somehow to approach the transcendent norm.

At the same time we may notice here an important formal difference between the two aspects of tradition. The fullness of tradition can only be seen on the "popular" level,that is, in the interaction and relativity of social life. The transcendent aspect ignores interaction, breaks down complementarity and absolutizes the single poles of purity, of the good and the high, of life (as against impurity, evil and death). By itself it can therefore be only partial, incomplete and indifferent, if not inimical, to social reality. Or in other words: whereas the "little tradition" is lived by the community the "great tradition" is fundamentally different in that it does not answer to any particular community. It is incomplete and can be only partially realized as an ill-fitting part of the little tradition, unsettling the delicate interactional balance.

This lengthy disquisition on tradition has not brought a practical definition any nearer. But perhaps the attempted analysis of its function may have laid bare something of its structure. The crux then is the conflict between the community-based tradition of complementarity and interaction on the one hand, and the search for transcendence and ultimate legitimation on the other.

[7]On the interdependence of vegetarian and meat-eating gods, see L. Dumont, "A structural definition of a Folk Deity of Tamilnad," *Contrib. Ind. Soc.*, III, (1959), pp. 75-87, esp 82 ff.

Here, I feel, we have come to the point where the field has been sufficiently cleared and the terms set for our treatment of power and authority in Indian tradition. Perhaps not surprisingly we shall find that the complex relationship between power and authority shows the same structure as tradition. At least that is what I shall try to argue.

III

At the start of our investigation of power and authority we should recall the terms in which Indian tradition formulates the problem: namely the relationship between *Kṣatra* and *Brahman*, or their representatives, king and Brahmin—a relationship that is well known but perhaps not so well understood. Here I should at once mention the important work of Louis Dumont, to which this relationship is of pivotal concern.[8] Dumont proposes to look at the hierarchical preeminence of the Brahmin over the king "not as a contingent trait for which a conjectural historical struggle might account, but as a necessary institution....In approximate, western, terms, the situation results from the distinction between the spiritual and the temporal being carried out in an absolute fashion." The Brahmin's pre-eminence is located on a different plane. Much as Dumont has done to place this and related problems in proper perspective, and much as I feel indebted to his views, I must differ with respect to their further elaboration. My point is that the absolute distinction between power and authority or between their representatives, king and Brahmin, involves a fundamental contradiction, which should not be explained away but made central to the argument. The well known tales of the struggle between king and Brahmin indeed do not relate historical events; they give expression to the contradictory relationship, as when the earth has to be returned to the care of the *Kṣatriyas* after they have been completely exterminated by that curious Brahmin, Paraśurāma. It is on this contradiction that I want to focus the discussion of power and authority.[9]

The ambiguity of the king-Brahmin relationship is felicitously

[8] I refer specifically to "Kingship in Ancient India," *Contrib. to Indian Socc.*, VI, (1962), pp. 48-77; French version in *Homo Hierarchicus*, Paris, 1966, App. C.

[9] *Op. cit.*, pp. 52, 54.

expressed in the words of the *Bṛhad Ār. Up.* 1.4.11., where the *Kṣatra* is said to have emanated from the Brahman as its foremost form: "therefore nothing transcends the *Kṣatra*; therefore the Brahmin sits below the *Kṣatriya* at the *rājasūya*; he bestows this homage only on the *Kṣatra*. But the Brahman is the womb of the *Kṣatra*; therefore, though he attains the highest status, he finally rests on the Brahman, his own womb; if he (the *Kṣatriya*) hurts him (the Brahmin,) he hurts his origin; in the same way as when attacking a superior, he is worsted." I think this contradictory statement, which makes the king supreme only to deprive him again of his supremacy, sums up the problem of the Indian concept of the state.

IV

Let us look more closely at the ancient Indian state. I think we should dismiss the deceptive appearances of a centralized unit held together by a bureaucracy reaching down from the king to the people at large. This certainly seems to be the ideal presented by the *Arthaśāstra,* but its reticence on chains of command and reporting would suggest otherwise. Instead we find an almost pathetic stress on the necessity of the officials' trustworthiness and a concomitant all-pervading spy system, which can only block administrative action and in the end reduce it to chaos. Moreover it is clear that the realization of a centralized bureaucratic set-up would require objective conditions, such as a high degree of monetarization, which would make it possible to separate the functions of government from rights in the soil. As it was, the ruler was mostly forced, like his feudal Western counterpart, to parcel out clusters of his own superior rights. Thus, for instance, Gupta inscriptions seem to suggest that many nominal officials were rather like feudal lords, whose official charges depended less on the ruler's orders than on their own landed power. After all, even France's absolutist *ancien régime* was hardly capable of the centralized bureaucratic control it attempted to achieve.

Nor should we think of a clearly defined territorial state, internally coherent and closed towards the outside. Already the fact that the well known seven elements include the ally indicates the openendedness of the state. It is equally signficant that territory, as a separate item, is not included. The term *janapada* (or, in some texts, *rashtra*) means the undifferentiated whole of people-cum-territory, in the same way as the French "pays" or the German "Land."[10]

I think we should interpret the situation as one where membership of the polity, in a greater or lesser degree, is not primarily defined by residence in a specific well-defined territory, but rather the reverse: certain differential rights in a territory arise from personal ties of kinship and dependency. Outsiders may be admitted, even welcomed—we noted already the characteristic open-endedness as expressed in the inclusion of the ally in the seven elements of the state—but their admittance has to be legitimized in terms of personalities or even kinship.[11] The state then is based on a network of personal relations in which rights in the soil are subsumed. This means that power and authority are situated at the crossroads, so to say, of the personal relations which make up the polity. Power and authority are dispersed. If there is a king he can only be the living expression of the balance of these relationships and their opposing pulls and pushes, which tie him down and prevent his acting on his own. He does not transcend the community by divine right or otherwise; at best he is a *primus inter pares*.[12]

[10]Cf. D.R. Bhandarkar, *Some Aspects of Ancient Hindu Polity*, Benares, 1929, 68f; recently H. Scharfe, *Untersuchungen zur Staatsrechtslehre des Kautalya*, Wiesbaden, 1968, 138ff. On the significance of the undifferentiated people-cum-territory as against the modern differentiation between nation and national territory, see L. Dumont, *Contrib. to Ind. Soc.*, VII, 1964, pp. 66-70. For the rise of the clearly defined and compact territory as the basis of national unity, the "*République une et indivisible*," see J.R. Talmon, *The Origins of Totalitarian Democracy*, reprint London 1966, 109f.

[11]One may compare E.R. Leach's observations on the use of the jural idiom of local group endogamy for legitimizing membership: "Anyone who was acceptable as a Pul Eliya landowner and was also acceptable in the capacity of brother-in-law to an existent Pul Eliya landowner would, in practice, be treated as "of our variga" (*Pul Eliya*, Cambridge, 1961, p. 303). Cf. also the *mutha*, or "clan" territory, as described by F.G. Bailey (*Tribe, Caste and Nation*, Manchester, 1960), actually a group of lineages living in the same territory and expressing this fact as conventional agnation (Cf. L. Dumont's remarks, *Contrib. to Ind. Soc.*, VII, 1964, p. 72).

[12]Compare, for instance, the remonstrances against the rulers (possibly strengthened by their alliance with the British) by their clan-brethren, to whom the ruler is only a *primus inter pares* in J. Todd, *Annals and Antiquities of Rajasthan*, 1829-32, (Appendix to Book. III).

V

Let me try to illustrate this point by a consideration of the *ratnins,* the "jewel holders," "the givers and takers of kingship," in the royal consecration ritual.[13] They have been taken to constitute a sort of bureaucracy, and the ceremony connected with them, the *ratnin* offerings, to indicate a significant advance in administrative organization.[14] However, as far as I can see, the texts do not indicate anything of the kind. At best the *ratnins* may be considered as household officials, who, of course, according to the needs of the moment, may be entrusted with all sorts of charges not covered by their designations. In fact, the commentator's inventiveness is hard put to explain these designations in terms of specific charges. More significantly, the underlying pattern seems to be connected not with a rationalized model of the state, but with cognate and affinal kinship.

The eleven or twelve *ratnins* take up residences arranged in a half-circle around the place of sacrifice. The king, taking his sacrificial fire with him, visits each *ratnin* in his residence,where a sacrifice is performed with materials provided by the *ratnin.* At the end of the whole series of visits (or alternatively after each visit) the king performs a sacrifice at the central place of sacrifice.[15] This reciprocal pattern of prestation and counterprestation—we should recall that the underlying model of the sacrifice in general is that of the generous reception offered to the guest—is indicative of the reciprocal ties binding king and *ratnins.* The sacrificial idiom of the *ratnin* offerings clearly covers the mutual acts of allegiance between each *ratnin* and the king, who by his return sacrifice makes himself the nodal point of all relationships.

If we now look at the mixed group of *ratnins,* the kinship character can be discerned. First there are the two or three consorts of the king, who represent in a direct way his affinal links with the people, whose "husband" he is elsewhere said to be. A similar relationship obtains in the case of Brahmin (or *purohit*) and king, the Brahman being generally considered as the womb of kingship, while the rela-

[13]Cf. My *The Ancient Indian Royal Consecration*, The Hague, 1957, Ch. VI.

[14]Thus R.S. Sharma, *Aspects of Political Ideas and Institutions*, Delhi, 1968, p. 145.

[15]The procedure can be compared with the yearly ceremonies described by A. Béteille (*History of Religions*, 5, 1965, p. 85), where the central temple is visited by parties carrying the *mūrtis* of the outlying temples and the *mūrti* of the central temple is carried to the associated temples.

tion between king and *purohit* is represented as a marriage-like bond. It may also be recalled that this relationship has its counterpart in the king's acting as bride giver to the officiating Brahmins at the *aśvamedha*—this being, in my opinion, the original meaning of the prescript that the king should give his wives to the chief officiants. More generally, the Soma sacrificer can by way of *dakṣiṇā* give his daughter in marriage to one of the officiants. The *senānī*, on the other hand, seems to represent the cognate kin, to wit the king's brother.[16] Possibly also the *rājanya* or *rājan* is a cognate,[17] he seems to correspond to the *bhrātṛvya* who, at first sight somewhat surprisingly, is one of the four anointers—a point to which we shall have to return.

The Brahmin, *senānī*, *rājan* (or *rājanya*) and the consorts form the first group in this and similar lists.[18] The distinct feature of the second group is that they form pairs: *sūta-grāmaṇī, kṣattṛ-saṃgrahītṛ, akṣavāpa-govikarta,* and (with the Maitrāyaṇīyas) the *takṣa-rathakāra* pair.[19] As the ritual texts never tire to explain, pairs mean pairing. That this is here equally the case appears also from the twelve "kingdom-bearing" (*rāṣṭrabhṛt*) oblations on the completed fire altar. These twelve oblations are offered in six rounds of two each,

[16] Cf. W. Rau, *Staat und Gesellschaft im alten Indien*, Wiesbaden, 1957, p. 107; also H. Scharfe, *op. cit.*, 158f.

[17] Or he is the king himself. This at least is the opinion of the *Satapatha Br.*, which has in the place of the *rājanya* or *rājan* the sacrificer. On the other hand, *Maitr. S.* 4.3.8 distinguishes the *rājan* from the sacrificer.

[18] Cf. especially the eight *vīras* who sustain kingship, *Pancaviṃśa Br.* 19.1.4., where we find king's brother, king's son, *purohit* and first consort, followed by *sūta*, *grāmaṇī*, *kṣattṛ* and *saṃgrahitṛ*.

[19] I refrain from translating these terms, since their actual content remains vague. So much is clear, however, that the names do not indicate specific administrative functions, but ritual rôles in agonistic potlatch-like festivals. Thus *sūta*, *grāmaṇī*, *saṃgrahītṛ*, *rathakāra* are clearly connected with chariot racing and chariot fighting. Perhaps also the *kṣattṛ* and the *takṣa* can be counted among the persons connected with the chariot (one commentary explains *kṣattṛ* as charioteer); but they rather seem to be connected, together with the *akṣavāpa-govikarta*, with dicing and the slaughter and cooking of the cow associated with it (or with the *odana* replacing the cow); for the *kṣattṛ*, Cf. *Royal Consecraton*, p. 145; Vādhūla fr. 70, W. Caland, A.O. IV, p. 176; for the *takṣan* as cutting off and receiving the head of an immolated animal—a custom eliminated in the classical *śrauta* ritual—Cf. *Maitr. Samh.* 2.4.1. Only the *bhāgadugha* and the *pālāgala* (the latter only in the *Śatapatha* and related texts) occur singly. The *pālāgala* seems to be connected with the fourth consort in the *aśvamedha*, the *pālāgalī*, and as such a (potential) affine; possibly the same holds for the *bhāga-dugha*, explained by *Baudh. Ś.S.* as *mahānasika*, to be compared with the *māhānasī dāsī*, the fourth consort in Baudh. 's *aśvamedha* description.

one to a male, the other to a female deity. The series is rounded off by a thirteenth oblation on a chariot, whereby the sacrificer is made to encompass the six couples.[20] The parallelism with the *ratnins* as regards name, numerical arrangement and intention is obvious. Moreover, the *rāṣṭrabhṛt* oblations are equally associated with an unction. I think we shall not be far amiss when we interpret the *ratnin* and *raṣṭrabhṛt* pairs as a representation of two moieties connected by the king who, as the third, is "born" from and dependent on their connubium.

This two-three scheme may also be at the root of the first group, but here another, related, numerical principle seems to have disturbed the arrangement, to wit the four-five scheme, used in the horse-sacrifice to organize the same personages. There we find four groups of guardians designated as *ratnins*,[21] round the royal horse which represents the king, to wit *rājaputras, ugras* (or *rājanyas*), *sūta-grāmaṇīs* and *kṣattṛ-saṃgrahītṛs*. Furthermore four royal consorts prepare the horse for immolation. Each of them is accompanied by a group of attendants, who are the female counterparts of the horse's guardians. These female attendants act again as partners of the four Brahmin officiants in the exchange of obscenities which should help the sham copulation of the chief consort and the immolated horse.[22] This numerical arrangement is also clearly expressed in the unction ceremony of the *rājasūya*. The king, in the centre, is anointed by four officiants standing round him to the four quarters; these anointers interestingly are an affine (*janya-mitra*) in the east, the Brahman priest in the south, a Vaiśya in the west and a cousin (*bhrātṛvya*) in the north.[23] Here again we find kinship as a basic principle.

[20] *Śatap. Br.* 9.4.1.

[21] *Āpastama S.S.* 20.5.9.

[22] *Śatap. Br.* 13.5.2.

[23] Cf. *Royal Consecration*, Ch. XIV. The list is the one of the Maitrāyanīyas. The other schools substantially agree. The four-five scheme, as an image of socio-political organization, seems to be fairly current in India. The epic relates that Yuddhiṣṭhira asked, by way of compromise, for a kingdom of only five villages, one for each of his four brothers, and one, presumably the central one, for himself. An example from reality is offered by S. Sinha's study of the principality Barabhum consisting of a central tract or *taraf* and four outlying *tarafs;* the *tarafs* are interpreted, following Risley, as original clan territories (*Man in India*, 42, 1962, p. 45). The four-five scheme offers a striking parallel with the Javanese *mantjapat* (Cf. F. van Ossenbruggen, *VMKAWL*, 1917). On the two-three and four-five schemes and their conjunction, see also P.E. de Josselin de Jong. *Minangkabau and Negri Sembilan*, Leiden, 1951, p. 106.

It is interesting that the four *varṇas*, though at first sight an obvious principle of classification, do not enter the picture of the *ratnins*. Only the *Śatapatha* half-heartedly tries to introduce the four *varṇa* scheme. Nor does it play a significant role elsewhere in the *rājasūya*, except in the dicing ceremony, where according to some texts the four players represent the four *varṇas;* but other texts mention, instead of them, kinsmen or *sūta-grāmaṇī* and *kṣattṛ-saṃgrahītṛ* as participants in the game.[24] The fourfold scheme here would seem to be a different, earlier conception of the classical four *varṇas*. The four parties are not *varṇas* in the classical sense of rigidly separated "castes," shunning intermarriage, but on the contrary marriage classes, whose essential unity is expressed by a circulative marriage system. It is interesting that the *sūta*, the *kṣattṛ* and the *ugra* are even in the *dharma* literature considered as the offspring of "mixed" marriages and, as the texts state, after a number of such marriages the fifth generation returns to the original *varṇa*.[25]

In short, the *rājasūya* in general and the *ratnin* ceremony in particular do not present the picture of a "state," but of a clan or segmentary system based on connubium.

VI

The analysis of the *ratnins* shows, if I am right, that kingship is constituted by the network of personal relations; it cannot transcend it, even to the extent that at least one school includes the king himself in the list of his *ratnins*. The basic paradigm of the network seems to be kinship and connubium spanning the whole quadripartite community. The king is only a *primus inter pares* who, even when consecrated, needs the concurrence of the *ratnins* for making a land grant to the Brahman officiant.[26]

This does not entail lack of hierarchy. On the contrary, as is already perfectly clear from the status difference between the consorts and the *ratnin* categories with whom they are associated, we can discern two, three or four hierarchical tiers. The interesting point

[24]Cf. *Royal Consecration*, pp. 143-145.

[25]Cf. G. J. Held, *The Mahabharata*, Leiden, 1936, pp. 89-97, who derives the *varṇa* system from a clan system, or more precisely "a circulative marriage system with a four-clan arrangement" (p. 95).

[26]Cf. *Āpastamba* Ś.S. 18.19, pp. 7 8

is that this hierarchy does not imply the absolute separation of the hierarchical groups, as in the classical *varṇa* theory. The hierarchy finds expression in kinship and marriage, like differences between older and younger, between the offspring of different wives or between bride-givers and bride-takers. But here we come up against a difficulty. Hierarchy based on circulative connubium (or: "generalized exchange") turns on a contradiction. As Lévi-Strauss observed about the Kachin: "*l'échange généralisé suppose l'égalité et il est source d'inégalite.*"[27] This contradictory situation is reflected among the Kachin in two opposed orders: the aristocratic *gumsa* order and the egalitarian *gumlao* order, analyzed by Leach.[28] Though shifts from one order to the other are represented in local history as the result of historical events, it appears from the analysis that the two orders are actually complementary. Each apart is unstable and incomplete, tending to shift into the other. A comparable situation has been analyzed for Minangkabau by de Josselin de Jong. There the aristocratic adat Katumanggungan and the egalitarian adat Parapatih exist side by side, while the followers of both orders can be considered as two opposing "phratries" (resp. Bodi-Tjaniago and Koto-Piliang).[29] Though the two phratries are conventionally associated each with a particular territory, while the third territory, that of the king, holds them symbolically together, the two adats are in fact "fairly evenly scattered over all Minangkabau."[30] It would seem that the complementarity of the two orders equally underlies the opposition of monarchy and "republic" in ancient India.[31] But not only in ancient India, for the same opposition between so-called aristocratic and democratic communities, again usually explained in terms of a historical sequence, seems to have considerably exer-

[27] C. Lévi-Strauss, *Structures Elémentaires de la Parenté*, Paris, 1967, p. 306.

[28] E.R. Leach, *Political Systems of Highland Burma*, London, 1964, esp. Ch. VI.

[29] P.E. de Josselin de Jong, *op. cit.*, 71ff.

[30] *Ibid.*, p. 105.

[31] There is thus, in my opinion, no need for a historical reconstruction of the different phases through which the republic developed out of elected kingship and finally ending up in a monarchical system, as proposed by J.P. Sharma, (*Republics in Ancient India*, Leiden, 1968, 17f). The admittedly hypothetical historical reconstruction can, however, as well be read as an attempt to account in a logical way for the interrelations between the two orders and their variants, instead of as a conjectural sequence of events. Moreover, as Sharma makes clear, the monarchical order existed all the time side by side with the "republican" one.

cised the minds of 19th century administrators and observers of the Indian "village community."[32]

VII

However, although the two orders are also in the classical Indian texts represented as opposed ideal patterns, in actual fact the difference is rather a matter of degree, since each of the two, as we saw, is ambiguous. The egalitarian order must needs lead to differences of rank. The king, on the other hand, cannot be an autocrat; his position remains embedded in the constituent relations of the community, whose unity he should represent. Power and authority are therefore not exclusively the king's; they are diffused throughout the community. Thus Leach observes that the Kachin chief in the aristocratic *gumsa* order has a role to play in judicial, military, economic and religious affairs, but this role is usually a minor one.[33] In this connection it seems significant that, for instance, in the Minangkabau example there is not one king but three *radjo,* each having a third part of the seat of kingship, Pagarrujueng, as his residence. The idea of multiple kingship can perhaps best be interpreted not in terms of differentiation of specific well-defined functions—this would seem to be rather a later and particularly a modern development—but in the sense of a basic diffusion of power and authority.

The idea of multiple kingship can also be noticed in India. Thus the *Taittiriy-Saṃhitā* says that the two kings of the gods, Agni and Soma, are honoured in the sacrifice in the midst of the gods, in order, as the text explains, to keep the gods apart.[34] This statement immediately recalls the two-three scheme. Indeed the parallel passage in the *Śatapatha* mentions Indra as the third. This text then further makes the interesting point that these three gods and the other gods reciprocally participate in each other so that "the gods came in a threefold way to consist of one deity"; " he who knows thus becomes singly the chief of his people."[35] Thus the single king or chief can only be so on account of reciprocal relations with his

[32]For instances, and for the theory of the village community, Cf. L. Dumont, "The Indian Village Community from Munro to Maine," *Contrib. to Ind. Soc.*, 1966, pp. 67-89.

[33]E.R. Leach, *op. cit.*, p. 184.

[34]*TS*. 2.6.2.1.

[35]*Śatapatha*. *Br*. 1.6.3, 18-22.

people. But , so as to take away, as it were, any illusion about the privileged position of the king as the connecting third, the text then continues paradoxically with the statement: "twofold in truth is this, there is no third,"[36] thus stressing the essential ambiguity of the situation.

The diffusion is also demonstrated in Dumont's exemplary study of a Kallar community. These Kallar sum up their unity in a conventional numerical formula: "4 chiefs (*Tevar*), 8 provinces (*nādu*), 24 secondary villages (*upagrāma*)." One of the four chiefs, sometimes styled *rāja,* is the highest in rank. The other three (or four, since some informants enumerate five chiefly lineages), considered as "ministers," characteristically derive their prestige, in descending order, from connubial relations with the first lineage. But at the same time all members of the community are styled *Tevar,* chief. As Dumont aptly observes: *"la notion de chef en tant que transcendante au groupe n 'existe pas."*[37] Under these circumstances the decline of the first chiefly lineage into near obscurity is perfectly understandable, even without the intervention of external factors.

I think that we should interpret in this way the statements on the divinity and sacral character of the king. Thus, according to the well known passages from Manu, the king does not represent a one and only king of the gods; there are eight of them who coalesce in the human king.[38] This statement in my opinion primarily means that the king is the connecting link of the eightfold dispersed kingship. The eight gods seem to represent the eight human *vīras* who in the *Pañcaviṃśa Br.* are said to support kingship. In other words the king is a mediator between the parts of the community.

Seen in this light it stands to reason that the king as mediator should also be the initiator and chief celebrant of festivals on which the general well-being is dependent.[39] We even find what amounts

[36] *Ibid.*, 23.

[37] L. Dumont, *Une sous-caste de l'Inde du Sud.*, Paris, 1957, 143f.

[38] Manu, 5.96; 7.4, 7; 9, pp. 303-311. It is interesting that in 7.7 these eight gods seem to be enumerated as four pairs; Agni and Vāyu, Sūrya and Soma, Yama and Kubera, Varuna and Indra. For the eight kings among the gods Cf. also the equally eight gods representing kingship among the gods in *BĀU.* 1.4.11. In other texts the number of gods is five, Nārada 18.26, Rām. 3.40.12, *MBh* 12.68. 41ff.

[39] Cf. J. Gonda, "Ancient Indian Kingship," *Numen*, III, 41f. One may also compare E.M. Forster's description, in *The Hill of Devi*, of the *Gokulāṣtamī* festival and the ruler's role in it.

to a "sacrificial theory of kingship."[40]

For all this, or rather because of it, the king does not transcend the community. The sacral or divine character of the ancient Indian king does not lie in his transcendence but in his immanence, in his representing the pivotal connection, as is graphically expressed in the enthronement ceremony. Seated on the throne, the centre of the universe, the king calls out to each of the four chief officiants sitting around him to the four quarters: "O Brahman." The addressed officiant answers: "Thou, O king, art *Brahman*," each adding an identification of the king with one of four deities Savitr, Indra, Mitra and Varuṇa.[41] If we take Brahman in the sense of "connection activated in dialogue,"[42] the meaning of the ceremonial dialogue stands out clearly: it signifies the dispersal and concentration of the "connection" by the king.

Thus the king does not rule by divine, in the sense of transcendent, right.[43] Depending on the circumstances, he may have more or less personal power, but he has no authority of his own, other than that derived from his participation in the reciprocal relations which make up the community.

VIII

So far the analysis has led us to the conclusion that authority, whether in the egalitarian or in the aristocratic order, is dispersed. It is enclosed in the network of personal relations. Its exercise is therefore bound up with the fluctuations of these relations and with the corresponding shifts in the actual distribution of power. The difficulty this involves is clearly reflected in Kauṭilya's advice on the number of councillors the king should have. If only two, they may combine against the king or they may fight each other; in both cases they will ruin him. Kauṭilya's advice therefore is for the king to have three or four councillors, but he concedes that even then such disastrous combinations or divisions are still possible. In fact there appears

[40]Cf. e.g. *Kauṭ. AŚ.* 1.19.33. The idea has already struck A.M. Hocart (see e.g. *Les Castes*, Paris, 1938, p. 29). Cf. also J.W. Spellman, *Political Theory of Ancient India*, Oxford, 1964, pp. 9-12.

[41]Cf. *Royal Consecration*, 141, p. 150.

[42]Cf. L. Renou, "*La notion de brahman*," *JA*, 237, 1949.

[43]Cf. P.V. Kane, *History of Dharmaśastra*, III, p. 25; J. Gonda, *op. cit.*, *Numen*, IV, p. 154.

to be no definitive solution. The problem is that the exercise of authority is beset with factional strife. In other words it would seem that the state is not based on harmony but on conflict; not on the horizontally layered order of *varṇa* but on the shifting vertical lines of faction.

This means that the state turned on institutionalized conflict. Though the classical ritual as we know it from the *śrauta* texts is certainly not intended to reflect socio-political realities, it conveys the overall impression of an underlying pattern of institutionalized conflict. The *śrauta* ritual exclusively stresses the single sacrificer, but we find many features and prescripts which can only be adequately accounted for by assuming an original dualistic and agonistic pattern.[44] Not surprisingly, the indications are clearest in the rituals bound up with kingship (*rājasūya, vājapeya,* and *aśvamedha*), where we find different types of contests, albeit in a strongly formalized and impoverished form, such as chariot races, raids, games of dice, debates. These are not just extraneous materials admitted in the solemn ritual as a concession to popular taste, they are the original features that have been refashioned in the classical *śrauta* ritual. For agonistic features and ideas are not limited to special sacrifices, but run through the whole *corpus rituale* even in its most systematized, seemingly non-agonistic parts, which serve as the basic models of the *śrauta* sacrifice. Thus, contrary to the exclusive stress on the single sacrificer, his rival, the *bhrātṛvya,* is well-nigh ubiquitous. According to the techniques of the systematized ritual he is dealt with *in abstracto*. But not always, for sometimes he is even given a *dakṣiṇa*. How this gift is to be effected is not explained, and in fact is inexplicable since the *bhrātṛvya* has no *locus standi* on the place of sacrifice, and *dakṣiṇās* are not to be given to those outside the place of sacrifice.[45] We even saw the *bhrātṛvya* take part in the unction of the king.

These and similar instances lead us inevitably to the conclusion that the original pattern of the ritual necessitated the participation of two opposing parties contending for the goods of life, like their mythical prototypes, *devas* and *asuras*. It is this pattern that forms

[44]I have dealt with this original pattern elsewhere, Cf. "Brahmin, Ritual and Renouncer," *WZKSOA*, VIII, 1964, pp. 1-31.

[45]An illustrative example of the original role of the rival is provided by the human head to be buried under the brick fire altar, Cf. "The case of the Severed Head," *WZKSOA*, XI, 1967, pp. 22-43.

the framework of the encyclopedia of Indian civilization, the *Mahābhārata*, which has been called by Mauss: "*l'histoire d'un gigantesque potlatch.*"

The outcome of the contest was not fixed once for all. When Yuddhiṣṭhira as a result of his victory has won the earth, as the "material sacrifice" (*dravyamayo yajña*, he is exhorted to stake anew the kingdom he has won.[46] It is therefore no matter for surprise that the *rājasūya* appears in fact to be based on a yearly renewed festival, like the Soma sacrifice in general. The king is not consecrated once for all. It is difficult not to think here also of the exiled king (*aparuddho rājā*), frequently mentioned in the ritual texts. Wealth and with it power and authority must periodically be redistributed through the institution of the contest. It is this pivotal institution that forms the origin of the ancient Indian ritual and that lies at the root of the polity.

This is still clear, notwithstanding its diametrically opposite inspiration, in the *Arthaśāstra*, where it deals with the seven elements of the state. The ally is included as the seventh element, but immediately after this and in the same context Kauṭilya deals with what seems an eighth one, the enemy.[47] The *Arthaśāstra* deals with the seven elements in the context of the *maṇḍala* theory of what is generally considered as "interstate relations." Obviously, however, we should not think here of the state in our modern sense. The *maṇḍala* theory schematizes the relations of alliance and rivalry that are part of the open-ended polity and that, as we have seen, are therefore included in the seven or eightfold definition of the "state." The ambivalence of the king's position and of power and authority is here expressed in the two forms—concentric and linear—of the *maṇḍala* theory. On the one hand the conquering king is represented as "the hub of a wheel" surrounded by the concentric circles of enemies and friends. On the other hand there is the linear representation where not the one king but two kings—the would-be conqueror and his enemy—form the centre.[48] In the first representation the king is in the centre, obeyed by his allies and subduing his rivals; the second is a dualistic scheme. But in neither does the king rise

[46]*MBh*, 12.8.34ff.

[47]Kaut. *AŚ*. 6.1.13. The state is said to consist of eight elements, however without specification of the eighth, Cf. *MBh*. 15.5.8.; 12.122.8 (var. lectio).

[48]Cf. H. Scharfe, *op. cit.*, pp. 123-126, where the two representations have been lucidly disentangled.

above the *maṇḍala*; his position remains dependent on the shifting outcome of the perennial contest.[49]

IX

Now all this does not seem to be peculiar to Indian civilization.[50] Perhaps it may illustrate or supplement what we know from elsewhere, but we have so far not gone beyond what may be termed the tribal condition of state and kingship. It appeared necessary, however, first to go at length into the common tribal condition, the better to do justice to what sets Indian tradition apart and gives it its special character. I refer particularly to the relationship between Kṣatra and Brahman. So far we have seen the Brahman only as the central "connection" holding the disparate whole together and which is again and again re-established in the contest.[51] We have seen how the king is made to represent the Brahman at his enthronement in a dialogue that looks like an impoverished "debate on Brahman" (*brahmodya*). It is interesting that the enthronement takes place after the chariot race and that the dialogue itself is closely associated with the game of dice. This means that the Brahman is not permanently fixed in any one person or group. In the dualistic scheme of the pre-classical contest it was exchanged between the contending parties. There is no room here for the rigid separation of spiritual authority and temporal power.

However the continual flux implied in this situation can hardly be satisfactory. It calls for its opposite, a fixed order, based on transcendent authority. Thus *dharma*, as we have seen, must be based on *śruti*, that is on transcendent revelation, however tenuously they are linked. The need for transcendent authority is also exemplified by the ideas of the Kallar, already referred to. The authority of the leading Kallar lineage is legitimized by a copper-plate charter granted by an authority transcending the community, the Nayak of

[49]Editor's note, Cf. de Casparis, pp. 123-124.

[50]We may think here, for example of the segmental lineage systems studied by Africanists, or of the "pyramidal" variety, as defined by A. Southall (*Alur Society*, Cambridge, 1956, p. 250), where the powers exercised at the different levels are virtually of the same type.

[51]On *Brahman* being inherent in the contest, specifically the verbal contest, Cf.L. Renou, *op. cit.*; also author, "On the Origin of the *Nāstika*," *WZKSOA*, XII-XIII, 1968, pp. 171-185.

Madurai. Even in the amonarchical view the Kallar, when offered a king by the Nayak, are said by one of Dumont's informants to have refused with the words: "We do not need a king; give us the four *Tevar*, we will obey them."[52] That is: the institution of the "four *Tevar*," though in fact based in the community, still needed the Nayak's transcendent legitimation.

The central problem was that of finding a way to lift authority from the continually shifting ground of personal relations and to establish a fixed order sustained by it. This problem would seem to be a universal one; each civilization must try to solve it in its own way. What concerns us here is the question how Indian civilization attempted to solve it.

The point where the problem was attacked was the ever-recurring struggle for power and prestige. This attack meant a fundamental change of "Weltanschauung"—a change that set the terms of Indian tradition. One must, of course, resist the temptation to make exuberant claims on behalf of one's own research preferences, if not out of the way hobby horses, but I would maintain that the fundamental change I am referring to found its clearest and most coherent reflection in the *śrauta* ritual, which resulted from the change of world view.

The ever-recurring struggle for the distribution of power and authority found its formal expression in the dualistic ritual of the periodic contest. From the ritual point of view, therefore, the main issue was the elimination of the contest. This was achieved by excluding the rival from the place of sacrifice. Instead of the interaction of the contending parties the single sacrificer, enacting alone and without rival the cosmic drama for his own benefit, was made the pivot of the ritual. The rival party, on whose "hostile friendship" the contest depends, is replaced by the corps of ritual specialists. The skills of contest and debate become the technical skills of the correct use of fixed formula, metres and chants; the counteraction of the rival is replaced by the technical mistake to be corrected by an equally technical expiation.[53] Indeed ritual competition itself is now simply a "mistake."

[52]Cf. L. Dumont, *ibid.*

[53]This is still visible in the ritual of the tenth day of the standard twelve day Soma sacrifice. Mistakes in recitation are to be declared by a "corrector" in a way which closely resembles a contest in improvisational verbal skill; Cf. *Āpastamba Ś S*, 21.9.7.9; *Nāstika*, p. 178.

What the ritual reformers had in mind is poignantly expressed in a passage of the *Jaiminīya Br.* that seems to contain the programme of ritual reform.[54] It describes how Prajāpati and Death fought each other by means of sacrifice. For long years the battle remains undecided, till at last Prajāpati discovers the symbolical and numerical equivalence. Thereby he is able to incorporate the rival sacrifice of Death into his own sacrifice and thus to eliminate him. The passage closes with the triumphal statement: "in our times there is no rivalry in sacrifice (*saṃsava*) any more; what was the second sacrifice, that came to nought; the sacrifice is only one, Prajāpati alone is the sacrifice."

The exclusion of the primordial rival, Death, and the assertion of the unopposed lord of life, Prajāpati, who is at the same time the prototype of the sacrificer, amounted to a revolution of the socio-religious system. However the price that had to be paid was equally momentous: complete divorce from social reality, a price incapable of being paid in full. The sacrifice was cut loose from the community. The place of sacrifice in the classical view is the ideally ordered world completely sealed off from the world of social relations.

In the individualized sacrifice the single sacrificer turns his back on society and strikes out in a world exclusively his own. His specialist assistants can only be there on the strength of the theory that they are fused with him in one single body, not in a subservient capacity but sharing alike in the benefits of the sacrifice. Even if the sacrificer has to give them *dakṣiṇās*, these gifts are not a salary; they should be entirely free gifts, without any strings of reciprocity attached. From the social point of view they should be irrelevant. Obviously, however, this ritual theory is insufficient. Sacrificer and officiant are fused into one single unit, but at the same time there is no relation at all. As I have argued elsewhere, the individualization of sacrifice could not stop at this point. It had to proceed to its logical conclusion, the complete interiorization of sacrifice which renders the specialists' services superfluous, as in the *prāṇāgnihotra,* and frees both sacrificer and officiant from their impossible bond. In other words, the individualization of sacrifice lies in the same line with renunciation of society. The ideal sacrificer, like the ideal Brahmin, stands outside society; he is a renouncer.

It was in this way that the problem of transcendence was attacked. It meant a dichotomy of the universe. On the one hand the worldly

[54] *JB*, 2.69-70; Caland, Auswahl, No. 128.

sphere of social relations, on the other the outer-worldly sphere of the individual, cut off from society and thereby transcending it.[55] It would seem that we touch here on the well known separation between the Brahmin's spiritual authority and the king's temporal power. We should however be careful not to construct this opposition simply as a complementary one. Authority could only be made transcendent on condition that it be free from involvement in the social world and its attendant struggle for the distribution of power. The dichotomy excludes in principle any relation between power and authority.

By the same token society stands condemned, because it lacks authority. The bearer of authority is the Brahmin, but he can be so only as long as he keeps himself free from involvement in the social world. In particular he should shun the holder of power. The texts have harsh things to say of the Brahmin who serves the king.[56] At best he is put on a par with the Kṣatriya.[57] Not surprisingly even the *ṛtvij*, the sacrificial officiant, is not a true Brahmin, but equally put on a par with the Kṣatriya.[58] In fact he should not be a priest at all, because this involves him in the social world, and in a subservient capacity at that. It was not, as is often assumed, the Brahmin, who by some inexplicable stratagem excluded the king from priestly and sacral office. It is the other way round: the Brahmin's withdrawal left the king alone with priestly and sacral responsibility.

X

If it be asked whether this dichotomy of power and authority is at all a feasible proposition, the answer is quite obviously and simply:

[55]On this dichotomy Cf. L. Dumont, "World-renunciation in Indian Religions," *Contrib. to Ind. Soc.*, IV, 1960, pp. 33-62. Dumont adheres to the usual view that sacrifice belongs to the social world. However, we should distinguish between the popular sacrifice or festival (in which the Brahmin takes no or only a marginal part) and the rigidly desocialized *śrauta* sacrifice. Equally the Brahmin is for Dumont, possibly led astray by the usual rendering "priest," part of the the social world. However, ideally he is a renouncer; he can only act as a priest at the expense of his outer-worldly status.

[56]Cf. for example, *Manu* 3.64, 153; 4.85f.

[57]*Manu* 12.46; significantly this passage brackets the *purohit* together with those engaging in contests as equal to Kshatriyas.

[58]*MBh*, 12.76.7.

no. In practical terms, the king's power can only be legitimized by the Brahmin's transcendent authority. But the Brahmin cannot involve himself with the king without jeopardizing his outerworldly status. On the other hand the Brahmin, however renunciatory he may feel, cannot live on transcendence alone, but must trade it for subsistence. The situation is certainly contradictory. However, such contradictions, it would seem, are at the core of every civilization. The point I want to stress here is a different one.

The divorce between social reality and transcendent authority left society unreformed. As in the case of the *śrauta* sacrifice, reform was only possible outside the social sphere. Conflict remained the central institution, as before. Authority having been siphoned off, the state lacked the means to rise above the essential instability of personal relations. For all the splendour of the courts that so much impressed unwary travellers, the state was atrophied in its development, at the mercy of the turns of the *maṇḍala*, the "circle" of kings, and without permanence.

Now it could be argued that a universalistic principle underpinning the state is given in the caste hierarchy which replaces conflict as the pivotal institution with a permanently fixed order. The caste hierarchy proceeds from the opposition between pure and impure.[59] It separates pure and impure so as to safeguard purity. At the same time the recognition of the transcendent ideal of purity by the impure provides for hierarchical cohesion. However, here we come up against the difficulty presented by the fundamental dichotomy. The point is that the opposition can not be a complementary one. In order to safeguard purity the opposition has to be absolute. As in the case of the king and the Brahmin, any relation between the two should be ruled out.

Equally the *varṇa* order can not form the basis for the cohesion that social reality requires. It is aimed at rigid separation. The great evil is *varṇasaṃkara*, the mixing of castes. One might, however, argue that, though the *varṇas* are separated, the internal cohesion of each *varṇa* will only be the stronger for it. But even so it will have to be conceded that this would hardly be helpful towards replacing the particularistic community as a basis for the state. For the king is on the one hand kept down by his essential equality with his Kshatriya brethren; on the other he is hampered in his relations with the

[59] I refer to L. Dumont's views, for example, *Homo Hierarchicus*, Paris, 1966, p. 78; *Contrib. to Ind. Soc.*, V, 1961, p. 34.

other *varṇas*. Quite apart from the fact that, as we saw already, authority is beyond his reach.

But even the internal cohesion of the *varṇa* is put in jeopardy. For the prohibition of marriage with *sapiṇḍa* relatives rules out any manageable system of connubium to cement the cohesion of the *varṇa*. Moreover marriage should be, according to the *dharma* texts, a free gift without any reciprocal obligation in accordance with the Brahminical theory of the gift in general.[60] As Lévi-Strauss has observed on this point, it is hard to see how a society could function under these circumstances.[61]

In other words, the *varṇa* order does not provide for any cohesion, nor is it intended to do so. Rather it is aimed at breaking it down. Clearly it can only be a theory, turning its back on reality, as the ideal Brahmin does. Reality left to its own devices remained based on personal relations. The basic paradigm, as we saw, would even seem to be connubium, witness the representation of caste as arising from intermarriage.[62] Caste in this sense, say *jāti*, corresponds to social reality, but it is very different from the *varṇa* theory. Belonging to the social world, it is liable to shifts and reversals. As such it is not even peculiarly Indian. The peculiarly Indian character of the situation is the coexistence of *jāti* practice and *varṇa* theory. The importance of the *varṇa* theory lies precisely in that it is aimed at overcoming the instability of the social world. It is based on outerworldly brahminical authority and therefore provides the terms in which reality must be legitimized.

Though it is common practice to speak of the caste system, we should realize that there are in fact two opposite systems: the social reality of *jāti* and the theory of *varṇa*. The linkage between the two is that the *varṇa* theory is there to provide the legitimizing idiom for the reality of *jāti*. The confusion of *varṇa* and *jāti* arises from the fact that social relations have to be legitimized in terms of a theory that denies them.

[60]On the Brahminical theory of the gift excluding any reciprocity Cf. M. Mauss, "*Essai sur le Don,*" *Sociologie et Anthropologie*, p. 243.

[61]C. Lévi-Strauss, *op. cit.*, p. 460. The author argues that the gift marriage theory will have arisen from a system of generalized exchange, the true nature of which was no longer understood. In the present case, I should like to go one step further: the theory of gift marriage does not seem to be a matter of incomprehension but rather of principle.

[62]Cf. *Manu* 10, pp. 6-61.

XI

Here, I think, we can take up again our discussion of tradition. What is commonly but vaguely referred to as Indian tradition is not a matter of a number of more or less antiquated, more or less harmful or useful institutions and concepts. Its essence is the contradictory coexistence of a social reality with a transcendent theory that denies reality not as a consequence of insufficient understanding but as a matter of principle. It is this situation that constitutes the specific nature of Indian tradition. To borrow Dumont's apt phrase about Hinduism: its "secret may be found in the dialogue between the renouncer and the man-in-the-world." Only it is a dialogue of contradictions.

This does not mean that Indian civilization was from the outset bogged down in contradiction. On the contrary, the contradictory situation leads to ever new attempts at bridging the intractable gap. In this way we can also understand the proverbial resilience of Indian civilization. Indian civilization has change built in. Foreign institutions and concepts do not present a direct threat to it, but can be accommodated and harnessed in new attempts at bridging the fundamental gap. In the same way, it would seem, the Western impact was not a destructive onslaught, but in fact offered new possibilities for attempts to reconcile the two opposite sides of tradition. Thus, for instance, the modern caste association[63] seems to be situated between the local *jāti* and the supra-local *varṇa*. The caste association is clearly connected with the local *jāti*, but at the same time it tends to replace the personal, vertical ties with the local community—which incidentally obstruct *jāti* unity and coherence[64]—with horizontal supra-local, supra-personal ties, and as such is in line with the *varṇa* concept.

On the face of it there is little that links the modern national state with the traditional political order. But on closer inspection it would seem that the obviously foreign Western model of the modern state has been subservient to the traditional dilemma of power and authority. Founding India's modern state was not just a matter of

[63]On the caste association, see L.I. and S.H. Rudolph, *The Modernity of Tradition*, pp. 30-36.

[64]On the vertical *jajmānī* ties preventing horizonal corporate unity, Cf. M.N. Srinivas, "The Social System of a Mysore Village," in M. Marriott (ed.), *Village India*, Chicago, 1955, pp. 19-32.

the gradual introduction of Western institutions. For these could and in fact did only create new and wider arenas for the interplay of factional power relations. They had to be supplemented by authority. And authority could only come from the renunciatory sphere. It can not be accidental that in the decisive period between the two world wars the national movement was dominated by a man whose extraordinary capacities were cast in the mould of the classical renouncer. In Gandhi the dilemma of worldly power and outer-worldly authority was manifested with tragic poignancy. It may even have been the deeper cause of his final undoing; whether by murderer's hand, as it actually happened, or otherwise, through neglect and irrelevance, as in fact also happened. But he bequeathed on India the dual structure, first exemplified in the Gandhian Congress constitutions,[65] of factional power relations in party and parliament counterbalanced by an extra-constitutional consensus-making body as the final national authority. It is obvious, however, even apart from the present bifurcation of the "Congress system," that the dilemma of power and authority has not been definitely solved, nor can it be. But neither has it been solved anywhere else, as we know only too well.

[65]On the Congress Constitutions, Cf. D. Rothermund, "Constitutional Reform versus National Agitation," *JAS*, 21, pp. 505-521.

5 Traditions of Statecraft in Ancient India

THOMAS R. TRAUTMANN

The purpose of this essay is the modest one of defining the traditions of statecraft in ancient India, and of describing their origins and interrelations. By statecraft I mean advice to the ruler put in literary form; thus "tradition" is here used in the special sense of intellectual traditions, not the administrative traditions of historical Indian states. The question of the influence of these intellectual traditions on actual practice will be largely, though not entirely, set aside. Even within these narrow bounds we must confine ourselves to the statecraft of kings, for while monarchy was not the only form which ancient Indian states assumed, it was the only mode for which there grew up a literature of statecraft. The *Arthaśāstra* does indeed include a section on republics and oligarchies, not however with the intention of comparing diverse constitutions, but rather to instruct the king on how he might deal with them, and if possible, destroy them; while throughout the book the king is the beneficiary of its teachings. Further, it is *Arthaśāstra* or the science of politics in general, and the *Arthaśāstra* ascribed to Kauṭilya in particular, which will be the centrepiece of this essay, partly because, of the Sanskrit literature on statecraft, it is the works of this science which are solely devoted to advising the king (whereas, for example, in the *Dharmaśāstras* statecraft is merely a branch of law), and partly because in Kauṭilya's *Arthaśāstra* we have the purest or perhaps one should say the most uncompromising expression of an important view of statecraft. It is with this work that we must begin.[1]

[1]It would be inappropriate to burden an essay of this sort with bibliographical details of the sources used, which in most cases will be well known to the specialist anyway. Suffice it to say I have used the most authoritative editions accessible to me, which in the case of the *Kauṭilīya* is that of Kangle. Critical editions of the *Nītisāra* and the *Nītivākyāmṛta* are desiderata; I have used Gaṇapati Sāstrī's (*Trivandrum Skt. Ser.*) and Pannālāla Sonī's (*Māṇikacandra-Digambara-Jaina-Granthamālā*) editions respectively. Lacking access to Nārada's text I have used Jolly's translation (*Sacred Books of the East*). Buddhist reactions

The *Arthaśāstra* of Kauṭilya is the oldest representative we have of what must have been a fairly extensive literature. Even if the many quotations of earlier authorities in the *Arthaśāstra* are largely fictive, devised for their literary effect, the existence of various older schools and works of *Arthaśāstra* can scarcely be doubted. In particular the works associated with the names of Bṛahaspati and Uśanas or Śukra must have been early and important treatises. These two are the preceptors of the gods and demons respectively and as such are invoked in the opening of Kauṭilya's *Arthaśāstra*; verses attributed to them may be found in numerous commentaries and compilations; and in modern times anonymous paṇḍits have paid their memory the compliment of repairing the loss of their works with the fabrication of a *Bārhaspatya Arthaśāstra* and a *Śukranītisāra.*

Besides these two works there were numerous other predecessors of the *Arthaśāstra* of Kauṭilya which are also lost to us except in so far as the works of a later age incorporate and transmit the best fruits of an earlier. Let us briefly try to fix the position of the work ascribed to Kauṭilya in the early *Arthaśāstra* tradition. I have argued elsewhere that the predecessors of Kauṭilya's work—or perhaps we should use the appellation of *Kauṭilīya* to distinguish it from other *Arthaśāstrs*—that the predecessors of the *Kauṭilīya* included not only finished *Arthaśāstras* covering the whole field but also monographs concerned with single aspects of the science of politics, and that the *Kauṭilīya* is a compilation, with some reworking, reorganization and the addition of some fresh matter, of these monographs, made most probably in A.D. second or third centuries.[2] Thus the *Kauṭilīya,* so far from being the original conception of a single intelligence, is rather the result of generations of discussion upon political subjects. The *Kauṭilīya* then is not an extreme or peculiar work but a somewhat more advanced yet very faithful representative of the tradition within which it was formed, which enhances its value for an historian of ideas. Some of the extremer views of its predecessors, indeed, are rejected, as when the *Kauṭilīya* ascribes to the Bārhaspatyas the opi-

to *Arthaśāstra,* are collected by E.H. Johnson in *J. of the Royal Asiatic Soc.* 1929, 77ff.

[2]"The Structure and Composition of the Kauṭilīya Arthaśāstra," Ph.D. thesis, University of London, 1968. Revised version published as *Kauṭilya and the Arthaśāstra: A Statistical Investigation of the Authorship and Evolution of the Text,* Leiden, E. J. Brill, 1971, in which questions of date and authorship are examined at length.

nion that Vedic religion serves only as a cloak to hide worldly self-interest (1.2.4). But if the *Kauṭilīya* sums up and transmits the best of the *Arthaśāstra* tradition it is also likely to have expanded its scope: for in some of its more important parts, especially its second book dealing with the duties of overseers of government departments, there are scarcely any signs of earlier authorities. In short, the *Kauṭilīya* filters, transmits, refines and augments the *Arthaśāstra* tradition, and in doing so the ancient works were superseded and lost.

Let us take a closer look at this *Kauṭilīya Arthaśāstra*. The work may be divided in two, the first half (Books 1–5) concerned with the conduct of the internal affairs of the kingdom, the second half (Books 6–15) with foreign relations. Book 1 opens with a "table of contents" and a discussion of the place of *Arthaśāstra* (or *daṇḍanīti*, as it is here more aptly called) among the sciences; it goes on to consider an assortment of topics such as the education of the prince, the testing of ministers, and above all, the employment of spies, *agents provocateurs* and assassins in the service of the king. Book 2, dealing with the duties of the overseers of government departments, is of exceptional interest both for the extent of its detail—it is the longest book of the *Arthaśāstra*—and the fact that it is practically the only disquisition on this subject in the whole of Sanskrit literature. The next two books (3 and 4) concern law, the first being a systematic dissertation on the eighteen "feet" of litigation (or the law of transactions), the second concerned with the suppression of crime. The fifth book is, like the first, a miscellany containing a number of unlikely bedfellows: the secret punishment of opponents, dubious means by which an exhausted treasury may be replenished, correct behaviour for courtiers and dependents of the king, and so forth.

Book 6 acts as an introduction to foreign affairs, which is the prime concern of the long Book 7, under the rubric of the sixfold policy. Book 8 deals with the various vices or calamities which may affect the king or the constituents of the state. The remaining books are largely devoted to war: the preparations for and conduct of war, the destruction of republican states, the means by which a weaker king may avoid being crushed by his enemies, how to capture a fort. Book 14 contains poisons, potions, and spells by which the enemy may be destroyed or deluded, or one's own army protected. Book 15 analyzes the rhetorical devices employed in the *Arthaśāstra*.

The *Kauṭilīya*, especially the latter half, abounds in lists of categories. Thus we have the four expedients, the five "limbs" of counsel, the six policies, the seven constituents of the state, the seven vices of which three arise from lust and four from anger, the twelve elements of the circle of states and the eighteen worthies. This is merely the common coin of statecraft. We are told that the six policies are peace and war, staying quiet and marching to battle, seeking refuge and duplicity. Then all the changes are rung: staying quiet after declaring war; staying quiet after concluding peace; marching after declaring war; marching after concluding peace; and so on. All combinations are tried, all contingencies are anticipated.

Another aspect of the *Arthaśāstra* is its straightforward, laconic and dry exposition, relatively unrelieved by similies drawn from the animal and vegetable kingdoms. Rather exceptional are these verses on fraudulent officials (2.9.32-4):

> Just as it is impossible to not taste honey or poison placed on the tongue, so impossible is it for treasury officials not to taste at least a little bit of the king's money.
>
> Just as it is impossible to know when fish swimming in the water are drinking, so impossible is it to know when officials carrying out their duties are embezzeling money.
>
> It is possible to know even the paths of birds flying through the sky, but not the ways of officials acting with their intentions concealed.

Throughout the *Arthaśāstra* the king is the unexpressed subject of every verb: he should cause this to be done, he should have that established. In only a few places is someone else's point of vantage, not necessarily identical with that of the king, taken. Thus, the conduct of a prince in disfavour (1.18), and the fitting behaviour of courtiers (5.4) and dependents (5.5) are considered, and a chapter is devoted to the steps the minister must take to secure the continuity of the state in the event of the king's demise (5.6); but only in the first of these topics might the advice given result in harm to the king, and a prince is after all a king in embryo. On the whole it is the king who is the agent.

How should he act, and to what end? If there is one thread which runs through the work from cover to cover it is the aggrandizement of the king's power and the promotion of his security. These two notes—power and security—must be struck in harmony or the whole venture of kingship will be lost. Let us take them up separately.

The *Arthaśāstra* rarely considers general questions of ends and means, but confines itself to concrete situations. When in the opening chapters it does speak philosophically the doctrines enunciated are lofty and in keeping with other works on statecraft: the object of the state is to achieve for the subjects security and well-being, or the triad of piety, profit and pleasure, or again the pursuit of Vedic religion, philosophy and economics, or yet again the king pursues wealth in order to bestow it on the worthy. The means to these noble ends is force or punishment (*dāṇḍa*), but force justly applied (*yathārhadaṇḍa*), being neither too harsh nor too lenient. Force protects the subjects from the invader and the criminal; the fear of punishment bends them to their duties. This philosophy with its characteristically low estimate of human nature is such as can be found in any *Dharmaśāstra.* Apart from these concessions to general considerations, however, the king's pursuit of power is everywhere assumed in the *Arthaśāstra,* and higher objects are discussed no further. Within the kingdom the king's power over his resources is acquired by a large well-organized bureaucracy, and the subjects are but the human variety of those resources; control over the bureaucracy is achieved by a large establishment of spies and agents of all kinds who search out fraud and test the loyalty of the king's officials as well as the populace generally, and report directly to the king.

In regard to other rulers the king is the *vijigīṣu,* one desirous of conquest. Hostility open or concealed is the normal relation between states. The neighbouring kingdom is one's natural enemy, because each is food for the appetite of the other; one's neighbour's neighbour is one's neighbour's natural enemy for the same reason, and thereby the *vijigīṣu's* friend, and so forth. No final end to the state of endemic strife thus implied is contemplated. Peace is merely the temporary suspension of hostilities; and the limits of the subcontinent are the only bounds placed upon the ambitions of the king.

The note of security is rung just as insistently. The king is advised in detail how his secret agents may remove his powerful enemies within the kingdom by intrigue and assassination. The people's discontents are to be quieted if possible by pious harangues on the divine establishment of kingship. The rules for the protection of the king's own person from the enemies' agents, his servants, even from his queens and his sons, suggest that personal safety was a constant preoccupation of the king in ancient India. But above all security is pursued by reflection and caution. All the risks are to be weighed before the start of any undertaking—it is a major purpose of the *Arthaśāstra* to weigh these for the king—and the greater risk is to be shunned. This is best illustrated by the doctrine of the four means: conciliation, bribery, separation and force. It is characteristic of this doctrine, as of *Arthaśāstra* teachings throughout, that force is the last resort, after having tried to win over an enemy by sweet words and gifts, or weakening him by having agents sow dissension in his camp. Force is to be avoided when possible, not because it is morally dubious, but because it involves expense and risk, and one's object may more easily be obtained through conciliation and the like, or through occult means. But where force must at last be resorted to, even then it would, by preference, not be naked force. For example, when all other expedients fail in dealing with a discontented retainer the king is advised to make him incur the hatred of the people by appointing him tax collector; after a while he may be secretly assassinated or killed in an inspired insurrection without fear of public outcry. The emphasis on the cool calculation of risk and the conservation of energy with which the quest for power is to be conducted leads inevitably to a preference for the devious, the cunning, the crooked or deceitful, all of which words could serve as equivalents for the name of the reputed author of the *Arthaśāstra*, the word representing the chief virtue or vice, depending on one's point of view, of the successful Indian minister.The selfish search for power and security is not a monopoly of the *Kauṭilīya* among Indian works of statecraft; what is unique is the harsh logic with which this premise is worked into a programme for the king, without hesitation or scruple, baulking at neither duplicity nor the fraudulent impersonation of the gods.

When we examine the *Arthaśāstra* works which follow the *Kauṭilīya* we find its dark counsels mitigated in one manner or another. The *Nītisāra* of Kāmandaka, which is largely a versified summary of the *Kauṭilīya*, does so partly by abridgement: the doctrines of its predecessor cannot seem quite so harsh when only a part is presented. It is true that Kāmandaka shows a preference for those parts of his original where the unscruplous pursuit of self-interest is most evident, ignoring almost entirely, like other later *Arthaśāstras*, the very important second book on the duties of overseers, which had perhaps become obsolete through the evolution of different administrative practices. Besides abbreviation, however, the *Nītisāra* offers the sanction of precedents from the legends of the epics for the more underhanded bits of advice, as a pap for those of tender conscience, and makes the occasional appeal to the higher ends of the state for the justifications of its less savoury means. In the *Nītivākyāmṛta* of Somadeva, a yet shorter condensation of the *Arthaśāstra*, there is a greater emphasis on pious ends and less said about doubtful means, while the whole is made more palatable by means of maxims and similes: "When unable to conquer the enemy in the battle of wits, he should resort to the battle of swords"; "Seeking shelter with a weak king from fear of a strong is like climbing a castor plant from fear of an elephant." There is nothing in it that would lead us to suspect that it is the work of a Jain monk. It emphasizes the superior role of Brahmins in society and the state: counsellors are to be Brahmins, not Kṣatriyas, for "the bearers of weapons should not be the bearers of counsel." Another maxim stresses the need to strike a balance among the claims of the three ends of man: "He who abandons love and wealth and pursues religion alone abandons cultivated fields to plough the wilderness."

Also of the *Arthaśāstra* tradition but constituting a genre of its own, employing the terms and teachings of *Arthaśāstra* but using a different vehicle, is the fable literature of the *Pañcatantra* and *Hitopadeśa,* and the collections of gnomic sayings ascribed to *Cāṇakya.*[3] The fable or the popular anecdote, with its amusing story culminating in a hard-bitten moral (which is sometimes far from moral), is an admirable device by which princes may be instructed in the iron necessities of successful kingship, and that is the avowed purpose of these works. It is the principle of the sugar-coated pill. Here is an illustration:

The mouse comes out of his hole at the foot of a banyan tree at sunset to seek his dinner. The cat on his nightly prowl has become ensnared in a trap set by a Caṇḍāla hunter. The mouse is delighted to see his ancient enemy thus rendered helpless; not only does he

[3]Professor Ingalls has shown (*J. of the Amer. Or. Soc.*, 86, 1966, 1 ff., in spite of Sternbach's reply, *ibid.*, 87, 1967, 306ff.) that the earliest of the Cāṇakya collections draws on the *Hitopadeśa*. The ascription to Cāṇakya of aphorisms and fables probably derives from some reader's natural but mistaken assumption that "Cāṇakya the wise" in the invocation of the *Pañcatantra* and its descendants was the main source of the *Pañcatantra's* fables, at a time when the *Kauṭilīya* had fallen into relative obscurity; whereas in fact the author of the *Pañcatantra* refers, under his more popular name Cāṇakya, to the reputed author of the *Kauṭilīya* from whom he had obtained not amusing stories and pithy sayings but the formal doctrines and categories of *Arthaśāstra*.

boldly come up and eat the meat with which the snare had been baited, but he scrambles on the cat's back out of pure joy. But suddenly he spies an owl ready to swoop down upon him should he remain where he is, and a mongoose who is sure to catch him if he flees. What is he to do? In a flight of oratory he persuades the cat to conclude the pact arising from their mutual distress: the cat will shield the mouse under his belly until the owl and the mongoose leave, and the mouse will gnaw through the bonds of the snare in return. Thereupon the mouse begins to gnaw, but he proceeds very slowly. He explains to the increasingly agitated cat:

> Nobody is the friend of another, nobody is another's well-wisher. Persons become friends or foes only from motives of interest; interest enlists interest just as tame elephants catch wild. Nor indeed after a task has been accomplished is the doer regarded; for this reason, all tasks should so be done that something remains to be done. (*Mbh.* 12.136. 104-105)

Dawn arrives, bringing with it the Caṇḍāla hunter and his hounds. The owl, blinded by the light of day, returns to its nest. The mongoose flees the approaching hunter. The mouse, now free of danger, honours the contract by gnawing through the last remaining thong, allowing just time enough for him to disappear down his hole and for the cat to climb a nearby tree without a thought for his empty stomach. Later when the trapper and his dogs have left with the empty snare, the cat offers the mouse life-long friendship. But the mouse demurs, observing:

> There is no such thing as a foe or a friend by nature. It is force of circumstances that creates friends and foes. (*Mbh.* 12.136. 132)

The tale is from the *Mahābhārata* but it represents the kind of tales found in this branch of literature, and in many other works as well.

When we turn to a different tradition of statecraft, that of the *Dharmaśāstra* (and by this I mean the legal portions of the epics as well as the *smṛtis*, both having equal authority as sources of *dharma*) the emphasis is displaced from the objects (*Arthaśāstra*) or implements (*daṇḍanīti*) of the king to his duties (*rājadharma*). The whole duty of the king is, in a word, to protect and to punish, the two being complementary aspects of the rod, symbolic of force. The rod, moreover, stands above the king, ready to strike him down if he misuses his power, for Daṇḍa is conceived as a great god, having a black hue and red eyes.

Again, the *Dharmaśāstra* tradition differs from the *Arthaśāstra* in the extent to which it provides the enterprise of kingship with a philosophical basis. The king wields the rod; the good are protected, the wicked punished, and all estates and stations adhere through fear of the rod to their proper duties. For the Brahmins this duty is sacrifice: they "pour upward" the oblations on which the gods subsist; the gods commend men to Indra, their king, and Indra "pours downward," sending the rain on which the kingdom depends for its prosperity. Through the benign actions of this "great chain of doing" alone can religion be secured, for the gods do not accept the sacrifices performed in an anarchic or ill-ruled land.[4] Just as the good king brings the seasonable rains, so where there is misrule or no king at all, the rains fail and the strong devour the weak as do fish when the pools begin to dry up. Such, indeed, had been the case in the primeval past when kingship was divinely appointed as the result and remedy of sin, to save the people from anarchy and to guarantee the gods their source of nourishment, the sacrifice. Furthermore, not only is kingship divinely established but the king himself is a representative of the gods on earth, and is even called a god in human form: Agni in his wrath, Indra in battle, Soma in benevolence, Yama in meting out justice and Kubera in his benefactions. "The king, even if only an infant, is not to be despised thinking, 'He is a mere mortal'; for he is a great deity in human form" (Manu 7.8).

This comprehensive philosophy, perfectly articulated if not always

[4]*Mbh.* 12.121. Most Hindu justifications of the state are extensions of the theory of the sacrifice. The absence of a specifically Vaiṣṇava or Śaiva doctrine of the state and the persistence of the great royal sacrifices long beyond the Vedic period in which they developed are perhaps the result of the individualistic and even asocial character of *bhakti*, meditation and *yoga*, in contrast with the public character of the sacrifice. I do not believe the problem has even been addressed, or even noticed. It might even be true to say that while there have been Vedic states, there have been no Vaiṣṇava or Śaiva ones, except perhaps in Southeast Asia where the *devarāja* cult obtained. A passage in the Pali canon shows that Buddhists were capable of conceiving of the state as a kind of secular contract entered into by the people with their elected (not divinely appointed) king in the immemorial past, solely as a remedy for anarchy, not the distress of hungry gods (*Dīgha Nikāya, Agañña, Suttanta*).

systematically expounded, justifies the sharp measures the king may be required to take both by the fear of anarchy if he should fail and the hope of prosperity and order should he succeed. The concrete measures advocated are, it is true, in many cases the same as those in the *Arthaśāstras*, on which the *Dharmaśāstras* did not hesitate to draw. Thus the employment of spies and the manipulation of the circle of states are treated in the legal texts, and their teachings, as indeed their very terms, find counterparts in the *Arthaśāstra* tradition whence they derive. On the whole, however, there is much less of what is morally questionable in the *Dharmaśāstra* tradition, and where it is retained the authorities betray a more sensitive conscience by adding some justification, appealing, for example, to the fear of anarchy or the divinity of the king. Such justification could serve to legitimize quite extreme royal powers. It would be hard to frame a pair of verses better designed to excuse the abuse of royal authority than these from Nārada (18.21, 22):

> Whatever a king does is right, that is a settled rule; because the protection of the world is entrusted to him, and on account of his majesty and benignity towards living creatures.
>
> As a husband though feeble must be constantly worshipped by his wives, in the same way a ruler though worthless must be (constantly) worshipped by his subjects.

But the *Dharmaśāstras* look to other sources for their statecraft as well: the battle codes, proscribing the immunity of one who joins hands in supplication or one who runs away "with hair flying," and the reminder that the Kṣātriya slain by a wound in the back takes on the sins of his leader, but one who dies honourably goes straight to heaven, all this seems to look back to the martial traditions of an heroic age, not the more cautious and less scrupulous *Arthaśāstra* tradition. Again, the emphasis on the prerogatives and exemptions of the Brahmin, especially the learned Brahmin, is nowhere as great as in the *Dharmaśāstras*. The Brahmin is not to be taxed, and on no account killed; he is to be protected and supported by gifts of goods and land which succeeding generations of kings must uphold unless they wish to become worms in ordure and fry in hell with their ancestors, according to the common formula of the copper-plate land grants.

It is of course the view-point of the Brahmin, that the *Dharma-*

śāstras represent, or more exactly the viewpoint of the paṇḍit, the man of learning. He depends upon the king's generosity if he is to be able to pursue both his studies and to eat. The scholar is ever anxious to increase the security of his class, dependent as it is on the benevolence of others, and in times of anarchy his knowledge gives him no protection. Susceptible to pride as are intellectuals of all ages the Brahmin calls himself *bhūdeva*, a god on earth; but recognizing the supreme importance to his calling and to the tradition he piously serves of a strong ruler, he reluctantly shares his claims to divinity with the king. In this way he and his tradition shore up the foundation of an institution which he can influence but cannot control. But kings do not always match their divine nature with god-like deeds; the learned Brahmin is subject to him and, as a subject, must sometimes share the common man's interest. Thus while he teaches the people obedience, the *Dharmaśāstra* instructs the king to hold his subjects' happiness above his own, and warns that the wicked king is crushed by the gods, or that the people will rise up and slay him like a mad dog.

Having determined that *Dharmaśāstra* is the expression of the paṇḍit we must ask of what class *Arthaśāstra* is the expression; the question is important since it has a bearing on the history of that tradition. I have said that *Arthaśāstra* serves the enlightened self-interest of the king, and this is doubtless what is meant when certain Buddhist works call it "the Kṣatriya science" (Kṣatriya-vidyā). But in one sense there is scarcely a more inappropriate designation, for the Kṣatriyas were originally the Vedic nobility, and nothing is further removed from the frank, impassioned and impulsive chiefs of that age than the calculating and devious teachings of the *Kauṭilīya*. Between these two poles lies a profound spiritual revolution, no less revolutionary for having been accomplished very gradually. The revolution was effected by a technique one of whose names is *indriyajaya*, victory over the senses, the assiduous application of which separates the concept from the deed by interposing reflective thought. *Indriyajaya* no doubt is an ascetic technique in origin, and always retains a moral import; but it is no accident that works of statecraft never fail to impress upon the king the need to subdue the senses.

Indriyajaya was at first a concern of ascetics, for whom salvation was essentially a problem of knowledge; but the scholarly Brahmin had well learned through long years of education to postpone gratification of the senses for higher ends. Now Brahmins of learning increasingly shared the counsels of the king, beginning with the *purohita* or house priest who from Vedic times, through the magical lore he had acquired during his studentship, secured the defence of the realm and the victory in battle of his king, to the Brahmin minister, *mantrin,* of later times. Brahmins were absent from the council of nobles who elected and anointed Karṇa as commander-in-chief of the Kaurava forces in the *Mahābhārata* war; but Somadeva, as we have seen, disqualifies the bearer of arms from bearing counsel. Between these two lies a history of the steady aggrandizement of the Brahmin's share in the counselling of kings, in that *mantra* of which *Arthaśāstra* speak so highly. The entire *Kauṭilīya* is *mantra* systematized and written down; it is an expression of the Brahmin minister whose loyalty has been proved, who is utterly devoted to the king, and on whom alone the welfare of the kingdom rests in that dangerous moment when the king dies and the succession must be secured. Rather than Kṣatriya-*vidyā* it might better be called *mantri-vidyā*.

The typical instrument and exponent of *Arthaśāstra* ideas in story is much more often the minister than the king. So frequent is his appearance that we are justified in recognizing a literary type which we may call "the cunning minister." Most kings in literature are provided with such a minister, especially if they have some dirty work to do (if they are good kings their ministers are likely to have more inclination to the *Dharmaśāstras;* in either case the minister gets the credit). The type has certain defining characteristics: he is nearly always a Brahmin; he is learned and of piercing intellect; he is in fact the intelligence behind the throne, a "king concealed within an image" (*bimbāntarito rājā*) as Hemacandra calls Cāṇakya, often deceiving his master in his master's best interest; and true to the doctrines of *Arthaśāstra* which he is fond of quoting, he prefers a stratagem, the more involved and unlikely the better, to the open use of force; his chief attribute is *kauṭilya,* or any other of a number of words meaning "crookedness" but denoting likewise fraud, deceit, cunning or subtlety.

Now this type, however improbable the figure he cuts in the stories, did not arise in a vacuum, from the free play of the imagination alone; he reflected more or less accurately an historical type with whose appearance the origin of *Arthaśāstra* must be closely connected. We see this type first perhaps in the Dīgha Kārāyaṇa and especially in the Vassakāra of the canonical Pali tales, the servants of the Gangetic kingdoms of Kosala and Magadha in the times of the Buddha. The states of this age are already of considerable size—Kosala, the largest, exercised hegemony over an area as large as France—and society was much more complex than in the Vedic age. Yet the kings still show that willingness to yield to impulse characteristic of an earlier stage of development and are quite unable on their own to devise such stratagems as that which Vassakāra, for example, hits upon to overcome the Vajjis for his lord, Ajātasattu of Magadha: he has Ajātasattu pretend to cast him out of favour for befriending the Vajjian interest; he is welcomed by the unsuspecting Vajjians and from this favourable position he succeeds in sowing such dissension amongst them (*mithubheda;* cf. the *suhṛtbheda* of the *Pañcatantra*) that they become fatally vulnerable to Ajātasattu's armies.

It would be extraordinarily difficult and perhaps impossible to prove the historicity of this particular figure but it is in any case reasonable to infer, coincident with the rise of the large Nanda and Mauryan empires, founded by ambitious usurpers of doubtful origin, the growing importance of a new type of statecraft and an enlarged advisory and ministerial class, together with the decay of an older aristocracy and the taming of the folk. Megasthenes attests a disarmed peasantry when he says the farmer ploughs his field unmolested by the clash of armies nearby, to a disarmed nobility when he says that horses and elephants were the monopoly of the Mauryan state, and throughout to a large bureaucracy. It is at this time too that Persian influence, hitherto a matter for pure speculation, becomes visible in the monuments of Mauryan art. One may ask whether there is not a Persian contribution in Indian statecraft.

The greatest of the surviving *Arthaśāstras* is linked, by the name of the greatest of the cunning ministers, Kauṭilya or Cāṇakya, to the Mauryan age. It matters little that this ascription puts the *Kauṭilīya* in its present form several centuries too early: the *Arthaśāstra* tradition was already quite old.

The tradition met with some considerable opposition from more pious circles. It may not be so significant that the Jains condemned the *Kauṭilīya*—they also condemned other Brahmanical works like the *Mahābhārata* and the *Rāmāyaṇa.* The Buddhist *Jātakas* (both in the Pali and in Āryaśūra's version), however, are well aware of a conflict between the requirements of *dharma*, and the teachings of *Arthaśāstra*, which they forthrightly condemn: it is the royal science in which the path of *dharma* is lost through following *artha* (*Jātakamāla* no. 9). In one passage the *Arthaśāstra* of Kauṭilya is alluded to by a play on the connotation of the author's name; so, too, Bāṇa, in his *Kādambarī*, when he has the pious minister warn the prince against the teachings of *Arthaśāstra* with the words:

> Is anything sacred to those (kings) for whom the treatise of crookedness (*Kauṭilyaśāstram*), exceedingly cruel in its precepts, is an authority?—whose teachers are priests with souls grown bloodthirsty from the practice of black magic; whose advisors are ministers whose sole end is to over-reach an enemy; who are infatuated with the Goddess of Fortune, cast off by thousands of kings; who practise the arts of death; and to whom brothers whose hearts are full of natural affection may be murdered.

There is indirect evidence as well that the harsher injunctions of *Arthaśāstra* were not everywhere well received. We have seen that the successors of the *Kauṭilīya* mitigated its harshness in various ways, by abbreviating or omitting the more offensive parts, by appeal to legendary precedent or the principle of need, or by clothing the doctrine in a more aggreeable form such as the fable—the technique of the sugar-coated pill. Further one has the impression that the *Dharmaśāstra* tradition was the stronger of the two, that it developed a more extensive literature and that it held the greater prestige. Its statecraft may have been less original, less consistent and less frank; it may have encouraged supine obedience to an oppressor and provided his ambitions with divine sanctions; but in its greater stress on the *dharmaraja*, the pious king, than the *vijigīṣu* of *Arthaśāstra*, it encouraged as well a gentler and more humane statecraft.

Before bringing these notes to a close I must, however, briefly, make some remarks about what I will call "the royal mystique." By this designation I intend what is not a system of well-defined and well-articulated concepts, but rather a network of interrelated symbols, and whose vehicle, therefore, is not so much the expository treatises of *Arthaśāstra* and *Dharmaśāstra* but works of art such as the courtly epics, royal biographies, and the ornate eulogies found in inscriptions. Dr de Casparis's intriguing paper deals directly with this topic and thus relieves me of the necessity to describe it at length.[5]

Perhaps the simplest way of describing the royal mystique is by providing a glossary of its terms. In the first place the ideal king is a *hero,* whose chariot is unopposed (though chariots may have ceased to be serious instruments of war); who conquers his foes by his unaided valour and heaven by his fame; whose two arms have embraced the earth and made her his lawful wife in the Kṣatriya tradition of marriage by capture or, varying the simile, who has been chosen as her husband by royal fortune in the Kṣatriya tradition of maiden's choice. Never mind that royal fortune is fickle, and will break the match when the whim siezes her, or that she has been enjoyed by thousands of kings in the past and is therefore, as the passage from Bāṇa quoted above implies, hardly the embodiment of virginal purity; there is plenty of time for the king to ponder those truths when he seeks the consolation of philosophy after having lost his throne to a usurper. Then, the king is a *cakravartin,* a universal emperor whose sway extends to the limits of the subcontinent (but, significantly, not beyond), whose victories are righteous in that he reinstates the conquered king as a subordinate, seeking only glory, not plunder and annexation. So potent is the aura surrounding the righteous king that the mere sight of him and of the wheel that proceeds his advance may be sufficient to cause the kings of the earth to submit. This is in the course of his *digvijaya,* his conquest of the four quarters, whereby he circumambulates the subcontinent in the auspicious sunwise direction, receiving submissions. Finally, he celebrates the Vedic royal rites, especially the *aśvamedha* or horse sacrifice, setting a consecrated stallion and a hundred other horses free to wander at will accompanied by an armed guard which enforces the submission required of a king into whose territory the sacrificial horse wanders.

The spirit of the royal mystique thus briefly sketched is archaising, preserving Vedic forms into times which had achieved more modern expressions of religion. It is martial, looking back to the heroic age for its paradigms, and would for that reason better qualify for the epithet of "Kṣatriya science" than does *Arthaśāstra,* if only it were a science, a corpus of doctrine rather than a corpus of symbols. Being symbolic, it is more accessible to the popular imagination

[5]Of the extensive literature on this subject I should also like to mention the excellent article by Professor J. Duncan M. Derrett, "Bhū-bharaṇa, Bhū-pālana, Bhū-bhojana: An Indian Conundrum," *Bull. of S.O.A.S. XXII,* I (1959), 108-123.

than abstractions can ever be, and by virtue of this has penetrated many regions of art and intellect. The story of the life of the Buddha, from the prophecy at his birth that he would become either a *cakravartin* or a *buddha,* to the interment of his ashes under *stūpas* to which a *cakravartin* was also entitled (an honour shared with him by Menander, if we are to credit Plutarch's story) is suffused with the royal mystique.

The poet's job was clear: it was to select those attributes of his patron's character and career which corresponded to the pattern and so arrange and adorn them that the pattern was as exactly reproduced as may be. In this way the king, poor contingent mortal that he was, and as such uninteresting to minds which strove for what is permanent, uncontingent and universal, was rendered immortal. The historian's task is the reverse: to find the suffering flesh behind the golden mask, to dismantle, in fact, the poet's edifice—and his sources are everywhere impregnated with the royal mystique. There is more than one instance in the history books where the poet has triumphed over the historian.

One may ask whether the royal mystique had any practical issue. Could not the kings have followed the grim counsels of *Arthaśāstra* while their poets dressed them up as *cakravartins*? They may have, but difficult as it would be to prove the point, I believe that the royal mystique did affect royal practice. It is true that the inscriptions of the humblest sub-feudatory, who because he cannot defend his lord against an aggressor will readily switch loyalties, nevertheless describe him as chosen by royal fortune for her very own; this is the small change of the inscriptions, much worn by passing from hand to hand. Again, the horse sacrifice was repeatedly performed, but often by kings of an otherwise blinding obscurity, whose pretentions only seem ridiculous to us. Still, the persistence of the *aśvamedha* does show that kings would make some efforts and run some risks to measure up to their portraits; for if the movements of the sacrificial horse could be guided by controlling the movements of the herd, there was yet the danger that it would wander into the lands of a more powerful king, and all the terrible calamities attending a broken sacrifice be rained down upon the unfortunate sacrificer. What of the conquest of the four quarters? Here, too, the poets served their patrons well, supplementing with fiction the sometimes paltry reality, taking the wish for the accomplishment, so that in extreme cases one suspects that delusions of grandeur were found as satisfying (and more easily attained) than the substance of power. But here again I am satisfied that kings aspired to resemble their portraits, that the royal mystique inspired policy. Take the case of Rājendra Coḷa. If a king in the extreme southern tip of India were to conquer the four quarters he would find himself crossing the ocean. Rājendra Coḷa did just that: to the west he moved against the Pāṇḍyas and Keralas, to the south he extended his father's conquests in Ceylon, and eastward he bore Coḷa arms against Śrī Vijaya, the Sumatran maritime empire which controlled the Malacca Straits, though there is no sign that this last expedition had any permanent effect. It is possible to provide each of these campaigns with a material motive—the subjugation of refactory vassals or possible enemies and the control of sea-going commerce—consonant with the teachings of *Arthaśāstra*, and without reference to the royal mystique in which these achievements, once accomplished, are clothed. However that may be, we are on reasonably certain ground when we assert that the expedition to the north had a purely symbolic value. Like the Śrī Vijaya campaign it entailed no lasting territorial or financial gains; but Rājendra's army brought back the sacred waters of the Ganges with which he was anointed and with which he raised a "liquid pillar of victory."[6]

It may even be the case that the royal mystique had a greater influence on the policies of kings than did the *Arthaśāstra* and *Dharmaśāstra* traditions, as the ancient period of Indian history drew to a close. It passed on the martial traditions of a simpler age now long dead; and perhaps in making of war a ritual it served to stultify them by the time the Central Asian invader made his decisive reappearance, now under the bannei of Islam. In any case, it fostered with a congenial imagery the doctrine of the divine appointment and nature of the king. Abroad, this was the Indian contribution to the *devarāja* cults of Southeast Asia; at home, this was the soil of Akbar's imperial cult; and long after the passing of the ancient order, this was perhaps the secret of that grandest of social successes, the Delhi durbar.

[6]Dr John Marr has pointed out to me that the spiritual superiority of the northern direction and the idea of conquest of the north has fascinated Tamil rulers from the Śangam age. For example, the poet states that his Cola patron carved the tiger-crest (or if a Cera, the bow-crest) with his sword on the flank of the Himālaya. Thus Rājendra's Gangetic expedition could equally be looked at in the light of a specifically Tamil royal mystique.

6 Inscriptions and South Asian Dynastic Traditions

J. G. DE CASPARIS

1. Inscriptions and Traditions

By and large inscriptions are the most important source for the early history of South Asia (here used to indicate the whole of the Indo-Pakistani subcontinent and Ceylon) from the 3rd century B.C. to the end of the 13th century A.D. Their particular value is due to the fact that, apart from some easily recognizable forgeries and a few more complicated cases, inscriptions can be taken to date back to the time at which they were promulgated. The date is in most cases accurately defined or can, in most of the remaining cases, be approximated on the basis of an analysis of such details as script, terminology, proper names, composition, etc. In addition, considerable numbers of inscriptions are available throughout the period under discussion for the politically or culturally most active parts of the subcontinent. In contrast, Indian historiographical texts, though of outstanding significance for certain areas, notably Ceylon and Kashmir (as well as Gujarat after A.D. 11th century), have only limited importance for the early history of most of the subcontinent. It is therefore proper to regard such texts as supplementary to the inscriptions which alone can provide us with a reliable historical frame. Other sources, such as coins and foreign notices, are even more limited in scope.

On account of their unique value as sources it is essential for the historian to acquire clear knowledge of the basic aspects of inscriptions, including their traditional contents. He may then hope to ascertain the changes and developments with which he is, above all, concerned. He must be able to discern even the slightest deviations from the norms set by tradition since these are likely to be historically significant. If, for instance, a king is mentioned in a certain inscription without the titles, honorifics and other epithets normally found in the period and in the dynasty to which he belongs then it is obvious that an explanation is required. By taking into account all possible factors the historian will try to decide whether the absence of a traditional title or epithet is due to a change in the position of the ruler (and, if so, how and why), or merely reflects a change in traditional patterns. There are, of course, other possibilities, too. The text may have been carelessly drafted or may belong to an outlying part of the kingdom where the precise protocol was unknown. On the other hand, the inscriptions are themselves essential sources for our knowledge of some aspects of Indian tradition which are insufficiently illustrated by the texts. Some of these form the main subject of this paper. Finally, it should be added that the composition of inscriptions is itself a form of tradition, followed with different intensity in different periods and areas of ancient South Asia. Thus, it started at a relatively late stage in the evolution of South Asian culture as a whole, as no inscriptions earlier than the time of Aśoka (middle of the 3rd century B.C.) have hitherto been discovered. Some areas, such as Sind and Kashmir, are poorly represented, which is remarkable especially for Kashmir with its glorious literary and historiographic tradition. Inscriptions, being a form of tradition, tend to follow their own norms and conventions, some of which are of a traditional nature: benedictory verses, methods of dating, etc.

From these comments it may have become clear that tradition is given a fairly wide scope in the present paper. It is taken to imply: "statements, beliefs or practices, transmitted (especially orally) from generation to generation."[1] Unlike customs, traditions are believed to be rooted in sacred knowledge or, at least, to go back to a remote past whence they have come down to later generations along an uninterrupted line of respectable teachers or other persons of authority. In the ancient Indian context such a definition would include not only the revealed sacred literature (*śruti*) but also other authoritative texts, such as the law books, epics and *purāṇas*. In addition, there are sectarian traditions such as those of the Bhāgavatas, Pāśupatas and, outside the Brahmanic pale, those of Buddhists, Ājīvikas and others. The Tamil Nadu of south India possesses its own vast body of traditional literature: the Śangam texts. As it is often impossible to draw a precise line between the sacred and the profane in South Asia it is not surprising to find that such branches of knowledge as grammar or even sexual love possess long traditions

[1]*Shorter Oxford Dictionary, s.v.*

of their own, which were laid down in authoritative texts at comparatively late stages.

Among the different types of South Asian traditions reflected in the inscriptions only one will be discussed here, namely the dynastic traditions. These are of particular interest as most political, economic and cultural life centred around the royal courts. Particular attention will be paid to those traditions on which only the inscriptions give us rich information, namely those concerning the origin and beginnings of royal dynasties, the succession of kings, and the use of consecration names. Finally, a few miscellaneous traditions, closely associated with the types mentioned above, may be briefly surveyed.

2. The Origin and Beginnings of Dynasties

The most important traditions are those relating to the origin and beginnings of royal dynasties. They had the important function of providing the ruling classes with some kind of legitimacy. In South Asia, as elsewhere, new centres of power emerged from time to time when local élites challenged the established authority and replaced it after some time. Or a collateral branch of a royal family revolted and later succeeded in imposing its supremacy over the earlier ruling line. The gradual expansion of Brahmanic culture into tribal areas (a process that has continued during millenniums and is not yet quite completed) brought new populations within the fold of Hinduism and thus gave rise to new political units. The first beginnings of political power are rarely very impressive and, in some cases, no doubt better ignored. After a few generations, however, the details tend to fade away to be gradually replaced by legendary episodes reflecting the ideals and motives of the later rulers. The nature of these episodes is invariably such that it may provide justification for the leadership. From about A.D. 7th century this was normally achieved by the composition of elaborate genealogies connecting the rulers with either of the great dynasties of the mythical past: the solar or the lunar dynasty. The inscriptions then contain endless lists of names of kings, from the Sun or the Moon to the heroes of the *Rāmāyaṇa* of the *Mahābhārata*, and from there to the immediate predecessors of the king under whose orders the particular inscription was composed. It is, however, striking that, although the solar and lunar dynasties have been known in Sanskrit literature since early times, it is not till after about A.D. 7th century that this type of genealogy becomes a regular feature of the inscriptions. And even from then till the end of the period under consideration there are many examples of unorthodox genealogies. It is the latter that will mainly require our attention. Although the precise interpretation of the traditions concerning the origin and beginnings of dynasties is beset with difficulties, some conclusions seem to emerge. An example may illustrate the problems of interpretation.

Some Pallava inscriptions mention or allude to a tradition about the origin of the dynasty, which is traced back to the union between the Brāhmaṇa hero of the *Mahābhārata:* Aśvatthāman, son of Droṇa, and a Nāgī. Much has been written about this legend,[2] in which many scholars have detected memories of a migration of Brāhmaṇas from the north (especially the areas with which the epic is mainly concerned), who would have intermarried with girls from south Indian families. It is, however, also possible that the story is no more than a sophisticated attempt by a court poet to provide his patron with a respectable lineage by connecting him with the renowned lunar dynasty of Hāstinapura. As the Nāgas are often regarded as the ultimate owners of the land it is plausible that the Nāgī should be taken to symbolize the south Indian roots of the dynasty, which alone could legitimize its authority in the area. It is true that the latter explanation does not necessarily exclude the possibility of an old tradition according to which the ancestors of the ruling king would originally have come from the north. It can be argued that if such a tradition had existed it would have facilitated the task of the court poet, who had merely to adapt and elaborate it for official purposes. Such an interpretation, though by no means necessarily the correct one, would account more satisfactorily for the principal features of the account. On the other hand, this example shows the kind of difficulties that are likely to arise in the analysis of the epigraphic evidence: what initially may have appeared as the account of a picturesque local legend turns out to be a highly so-

[2]According to the Velurpalalayan Plates of Pallava Nandivarman III (see the edition by H.K. Sastri, *South Indian Inscriptions*, II, No. 98, pp. 507f.), v. 6; Vīrakūrcha who "simultaneously with the hand of the daughter of the chief of the serpents, also grasped the complete insignia of royalty and became famous." Cf. R. Gopalan, *History of the Pallavas of South India*, 1928, pp. 50 ff., 196ff. Cf. also L. de la Vallée Poussin, *Dynasties et Histoire de l'Inde*, 1935, pp. 260f.

phisticated effort to legitimize the authority of the ruling dynasty either by the invention of an elaborate lineage or, more probably, by the transformation of a local legend into an account emphasizing the major preoccupations of the later kings. What seems to emerge from this discussion is that, if the account is based on some local legend, it shows us the latter after such a thorough revision that it is impossible to get an idea of its original form.

Whatever its precise origin, the tradition of the Brāhmaṇa and the Nāgī did not remain confined to South Asia. In an inscription of Prakāśadharma Vikrāntavarman I, found near Mi-son E.6 in ancient Campa (present Quang-nam province of Vietnam) and datable to the latter half of A.D. 7th century, the king's lineage is traced back to the mythical founder of the early Indianized kingdom of Fu-nan, the Indian Brāhmaṇa Kauṇḍinya. According to this version Kauṇḍinya came ashore in southern Cambodia, carrying a javelin that had once belonged to Aśvatthāman, son of Droṇa, and had come down to him along an uninterrupted line of generations. After Kauṇḍinya had set foot on Cambodian soil he lifted his javelin and hurled it far away. The centre of his future capital was to be at the precise spot where the javelin descended. At that very moment he had an encounter with Somā, daughter of the Nāga king, who had been watching at a distance. It is from this union that the later rulers of Fu-nan, to which also Prakāśadharma was affiliated, derive their origin. The main features of this tradition are already attested to by K'ang-T'ai, a Chinese envoy reported to have visited Fu-nan in the middle of A.D. 3rd century.[3]

In both versions of the story there is an apparently significant feature: the founder of the dynasty is represented as a Brāhmaṇa whose way of life did not conform to the established pattern for his caste but rather to that of the Kṣatriyas. The choice of such an ancestor reflects the fact that the Pallavas are described in the inscriptions as Brāhmaṇas of the Bhāradvāja *gotra*. The javelin tradition is therefore clearly an attempt at justifying the royal dignity for a Brāhmaṇa clan. The Cambodian version becomes no less

[3]L. Finot, "Inscriptions de Mi-sön," *B.E.F.E.O.*, IV, 1904, p. 923; J. Przyluski, "*La Princesse a l'odeur de poisson et la Nāgī dans les traditions de l'Asie orientale*," *Et. Asiat. E.F.E.O.*, II, 1925, pp. 265-284; Év. Porée-Maspéro, "Nouvelle Etude sur la Nāgī Somā," *Journ. Asiat.*, 1950, pp. 237-267; R.O. Winstedt, "Indra and Saktimuna," *Journ. Mal. Br. R.A.S.*, XXIII, 1950, p. 151f.; J. Boisselier, *La Statuaire du Champa*, 1963, p. 25; Év. Porée-Maspéro, *Etude sur les rites agraires au Cambodge*, I, 1964, pp. 164 ff.

significant if one reflects that the royal family there used to intermarry with the chief priestly families, in particular with that entrusted with the *devarāja* ritual.[4] There can therefore be little doubt that existing traditions were tailored to the requirements of royal families. The local element is not altogether absent. It is symbolized in the figure of the Nāgī in both versions. Nāgas are often regarded and worshipped as the ultimate owners of the land and their favour would be particularly important if, as in the case of both the Pallavas and the rulers of Fu-nan, the founders of ruling families did not originally belong to the country over which they ruled. Finally, it is interesting to note that tradition is here almost materialized as a javelin transmitted from generation to generation from legendary past to historical times.

After this detailed discussion an attempt may be made to classify the traditions concerning the beginnings of royal dynasties. The most promising type of division is probably one based on the strength of non-historical elements, such as those borrowed from the epics and *purāṇas* or from local folklore. Four general groups can be distinguished. The apparently simplest type is that laid down in brief, matter-of-fact genealogies at the beginning of inscriptions or engraved in special seals. The second type consists, in complete contrast, of very elaborate accounts in which some genuine traditions are almost completely submerged in epic and *purāṇic* matter. In the third type epic and *purāṇic* matter still predominates but it is transformed to account for local traditions, ideological factors or other considerations. Finally, in the fourth type, in many respects the most interesting one, the epic or *purāṇic* element is weak or almost negligible, but there is a strong folkloristic tradition which is only partly "sanskritized."

(1) We have many examples of relatively brief genealogies in inscriptions and seals mainly from the period from A.D. 3rd to 8th century. They are invariably retrospective in that they trace back the descent of the particular ruler in whose reign they were issued. They all give a list of kings from generation to generation, including the names of their main queens but excluding any collateral branches to which some of the earlier rulers may have belonged. In addition to names they also give some titles and epithets, but not those of

[4] L.P. Briggs, "The genealogy and successors of Śivāchārya," *B.E.F.E.O.*, XLVI, 1, 1952, pp. 177-185; Cf. G. Coedès, *Les états hindouisés d'Indo-chine et d'Indonésie*, 3rd edition, 1964, pp. 253f.

the exuberant kind usual in inscriptions. Some typical examples are the Gupta seals of Bhitari and Nālandā,[5] as well as the corresponding passages in Gupta inscriptions,[6] the seals of Harṣavardhana,[7] Śarvavarman Maukhari,[8] and Bhāskaravarman[9] at Nālandā, the Haraha inscription of Īśānavarman,[10] the Aphsad inscription of Ādityasena,[11] the Khalimpur inscription of Dharmapāla,[12] and a few others. The absence of supernatural elements or of grossly exaggerated praise creates confidence in their historical reliability as genuine traditions about the previous rulers. The fact that these genealogies occur so often on seals which, attached to royal edicts, guaranteed their authenticity, indicates that the genealogy was meant to emphasize the legitimacy of the king who issued the edict and, consequently, the lawfulness of the order.

Yet, closer examination of these genealogies reveals a curious feature, which has not received the attention it deserves. At the beginning we regularly find a few names (nearly always two) of kings preceding those that are clearly historical. The earliest example is that of the Gupta inscriptions, which mention two names, Gupta (or Śrī Gupta) and Ghaṭotkaca, before the first real Gupta emperor: Candra Gupta I.[6] The inscriptions clearly indicate the lower status of the first two rulers by omitting the full imperial titles as well as the names of their queens. Once one's attention is focused on this feature one can find a number of similar examples. Thus, the Cālukya inscriptions mention the names of Jayasiṃha and Raṇarāga before the first truly historical figure of the founder of Vātāpi: Pulakeśin I.[13] The Pāla inscriptions mention Dayitaviṣṇu and

[5]D.C. Sircar, *Select Inscriptions*, 2nd edition, 1965, pp. 329f. (=Book III, No. 32); Hirananda Sastri, "Nālandā and its Epigraphic Material," *Mem. Arch. Surv.*, LXVI, 1942, pp. 65f. (Pl. VIII, d-e).

[6]Allahabad Pillar Inscription of Samudra Gupta (J.F. Fleet, *Corp. Inscr. Ind.*, III, 1888, pp. 6 ff.), 11. 28f. (Sircar, *Sel. Inscr.*, p. 267); Bilsad Inscription of Kumāra Gupta, I, 11. 1-6 (Sircar, pp. 285 f.); Supia Inscription of Skanda Gupta, 11. 1-8 (Sircar, pp. 317 f.); Bhitari Inscription of Skanda Gupta, 11. 1-8 (Sircar, pp. 321 f.).

[7]Hirananda Sastri, *Ep. Ind.*, XXI, 1931-32, p. 74; "Nālandā," pp. 68 f.

[8]Hirananda Sastri, "Nālandā,", pp. 67 f.

[9]Hirananda Sastri, "Nālandā", p. 69.

[10]*Ep. Ind.*, XIV, 1917-18, pp. 110-120; Sircar, *Sel. Inscr.*, pp. 385-389.

[11]Fleet, *Corp. Inscr. Ind.*, III, 1888, pp. 200 ff.

[12]F. Kielhorn, *Ep. Ind.*, IV, 1896-97, pp. 243-254.

[13]F. Kielhorn, *Ep. Ind.*, VI, 1900-01, pp. 1-12.

Vāpyaṭa as predecessors of Gopāla,[14] the king whom his subjects elected to make an end to the chaos. In a similar manner the Candra inscriptions mention Pūrṇa Candra and Suvarṇa Candra,[15] and the Sena inscriptions Sāmanta Sena and Hemanta Sena.[16] In none of these five cases do we have any inscriptions or coins[17] of these early rulers, while the later inscriptions recording their names never give any details except merely conventional epithets. This suggests that such rulers were no more than local chiefs whose importance became apparent only in retrospect. The real reason why these names were mentioned at all seems to be the need of "anchoring" the real founders in an historical or regional context.

(2) The same aim is achieved by totally different means in the inscriptions of the second group with the very elaborate accounts in which hardly any real historical tradition can be detected among the mythical material. Such genealogies became usual in northern India and in the northern Deccan after about A.D. 7th century. In principle, most historical dynasties were connected with the solar and lunar dynasties of the epics and *purāṇas* via endless lists of mostly mythical, partly entirely fictitious names (or so it seems to us). Examples abound especially with the proliferation of royal dynasties in the 10th to 12th centuries. Thus, the Yādavas of Devagiri in Maharashtra trace their ancestry back to Yadu of the lunar dynasty, one branch of which would have migrated to the Deccan.[18] Most of these genealogies have little general interest, except in so

[14]Khalimpur Inscription (see footnote 12 above), vv. 2-3.

[15]For the Candra inscriptions Cf. the discussion and references by A.M. Chowdhury, *Dynastic History of Bengal*, 1967, pp. 154-189. The first king with full imperial titles is Trailokya Candra.

[16]Deopara Inscription of Vijaya Sena, *Ep. Ind.*, I, pp. 305 ff., especially vv. 5 ff. Sāmanta Sena is said to have retired to an *āśrama* on the banks of the Ganges after a career of warfare in Karṇātaka. This last example is different from the others in that it gives concrete details about the two first rulers, but it agrees in omitting any references to real rulership for Samanta and Hemanta Sena. It is also much later than the others.

[17]Ghaṭotkaca is a possible exception, although it seems at present more likely that not only the Basarh seal with the inscription *śrı-Ghaṭotkacaguptasya* but also the "St. Petersburg" coin with *ghaṭoguptaḥ* should be attributed to Ghaṭotkaca Gupta of the Tumain inscription rather than to the father of Candra Gupta I, whose name is spelt without *-gupta* in the inscriptions.

[48] A.S. Altekar, "The Yādavas of Seunadesa," in Yazdani's *History of the Deccan*, II, 1960, pp. 515f. For the complete genealogy Cf. for example, L.D. Barnett, "The Thana Plates of the time of Yadava Ramacandra," *Ep. Ind.*, XIII, 1922-23, pp. 198-206.

far as the choice of particular legendary ancestors may give us clues about prevalent attitudes among the later rulers. Such attitudes are, however, more pronounced in the case of the less stereotyped accounts.[19]

Owing to the tremendous prestige of the epics and *purāṇas* one would have expected the great majority of dynastic traditions to correspond to the norms laid down in these authoritative texts. Yet, there are not so many examples before the 10th century, and even in later times there are still a few examples where the influence of the epics is apparently weak, for example, in the Sena inscriptions. This point may not be without interest as it can give an impression of the influence of texts on prevalent concepts and attitudes of ancient Indian government.

(3) There are a small, but interesting, number of dynastic traditions in which epic and *purāṇic* material, though predominating, is combined with other elements. The Pratihāras of Kanauj and Mandor traced their lineage back to Lakṣmaṇa, Rāma's youngeı brother, who could be called his "doorkeeper" (Pratihāra).[20] A completely different explanation of the name Pratihāra is offered in the Sangam plates of the Raṣṭrakūṭa king Amoghavarṣa I (A.D. 871), in which the term is taken to reflect the Pratihāra ruler's subordinate status in respect of Rāṣṭrakuta Dantidurga (C.A.D. 754).[21] It is now believed that neither explanation is correct and that the name represents the sanskritization of a tribal or ethnic designation, possibly connected with the area round Mount Abu (Arbuda), Rajasthan. Thus transformed, the court poets of the Pratihāras could use it as a link with the legendary solar family while their southern rivals interpreted it as evidence for their earlier subordinate status.[22]

The Pallava tradition of Aśvatthāman and the Nāgī, discussed

[19]It would seem, for instance, that the well known reference to Gopāla being chosen as a king to make an end to the *matsyanyāya* (Khalimpur inscription, v. 4) reflects certain preoccupations in the reign of Dharmapāla. It may have been an attempt at legitimizing the rule of the Pālas by basing it upon the Buddhist tradition of the Mahāsammata (Aggaññasuttanta of the *Dıghanikāya*). The Khalimpur inscription itself is clearly Buddhist.

[20]Cf. the Yodhpur Prasasti of Bāuka (*Ep. Ind.*, XVIII, 1925-26, pp. 87-92), v. 4; Gwalior Prasasti of Mihira-Bhoja (*ibid.*, pp. 99-114), v. 3. Also B.N. Puri, *The History of the Gurjara-Pratihāras*, 1957, pp. 19f.

[21]Cf. the Sanjan Copper-Plate Inscription of Amoghavarṣa I, *Ep. Ind.*, XVIII, 1925-26, pp. 235-257, v. 9.

[22]Cf. especially B.N. Puri, *op. cit.*, pp. 1-18. For "sanskritization" Cf. M.N. Srinivas, *Social Change in Modern India*, 1969, pp. 1-45; F.G. Bailey, *Tribe,*

earlier in a different context, is essentially of the same type, though somewhat farther removed from the epical account than the Pratihāra tradition.[23]

(4) Four examples of the last type, which is by far the most interesting, may be discussed.

First, the Buguda plates (probably A.D. 8th century) give us the following story about the origin of the Śailodbhava dynasty of Kongoda (Orissa):

There was a famous personage among the people of Kalinga (Kaliṅgajanatāsu) whose name was Pulindasena. This man, although endowed with many personal virtues, for example, a lofty stature, strong arms and a broad chest, did not covet sovereignty for himself (*neṣṭaṃ bhuvo maṇḍalam*), but he worshipped Brahman so that the god might be pleased to create a fit ruler for Kalinga. The god granted his wish and created, apparently out of pieces of rock (*śilā-śakala*), the lord Śailodbhava, who thus became the founder of a distinguished dynasty (*parikalpita-sad-vamśah*).[24]

This is certainly a curious tradition. The term Pulinda is used in India and Ceylon to denote various primitive forest tribes. However gifted this particular tribesman may have been he was hardly the kind of man whom the later kings of Kalinga would have been proud to count as their ancestor. And, indeed, this man of the jungle did not become the progenitor of the illustrious Śailodbhavas but merely prayed for one in order that Brahman might create a hero out of pieces of rock. It is difficult to understand Pulindasena's function in the legend, unless it is based on an earlier version in which Pulindasena was the actual founder of the dynasty. Later, when a more respectable pedigree was required, the legend was sanskritized and the part of the creator transferred to Brahman. Perhaps the most striking feature of the tradition, however, is the strength of the local attachment of the dynasty, symbolized not only in the figure of

Caste and Nation, 1960, p. 188, who defines the term as "social climbing by conforming to an all-India standard of respectable behaviour."

[23]Cf. footnote 2 above.

[24]I quote from R.G. Basak, *History of North-Eastern India* (*c. A.D. 320-760*), 1934, p. 172, based on the edition and translation by F. Kielhorn, "The Buguda Plates of Mādhavavarman," *Ep. Ind.*, III, 1894-95, pp. 41-46. Cf. also R. D. Banerji, *History of Orissa*, I, 1930, pp. 120 ff. There are still some tribal communities left in Orissa till the present day. One of these, the Kond in Kondmal in the hills west of Bhubaneswar, is the subject of F.G. Bailey's above mentioned study (*Tribe, Caste and Nation*).

Pulindasena but even more convincingly in the rocks out of which the actual progenitor was made.

Secondly, the inscriptions of the Śilāhāras of Konkana (Maharashtra) present an interesting tradition about the origin of their dynasty. Their lineage is traced back to Jīmūtavāhana, lord of the Vidyādharas, who rescued the Nāga king Śankhacūḍa from Garuḍa by offering the celestial eagle his own body instead.[25] It is quite clear that the legend represents first of all an attempt at explaining the name of the dynasty, which can be interpreted as "food (*āhāra*) of (on) a rock (*śilā*)" or as "rock food." Etymologically there are at least two other possible explanations of the name. One could, for instance, translate it as "fetching (*ā-hāra*) stones (*śilā*)" or as "stone necklace (*śilā-hāra*)." It is, however, as Fleet has suggested,[26] likely that the name represents the sanskritization of Kannaḍa Seḷaṛa. In that case one could think of even more possibilities of sanskritizing and interpreting the name. The final choice cannot have been arbitrary, although it may not now be possible to find out all its reasons. The story of the offering of one's own body is well known, above all from the moving Śibi-*jātaka*.[27] In any case, it has a strong Buddhist flavour, by no means surprising as the Śilāhāras ruled in an area which was once a great centre of Buddhism. Here again we find a strong emphasis on "stone" or "rock," no doubt reflecting the local attachment of the dynasty.

Thirdly, there is the legend of the "fire pit" (*agnikuṇḍa*), about which so much has been written that there is no need for a detailed discussion here.[28] Only a few points need be noted. It is quite clear that the original story has been much more intensively sanskritized than the traditions discussed above. The spiritual ancestor of the dynasty is, in fact, one of the great Vedic seers, Vasistha, while the creation out of the fire pit of the four eponymic heroes of the Rajput dynasties takes place during the performance of a Vedic sacrifice.

[25]F.D.K. Bosch, *De legende van Jīmūtāvahana in the Sanskrit-litteratuur*, Leiden, 1914. The legend, which is probably best known from Harṣa's *Nāgānanda* and from the *Kathāsaritsāgara*, is based on a Buddhist *avadāna*.

[26]J.F. Fleet, *Dynasties of the Kanarese districts*, 1896, p. 536.

[27]Sibi Jataka (No. 499), Fausboll (ed.), *P.T.S.* IV, pp. 401-412. The Śibi (sivi) king gave his eyes to Sakka, disguised as a Brāhmaṇa. Cf. the story of Mānavamma in the *Cūlavaṃsa*, LVII, vv. 4 ff.

[28]The legend is recorded in very late texts such as the *Pṛithvīrāja Rāsau*, as well as in inscriptions of the Paramāras of Dhārā. Cf. G. Buhler, "The Udaipur praśāsti of the kings of Mālva," *Ep. Ind.*, I, 1893-94, pp. 222-238, vv. 5-7.

Here, again, the mountain is quite prominent: the Arbuda (Mount Abu), symbolizing the local roots of the dynasties concerned. A comparison with the dynastic legends of the Śailodbhavas and Śilāhāras, with which it has many basic features in common, seems to invalidate the earlier view that the *agnikuṇḍa* tradition commemorates an ancient ritual by which foreign tribes could be accepted into Hindu society.[29]

Fourthly, it may be useful to consider another dynastic tradition in close connexion with the foregoing examples, although it is not reflected in inscriptions. It shows some interesting and uncommon features. This is the account of Paṇḍukābhaya, narrated in the *Mahāvaṃsa* and other texts of Ceylon.[30] It reads like a fairy tale. Paṇḍukābhaya, though of royal blood, was conceived in secret. Following a prophecy that the boy would later kill his uncles for the sake of the throne he was brought up far from the capital. The uncles did all they could to find the boy but their efforts proved unsuccessful. When he grew up Paṇḍukābhaya became a rebel, recruited an army, or rather a band of followers, which made the countryside unsafe. This brought him into conflict with the army but Paṇḍukābhaya proved victorious and, after many complicated intrigues, later acceded to the throne.

In this account one can detect different influences. The Kṛṣṇa legend may have been its main source of inspiration, although some details can be traced back to *Jātakas*. The most interesting aspect of the tradition is, however, that it may seem, at first sight, far removed from the lofty ideals of *dharma*. Yet, it somehow reflects the power of the laws of *karman,* closely associated with *dharma*. Throughout the *Mahāvaṃsa* account one is aware that Paṇḍukābhaya is "chosen" to become king—chosen not by any human or divine agency but by the inescapable power of *karman*.

Some elements of the Paṇḍukābhaya tradition can be found back outside Ceylon. The Talgunda inscription of Śāntivarman of the Kadamba dynasty contains an interesting account of the rise

[29]James Tod, *Annals and Antiquities of Rajasthān*, 1829, pp. 89 ff.; V.A. Smith, *The Early History of India*, 4th edition, 1924, pp. 422-431. V.S. Pathak, *Ancient Historians of India*, 1966, pp. 157-172.

[30]*Mahāvaṃsa*, chapters IX and X; *Vaṃsatthappakāsinī*, G.P. Malalasekera (ed.), I, 1935, pp. 274-297; Cf. L. Perera in H.C. Ray and others, *History of Ceylon*, Vol. I, Pt. I, 1959, pp. 105-111. It is interesting and probably significant that the *Dīpavaṃsa* and the *Sāmantapāsādikā* give only a brief account of the reign of this ruler, whom they call Pakuṇḍa. Cf. especially L. Perera, *op. cit.*

to power of Mayūraśarman, the founder of the dynasty.[31] Mayūraśarman was a Brāhmaṇa attached to the court of the Pallavas of Kāñcī. After a quarrel with the king he left the capital and sought refuge in the forest. There he gradually became powerful (the inscription does not explain how) and levied tribute from the Bṛhadbāṇas [32] and other kings (or rather tribal chiefs). He successfully resisted all efforts by the Pallavas to bring his activities under control till he was recognized as an independent ruler of Kuntala (northern Mysore). In contrast to most of the other traditions the account of Mayūraśarman's rise to power gives the impression of being an authentic tradition. The sequence of events seems plausible in the known historical context of about A.D. 4th century. The impression of reliability is further strengthened by the relative precision of the account of the militant scholar. Just before this important account in the Talgunda inscription there are a few less factual features, such as the verses dealing with the unique Kadamba tree after which the family was named. Comparison with the other dynastic traditions tends to show that this tree is not merely a picturesque detail added to explain the name of the dynasty but rather a sophisticated device by which the family is "anchored" to the land which they ruled. It thus serves the same function as the mountain or rock in the traditions of the Śailodbhavas, Śilāhāras and *agnikuṇḍa* dynasties. Combined with the illustrious ancestry of Mayūraśarman,[33] his prowess and, especially, the recognition of his independence by the then prevalent power of the Pallavas, this feature gives the Kadambas a very strong claim to legitimacy.

This survey may have given as impression of the great variety of traditions concerning the origin of royal dynasties. This diversity stands in sharp contrast to the theories laid down in the *Pūrāṇas*, according to which there are only two legitimate dynasties: those of the sun and the moon. The analysis shows the influence of the doctrine but mainly at a later stage when the existing traditions were gradually harmonized with the texts. Some of the compromises

[31]D.C. Sircar, *Select Inscriptions*, 2nd edition, 1965, III, No. 69, pp. 474-79, pp. 4-24, where also earlier editions are mentioned.

[32]They are located in Perumbāṇappāḍi, "the Great Bāṇa country," north of the Palar river. Cf. K.A. Nilakanta Sastri, *The Cōḷas*, 2nd edition, 1955, p. 126.

[33]According to the inscriptions he belonged to the *Mānavyagotra*. The Talgunda inscription (V. 19) suggests that the Pallavas at one stage made him an army commander and provincial governor, taking into account his energy and high descent (*labdhvā pratāpānvayāv-api*).

were quite complicated, with strong emphasis on local roots no less clearly pronounced than descent from one of the illustrious royal families of the mythical past. Although the results show the strength of local traditions as well as the gradual predominance of the scriptural tradition one may doubt whether the elaborate accounts in the inscriptions can still be regarded as traditions. But, whatever their origin, once they were adopted they grew into traditions within the individual dynasties, where they were handed down from generation to generation with only minor alterations.

3. Royal Succession

The ancient Indian texts give us little precise information on the laws or rules on which royal succession was based. This important topic receives remarkably little attention in the *Arthaśāstra,* which discusses it *en passant* twice, in different contexts. Both passages suggest a certain flexibility, though clear preference is given to the eldest son.[34] The *Agnipurāṇa* is somewhat more explicit but the rules given there lack precision.[35] The vagueness of the most authoritative texts suggests that the succession to the throne was based less on the doctrines laid down in the *śāstras* than on tradition or, rather, traditional practices in vogue in particular areas or within individual royal dynasties.

For Ceylon it has been argued that there was, at least during the Anurādhapura period (until A.D. 11th century), a real "law of succession" which prescribed that the royal office should devolve upon the deceased ruler's younger brother, if there was one. Only after the death of the last brother did the eldest son of the eldest brother ascend the throne.[36] The are, however, sufficient excep-

[34] *Arthaśāstra*, I, 17, 52: *anyatrāpada aiśvaryam jyeṣṭhabhāgi tu pūjyate*, "except in case of a calamity, sovereignty passing on to the eldest son is praised" (R.P. Kangle, *The Kauṭilīya Arthaśāstra*, II, 1963, p. 48). The use of *pūjyate*, "is praised" suggests that it is a practice to be recommended without however being a hard and fast rule. The topic is discussed again in V, 6, 18-44, from the point of view of the minister but the latter discussion is less interesting except in so far as it may suggest considerable flexibility in the application of the rules (if there were any).

[35] Cf. B.B. Mishra, *Polity in the Agnipurāṇa*, 1965, pp. 46-51. Here the topic is discussed in connexion with the royal consecration ceremony.

[36] W. Geiger, *Cūlavaṃsa* Translation, I, Introduction, pp. XV-XXIV; W.

tions to make the term "law" seem inaccurate, the more so as there is no scriptural authority for it. The practice is therefore to be regarded as a tradition that was normally allowed because it was in harmony with Sinhalese social order.

If one accepts the principle of primogeniture on the basis of the *Arthaśāstra* (*aiśvaryam jyeṣṭhabhāgi*), one has to account for a surprising number of exceptions, among them, perhaps not unexpectedly, some of the greatest names of ancient India, for example, Aśoka, Samudra Gupta, Candra Gupta II, Skanda Gupta, Harṣavardhana of Kanauj, Pulakeśin II Cālukya, Vikramāditya VI Cālukya, and Harṣa of Kashmir. In many cases we have evidence or indications of a real struggle for power. It would be incorrect to regard these cases as examples of unlawful or illegitimate succession as long as we have no evidence that they were, in ancient India, condemned as contrary to *dharma*. The laws of *karman*, as well as the proverbial fickleness of the goddess of royal sovereignty, or even pure fate, provided full justification.[37]

The inscriptions establish, however, that, in the absence of a law of succession, there were strong guiding principles which were rarely disregarded. The succcssor should not only be closely related to the ruling king but should also be approved by him. In any case he should belong to the royal clan, or in some cases, to one of the acknowledged royal clans.

It has been noticed above that the official genealogies found in inscriptions are invariably retrospective and do not take collateral branches into account. What is emphasized is that the king who issues the edict is a descendant from the founder of the dynasty via a recognized line of rulers and their chief queens. It is never stated that the successor is the eldest son of the previous ruler, but it is usually noted that he had been "approved by him" (*tat-pāda-pa-*

Geiger, *Culture of Ceylon in mediaeval times*, by H. Bechert (ed.), 1960, pp. 114-117. This type of succession is occasionally found elsewhere, too, notably among the Maitrakas of Valabhī, where Bhaṭārka is succeeded by his four sons in succession. Harṣa's succeeding his elder brother Rājyavardhana at Sthāṇvīśvara (Cf. D. Devahuti, *Harsha, A Political Study*, 1970, pp. 69 ff.) may perhaps be added, although this rather seems an isolated type of succession among the Vardhanas.

[37]The *Rājataraṅgiṇī* is the most interesting text in this respect. Cf. especially the analysis by A.L. Basham, "The Kashmir Chronicle," *Historians of India, Pakistan and Ceylon*, 1961, p. 64. Kalhaṇa's emphasis on *daiva* suggests that this author was well aware of the absurdity of so much that happened in history.

rigṛhīta)[38] as the future successor. This may have implied a kind of blessing but in some cases it involved formal consecration as a crown prince during his father's reign.[39]

A much more stringent principle was that the successor should belong to the royal clan or, in some cases, one of the royal clans. This follows directly from the form of the genealogies in the inscriptions, which invariably emphasizes that the king issuing the order is a direct descendant from the founder of the dynasty. It is more clearly reflected in the fact that the relationship of the particular king with the founder of the dynasty is often expressed with such vague terms as *tad-vaṃśa-ja*, "born in his clan."[40] The clearest indication, however, is the use in inscriptions of names of clans in the genitive plural, often preceding the name of the individual king. A characteristic example is found in the Chandravalli stone inscription of Kadamba king Mayūraśarman (c.A.D. 330-360) beginning with: *Kadaṃbāṇaṃ Mayūrasammaṇa vinimmiaṃ taṭākaṃ*, "By Mayūraśarman of the Kadambas (this) irrigation reservoir was

[38]These genealogies are often as interesting for what they omit as for what they mention. Instead of *tatpādaparigṛhīta* one finds more often *tatpādānudhyāta*. The best explanation of the difference between the two terms is that brought forward by D.C. Sircar, *Indian Epigraphy*, 1965, pp. 349-351.

[39]For the *yauvarājyābhiṣeka* Cf. B.B. Mishra, *Polity in the Agnipurāna*, 1965, pp. 46ff. It is well known that *yuvarāja* consecration was traditional within some dynasties, such as that of the Colas, where regnal years were reckoned from this ceremony, not from the date of accession. Thus, the inscriptions of Rājādhirāja II are dated in regnal years from A.D. 1163, although the reign of Rājarāja II continued probably till A.D. 1173 (K.A. Nilakanta Sastri, *The Cōlas*, 2nd edition, 1955, pp. 359 f.). Similarly, the regnal years of Vijayabāhu I are reckoned from 1055/56 when Kitti/Vijayabāhu became king of Rohaṇa, not from 1070; Cf. C.W. Nicholas in H.C. Ray, *History of Ceylon*, II, 1960, p. 423. In the latter case, no particular consecration ceremony is mentioned in the *Cūlavaṃsa*, but he is given the name Vijayabāhu from then on (Chapter LVIII, 1), although he is still mentioned as *yuvarāja* (Cv. LVIII, 1) and *mahādipāda* (Cv. LVIII, 7) but in the very next verse (8) as king (*rājā*).

[40]This is, in fact, the most frequently found method, often involving a huge leap in time. Thus, in the above mentioned Buguda plates of Mādhavavarman (*Ep. Ind.*, III, 1894-95, pp. 41-46) we read after the legend of the foundation of the dynasty in V. 6: *Śailodbhavasya kulajo Raṇabhīta āsīt*, "born in the family of Śailodbhava (there) was Ranabhita." In the Gwalior Inscription of Mihira-Bhoja (by R.C. Majumdar (ed.), *Ep. Ind.* XVIII, pp. 99-114), V. 4, we read, after the praise of Lakṣmaṇa, *tadvanśe* [*sic*]....*devo Nāgabhaṭah purātanamuner babhūva*, "in his family, that of the ancient sage, there was king Nāgabhaṭa(I)." It is not until much later that we find the endless lists of names.

(caused to be) made."[41] In this case it is quite clear that the Kadambas are not a tribe or a people but a clan, usually indicated as *Kadamba-kula*. Another royal clan is that of the Vākāṭakas, where the inscriptions contain expressions such as *Vākāṭakānāṃ mahārāja-śrī-Rudrasenāgramahiṣī*, "Chief queen of His Majesty, king Rudrasena of the Vākāṭakas." Similarly one finds: *Palavānaṃ Sivakhadavammo*, "Śivaskandavarman of the Pallavas." The names of the Guptas, Maitrakas, Mukharas (Maukharis) and others are used in the same manner. An early example occurs in one of the Barhut inscriptions (B.C. 1st century), where a foundation takes place *suganaṃ raje*, "in the kingdom of the Śuṅgas."[42]

In ancient Ceylon the king should belong to one of three clans, preferably the "royal clan" (*rāja-vaṃsa*), also called the Kāliṅga clan, traced back to the semi-legendary Paṇḍu Vāsudeva, who would have come from Kaliṅga. Thus, Niśśaṅkamalla (1187-1196), though apparently unrelated to any of the previous rulers of the Island and presumably belonging to a minor branch of the Gāṅgas of Orissa, bases his claim to the throne of Ceylon on his descent from Okāvas, that is, Īkṣvāku, as the kings of the royal clan did. Accordingly he is given the title *Lakdivpolo-yoma parapuren himi*, "lord of the maiden, the earth of Laṅka, by right of descent." The term *parapuru*, corresponding to Sanskrit *paramparā*, is significant as it implies an uninterrupted line.[43]

The idea that sovereignty was sometimes considered to belong to a royal clan rather than to an individual king is clearly mentioned in the *Arthaśāstra*, where it is stated in connexion with attitudes to be adopted towards royal princes: "Or, the kingdom should belong to the (royal) family; for a family oligarchy is difficult to conquer, and remains on earth for ever without (having to face) the danger

[41] D.C. Sircar, *Sel. Inscr.*, p. 473.

[42] Poona Copper Plate Inscription of Prabhāvatī Guptā, *Ep. Ind.*, XV, 1922-23, pp. 41 ff. (1st Plate, 1.9) and *Sel. Inscr.*, p. 436; Hirahadagalli Plates of Śivaskandavarman, *Ep. Ind.*, I, 1893-94, pp. 5 ff. and *Sel. Inscr.*, p. 462 (1st Plate, 2nd Side, 1.2); B. Barua and K.G. Sinha, *Barhut Inscriptions*, 1926, pp. 1 ff. and *Sel. Inscr.*, p. 87.

[43] S. Paranavitana, "The Dambulla Rock Inscription of Niśśaṅkamalla," *Ep. Zeyl*, I, 19, pp. 121-135. On the so-called "law of succession," Cf. W. Geiger *Culavaṃsa Translation*, I, 1928, Introduction, pp. XV-XXIV; W. Geiger, *Culture of Ceylon in Mediaeval Times*, 1960, pp. 111-113; Lakshman S. Perera, "The royal lineage in the *praśastis* of the 8th-10th inscriptions," *Ceyl. Hist. Journ.*, II, 1952, pp. 229-236. For a different but unconvincing view Cf. M.B. Ariyapala, "Succession to the throne in Ancient Ceylon," *Univ. Ceyl. Rev.*, XII, 1954, pp. 195-216.

of a calamity befalling the king."[44] The precise translation of this verse raises problems, especially the meaning of *kula-saṃgha*. It is quite clear that this term does not indicate the oligarchies or republics discussed in Book XI, where they are denoted as *saṃgha*, but rather a "ruling council consisting of all male members of the royal family."[45] If this interpretation is adopted the passage does not necessarily refer to the tribal republics alone but would include also some monarchies such as the Nanda kingdom.[46] For a relatively late south Indian dynasty, the Hoysaḷas of Dvārasamudra, it has been pointed out that "the joint family to which the king, like his subjects belonged, had the *rājya*, or kingdom, as a joint family asset, in which all male members of the undivided family took a right by birth."[47]

4. CONSECRATION NAMES OF KINGS

The texts, including the *Dharmaśāstras* and the *Arthaśāstra*, give us little idea of the principles that determined the choice of consecration names of kings. According to such texts personal names, in general, reflect the *varṇas* to which their bearers belong: names ending in *-śarman* for Brāhmaṇas, those in *-varman* for Kṣatriyas and so on. The inscriptions make it clear, however, that while *-varman* is used by many royal dynasties (including also the Pallavas and Kadambas who were Brāhmaṇas) other name endings are characteristic of particular dynasties. In accordance with this usage we speak of the Guptas, Vardhanas, Pālas, Candras, Devas, Senas, Khaḍgas, Bhañjas, Karas, Nandas, Dhavalas and a few others. Except for the Vardhanas, who belong to the Punjab, this usage is limited to eastern India, in particular Bengal and Orissa. It would therefore

[44] Kangle's translation of *Arthaśāstra*, I, 17, 53.

[45] R.P. Kangle, *The Kauṭilīya Arthaśāstra*, II, Translation, note 52 to p. 48, rightly rejects for *kula-saṃgha* the interpretation as a council formed by a number of noble families (as in the "republics"). There is therefore no inconsistency between this passage, suggesting the invincibility of the *kula-saṃgha* and Book XI explaining the methods of bringing the "republics" under control.

[46] This seems to be the only reasonable interpretation of the twenty-two years' rule of the Nine Nandas (*Mahāvaṃsa*, V, 15; *Mahābodhivaṃsa*, Strong (ed.), 1891), although this is not in agreement with *kamen' eva* and its interpretation as *vuddha-paṭipātiyā* in the *Ṭīkā* (*Vaṃsatthappakāsinī*, G.P. Malalasekera (ed.), I, 1935, p. 179).

[47] J. Duncan M. Derrett, *The Hoysaḷas*, p. 178.

seem that these particular dynastic traditions have a local basis. They stand in contrast to other parts of the sub-continent where, at most, a preference for certain types of names is apparent.

Another interesting traditional feature, in this case limited to the east coast of south India and Ceylon, is the use of alternating consecration names. Thus we find among the eastern Gāṅgas of Kaliṅga that the names Anantavarman and Devendravarman alternate; among the Coḷas: Rājakēsari and Parakēsari; among the Pāṇḍyas: Jaṭāvarman and Māravarman; in Ceylon: Abā Salamevan and Siri-saṅgabō (Pali: Abhaya Silāmeghavaṇṇa and Siri-saṅghabodhi); finally, but less regularly, among the eastern Cālukyas: Viṣṇuvardhana and Vijayāditya.[48]

It is curious that both the use by kings of one dynasty of the same name endings and that of alternating names are limited to, or, at least, clearly predominant in eastern India—but the former in its northern section (Bengal and Orissa), the latter southward from Orissa. This strongly suggests that both must have a local basis and may reflect regional traditions of name-giving among certain sections of the population. As little serious research on proper names in ancient India has hitherto been carried out it is not possible to understand the full implications of these data. A most promising survey has been made by D.C. Sircar, who points out the popularity of family names in eastern India and calls attention to the gap between the theories set out in the *śāstras* and the data found in the inscriptions.[49]

5. Some Miscellaneous Traditions Concerning Kingship

In the last part of this paper it may be useful to mention briefly some other traditions closely associated with the royal dynasties, on which the inscriptions supply interesting information. As most of these data are well known there is no need for a detailed discussion.

There are a number of instances of revival of older dynasties after a (sometimes very long) period in which nothing is heard of them.

The Cālukyas of Kalyāṇī trace their lineage back to the Cālukyas

[48] In the last case, that of the Cālukyas of Andhra Pradesh, it seems as though the title alternates in generations. Cf. the table in K.A. Nilakanta Sastri, *A History of South India*, 1955, pp. 198 f.

[49] *Indian Epigraphy*, 1965, pp. 420-425.

of Aihole Vātāpi in spite of a gap of more than two centuries during which the area over which they had ruled was in control of the Rāṣṭrakūṭas of Mānyakheṭa (Malkhed). The connexion is made not via the last king of Vātāpi overthrown by the Rāṣṭrakūṭas, but via a certain Bhīma, a son of king Vijayāditya (A.D. 696-733), who did not, however, reign himself.[50]

The rule of the great Mauryas came to an end in about 184 B.C. Then, after a gap of seven centuries, we get information about a long line of Mauryas of Koṅkana from A.D. 6th to 11th century. Another line of Mauryas, perhaps related to the above, is known from southern Rajasthan and Malwa in A.D. 7th and 8th centuries. It can hardly be a coincidence that there was also a king Candragupta among the latter.[51] In Ceylon, too, there was a Maurya (Moriya) dynasty, members of which occupied the throne of Anurādhapura in parts of the 5th, 6th and 7th centuries. Traditionally, these Moriyas are descendants of some of the princes that accompanied the Bodhi tree to the island.[52]

The dynasty of the Imperial Guptas was continued by the Guptas of Magadha (A.D. 6th to 8th century) but the precise relationship, if any, is unknown. Even as late as the 12th and 13th centuries we get evidence for a Gutta dynasty of Guttal on the Tungabhadra in south India. Although the dynastic name is "prakritized" there is no doubt that these Guttas regarded themselves as successors of the great Guptas. They trace their descent back to Candra Gupta through Vikramāditya of Ujjayinī, use the Garuḍa banner (*Garuḍa-dhvaja*), and adopt the titles *Ujjayinī-pura-varādhīśvara* and *Pāṭali-pura-varādhī-śvara*, recalling the two known Gupta capitals.[53]

An interesting dynastic tradition, not limited to any particular area or period, is the close relationship between the king and the

[50]See *The Early History of the Deccan*, G. Yazdani (ed.), 1960, in particular, Part IV; K.A. Nilakanta Sastri, "The Chālukyas of Bādāmī," I, pp. 201-246; Part VI; K.A. Nilakanta Sastri, "The Chālukas of Kalyāṇī and the Kalachuris of Kalyāṇī," I, pp. 315-468; Part VII: K.A. Nilakanta Sastri, and N. Venkaṭaramayya, "The Eastern Chālukyas and the Chālukyas of Vemulavāḍa," II, pp. 469-512.

[51]D.C. Sircar, "A fragmentary Maurya Inscription from Mathurā," *Ep. Ind.*, XXXII, 1957-58, p. 207.

[52]W.A. Jayawardana in H.C. Ray (ed.), *History of Ceylon*, I, 1959, pp. 294f; W. Geiger, *Culture of Ceylon in Mediaeval Times*, H. Bechert (ed.), 1960, pp. 111-113; H. Ellawala, *Social History of Ceylon*, 1969, p. 32.

[53]Cf. D.C. Sircar, *Sel. Inscr.*, 2nd edition, 1965, note 2 to p. 264.

goddess Lakṣmī-Śrī, who became the real symbol of royal majesty. In accordance with this conception we find the goddess depicted on the reverse of coins from the Gupta period. This symbolic value is expressed even more clearly by terms in the inscriptions such as *śrī-hasta* or *śrī-nirīksita*, used to confirm the authenticity of grants.[54] From the Gupta period onwards we regularly find in inscriptions more or less elaborate similes representing the goddess as the king's mistress. Following the ancient epic tradition of the *svayaṃvara*, she chooses herself the king on which she bestows her favours but, fickle by nature, she easily abandons him for a more promising partner. Only the strongest kings may hope to keep her as a faithful spouse. This theme is endlessly elaborated in inscriptions, partly perhaps because it enabled the poets to show off their skill. On the other hand it seems that it was in some cases used as a deliberate device to explain, or even to condone, serious irregularities, elsewhere attributed to *karman* or fate (*daiva*). One of the earliest and best known examples occurs in Skanda Gupta's Junagarh inscription (A.D. 457), where it is said of the king that Lakṣmī chose him herself, discarding all the other princes.[55]

It may be useful to call attention here to a much more elaborate version of this tradition, found not in an inscription but in a literary text. In a most stimulating analysis of the *Harṣacarita* V.S. Pathak has demonstrated that this text represents the relationship between Harṣavardhana of Kanauj and his sister, who bears the symbolic name of Rājyaśrī, as one that connoted Harṣa's attainment of sovereignty. This brother-sister relationship, of which no other examples are known to me, somehow seems to render Harṣa's position stronger as it excludes the fickleness usually associated with sovereignty.[56]

Another matter on which inscriptions provide more interesting information than texts is that concerning traditional South Asian ideas of the shape and extent of the kingdom. According to the well known *maṇḍala* concept of the *Arthaśāstra* the kingdom is naturally surrounded by several circles of other kingdoms, each standing in different relationships to the central one. Some are allies, others

[54]D.C. Sircar, *Indian Epigraphy*, 1965, p. 150 (the former is often abbreviated to *śrī-ni*).

[55]*Corp. Inscr. Ind.*, III, 1888, pp. 58 ff., V. 5.

[56]Cf. the interpretation by V.S. Pathak, *Ancient Historians of India*, 1966, pp. 30-55; D. Devahuti, *Harsha, A Political Study*, 1970, p. 159.

enemies, others again are neutral. By deliberate policies, often of a Machiavellian character, the king of the centre, who is ambitious (*vijigīṣu*), sets out to enlarge his kingdom. By contrast, the inscriptions convey a more vivid and also more flexible idea of the kingdom. The term "state," though generally used in works dealing with ancient South Asian political thought, may suggest an "existence-by-itself" that the *rājya* did not possess; it was no more than the field of activity of the king, existing only by virtue of his majesty or *tejas*. This "radiant energy" is a quality which the king has in common with the sun or, in a milder degree, with the moon. It is therefore no coincidence that, as set out above, most ancient South Asian royal dynasties in the early medieval period trace their origin back to one or other of these celestial bodies. The analogy can be carried further. The *tejas* concept seems to imply also certain limitations, as the radiant energy does not penetrate everywhere with the same force. If the total kingdom is defined as the area in which the king's *tejas* is perceptible then it follows that its effect at the borders (*pratyanta*) must have been faint. The idea of the *maṇḍala* is perhaps primarily a systematization of the *tejas* idea, whereas the inscriptions try to interpret the actual state of relationships on the basis of this general idea.

The famous Allahabad Pillar Inscription of Samudra Gupta[57] gives in lines 17-28 what is usually defined as an account of conquests, in the opinion of some scholars even in the order in which they were made. A closer analysis of the wording of the inscription can, however, leave little doubt that the passage should rather be interpreted as a description of Samudra Gupta's empire as seen from the centre. It defines the different parts of the sub-continent (including Gandhāra, Nepal and Ceylon) in their relationships towards the centre. It is therefore not surprising that the list includes not only the completely annexed states and those that were made tributary, but also the border kingdoms, regarded as subordinate allies, and even those beyond the border which accepted certain obligations.

This particular concept of the ancient Indian *rājya* can be traced back to very early times, certainly to the age of the Brāhmaṇas with their different rankings of kings (such as *rājan*, *virāj*, *samrāj* etc.). It is clearly implied in Aśoka's Thirteenth Rock Edict, where the emperor claims that his *dharmavijaya* has pervaded not only his

[57] See note 6 above. Cf. also S.R. Goyal, *A History of the Imperial Guptas*, 1967, p. 132.

kingdom proper but also the domains of the Greek kings, the ancient kingdoms of south India, and the tribal areas in different parts of the sub-continent. Although Aśoka's *dharma* is a moral concept it is evident that its degree of penetration reflects the king's authority. Aśoka's *dharma* is not so different from Samudra Gupta's *tejas* as it may seem at first!

The foregoing observations suggest a conclusion concerning the nature of kingship in ancient South Asia. In contrast to Western political thought the "state" was not conceived of as a static unit but as one that was naturally dynamic. It is surprising that in a country so closely identified with non-violence the kings are invariably seen as conquerors. As their kingdoms lacked boundaries sanctioned by treaty or custom the kings' ambitions were contained not by inter-state laws but by available human and material resources, geographic barriers and, above all, similar designs of their neighbours. The king, as depicted in the inscriptions, is by definition a conqueror reducing all his rivals to submission. His conquest of the four quarters of the universe (*digvijaya*) is common-place. The inscriptions normally describe the traditional picture of the ideal king—more or less adapted to the particular ruler with whom the court poet is concerned.

How closely the idea of victory is associated with kingship appears also from the inscriptions of Aśoka.[58] There can be no doubt that Aśoka was a unique king. Yet his ideas, though original, are firmly rooted in Indian tradition. All individual elements of Aśoka's doctrines can be identified in Brahmanic or Buddhist texts, in most cases in both. The real innovation is the particular combination of traditional elements which are given a new meaning. Thus, in a famous passage of the Thirteenth Rock Edict Aśoka renounces victories by force and replaces these by ideological victories

[58]Aśoka regularly calls his empire "that which has been conquered" (*vijita*, e.g. Rock Edict II, line 1). J. Bloch, *Les Inscriptions d'Asoka*, 1950, notes that the term is used although Aśoka did not have to conquer his empire himself (note 2 to p. 93). It is true that *vijita* is used also in the Pali Canon for "kingdom," for example, *Majjhimanikāya*, No. 86, ed., Lord Chalmers in P.T.S. 1898, II, p. 97: *Tena kho pana samayena rañño Pasenadissa Kosalassa vijite coro Aṅgulimālo*... "At that time, in the kingdom of the Kosala king Pasenadi, the thief Aṅgulimāla....." Yet, one would be inclined to attach some importance to the use of this term (instead of *rajje* etc.), especially because *vijita* is often used in the sense of conquered, e.g. at the beginning of R.E. XIII: *Kaliṅgā vijitā*.

(*dhammavijaya*).[59] He also orders that all kinds of formal ceremonies (*bahu maṅgalam*) be transformed into the ceremony of righteousness (*dhamma-maṅgalam*),[60] while he sets a good example by substituting "tours in connexion with righteousness" (*dhamma-yātrā*) for the "pleasure tours" (*vihāra-yātrā*) of the earlier kings.[61] In many respects, Aśoka's policies, as set out in his inscriptions, are a reinterpretation of traditional lore.

The inscriptions also contain a number of other dynastic traditions, two of which require acknowledgement here, though there is no space to consider them: first, that of the idea of a king chosen to make an end to anarchy; and secondly, that of the old king withdrawing to a hermitage in the forest when he can entrust the kingdom to one of his sons.

6. Conclusion

The aim of the present paper has been to call attention to the importance of the study of inscriptions for our knowledge of the particular traditions connected with the royal dynasties of ancient South Asia. One of the conclusions that emerges from this study is that these traditions are based on three different sources:

(1) authentic historical materials of the type preserved in archives, relating mainly to genealogical matters and other basic details about the earlier kings;

(2) local traditions, mainly legends and other stories relating to the origins of the ruling dynasty or adapted in such a manner that they could be related to the ruling dynasty;

(3) epic, *purāṇic* or other literary traditions by which rulers could be connected with the ancient dynasties of the sun and the moon.

[59]R.E. XIII, line 11 (Shahbazgarhi version), *Sel. Inscr.*, p. 36. *Dharmavijaya* is normally translated as "conquest through *Dharma*" (=*dharmeṇa vijayaḥ;* e.g., D.C. Sircar, *Inscriptions of Aśoka*, 2nd edition, 1967, p. 58) but this seems less satisfactory in this context, where the term is clearly used in contrast to an ordinary conquest, in this particular case the conquest of Kalinga.

[60]R.E. IX, line 4 (Mansehra version), *Sel. Inscr.*, p. 28. The former are defined as ceremonies performed in the case of disease, marriage, etc., the latter as courtesy towards slaves and servants, gifts to Brāhmaṇas etc.

[61]R.E. VIII, beginning.

In general the order given here seems to reflect the chronological order in which the different types become prevalent, but the actual picture is more complicated owing to the immensity of the sub-continent and the occurrence of different compromises by which the different sources are harmonized. Many of the individual topics require more detailed investigation, which may enable us to correlate the data discussed here with other aspects of early Indian history.

7. The Mughal Imperial State

SHAIKH ABDUR RASHID

EARLY DEVELOPMENTS IN MUSLIM POLITICAL THEORY[1]

It has been written that:

> The ten years of the Prophet's rule in Medina (622-31 A.D.) and perhaps the thirty years following his death constituted the age in which human society had come as near perfection as could be hoped for. So the institutional, legal, financial, and of course, religious precedent of that period was to yield the terms, concepts, and prescriptions of that perfect order which was Allah's.[2]

But as Islamic armies spread over Persia and northern Africa and new lands were conquered and new people brought under the government of the Muslims, the need was felt for a strong and effective system of administration. Though the injunctions of the Quran and the precedents of the first four Caliphs (A.D 632-61), were accepted as guides for the evolution of new administrative institutions, Persian and Byzantine principles and practices of government were accepted and incorporated in Muslim political theory in order to meet the needs of government over a vast empire, comprising people of different faiths and races and speaking different languages. Political expediency and anxiety to bridge the gulf between "the normative dreams of the lawyers and actual conditions of life" caused the Muslim community to accept and adopt in the sphere of political organization the customs, usages and practices of pre-Islamic rulers whom it displaced. This led some of the more conscientious jurists to an

[1]Editor's note: For a useful brief analysis of pre-Mughal political theory, see also P. Hardy, *Partners in Freedom and True Muslims: the Political thought of some Muslim scholars in British India, 1912-47*, Scandinavian Institute of Asian Studies, Monograph No. 5, 1971, pp. 7-19.

[2] G.E. von Grunebaum, *Medieval Islam*, 2nd ed., Chicago, 1953, p. 143.

attitude of withdrawal with respect to the state, "leaving the field to their more time-serving and less scrupulous brethren"[3] among the *ulema*. The new ruling class that emerged with the rise of the Umayyads (661-750) and grew in power, prestige and pelf under the Abbasids (750-1258), evolved its own theory of the state and administrative institutions. The later theologians and jurists realized the hopelessness of achieving the perfect form of the ideal state in a world of imperfect realities and of maintaining the politico-religious organization of the city-state of early Islam. They set about justifying the state as it had evolved and then existed. Muslim political philosophy therefore grew up in the midst of a disillusioned society, and it is based mainly on post-facto deductions in order to make political organization correspond, as far as practicable, with the injunctions of Islam and the requirements of the *millat*.

Monarchy as an institution, though unknown to the *shariat*, was generally accepted in all Islamic countries and by all Islamic people as a necessary evil, and recognized as a legitimate form of government. The political institutions and even the personnel of the displaced governments had to be accepted under the compulsion of circumstances and this acceptance affected the ideas and the practices of the ruling class. The *khalifas* at first claimed to be the religious leaders of their people as well as their temporal rulers. The duties and functions prescribed for the *khalifa* and later for the sultans represent a compromise between the ideal norm and political reality.[4] Though this duality of powers theoretically placed unlimited authority in the hands of the *khalifa*, with the decline of the political power of the Abbasids the *khalifa* was divested in practice of all temporal authority, which was now exercised by his officers at the capital and the governors in the provinces. The *khalifat* as an institution remained merely a symbol of the unity and solidarity of the *ummat*, universal and supra-national in its outlook.

In early Islam differences about the dogmas of the faith did not in themselves form the ground for dissensions. The main differences arose because of the conflict between the interests of the state and the interests of private persons, and the complex problems of governing the conquered people and integrating them in Muslim society. The *khalifas* gradually became not merely the heads of the Muslim com-

[3]H.A.R. Gibb, *Mohammadanism*, 1949, p. 16.

[4]E.I.J. Rosenthal, *Political Thought in Islam*, Cambridge, 1958.

munity but rulers solicitous of the welfare of their subjects[5], whatever their religion, race or language. The claim of the *khalifa* to be the head of the community as representative of the Apostle of God gave place to the conception of his being "representative of God on earth."[6] This was bound gradually to make the *khalifa* a successor to pagan and Christian rulers by divine grace, assuming their powers and prerogatives and adopting their court and household ceremonies and etiquette.[7]

MUSLIM THEORY AND THE INSTITUTION OF MONARCHY

After the fall of Bagdad (A.D. 1258) some of the Muslim jurists and theologians justified the acceptance of Mongol authority by giving the verdict that "tyranny was better than anarchy."[8] The quest for security of life, property and the honour of women runs like a red thread through the political and social fabric of those troubled times. A strong government was considered the only guarantee of peace, progress and prosperity. Thus the natural contradictions in the acceptance of an irresponsible, autocratic, omnipotent monarch—an admittedly non-Islamic conception of kingship—are explained away by jurists and political thinkers on the basis of expediency and painful political necessity. This conception of sovereignty in complete disregard of the traditional idea of *imamat*,[9] quite foreign to Islam, is based on Sassanian tradition and the Persian conception of kingship. In the struggle for survival a compromise was made by stating as a law what was a fact.

Ziya al ud-din Barani (*c.* 1286-*c.* 1357), an Indo-Muslim writer on government under the Delhi sultanate and boon companion of Sultan Muḥammad Bin Tughlug (1325-51), gave an account of the

[5]The Umayyad dynasty, which created one of the greatest empires of the world, did not produce one single military ruler.

[6]Abdul Malik (A.D. 685-705) is reported to have assumed the title "Caliph of God" on his coins. Mamun (813-833) began to style himself "Representative of God." See Amir Hasan, *Kingship and Caliphate in Medieval Persia*, Lahore, 1942.

[7]Muawiya is said to have been the first king (*malik*) in Islam, but Walid I was the first to surround himself with imperial pomp (*ibid*).

[8]*Al-Fakhri*, translated by C.E.J. Whitting, 1947, p. 14.

[9]The general authority that the successor of the Prophet holds in the sphere of religious and imperial affairs.

circumstances in which Iranian Muslims accepted the institution of monarchy:

> Now, between the traditions (*sunnah*) of the prophet Mohammad and his mode of life and living, and the customs of the Iranian Emperors, and their mode of life and living, there is a complete contradiction and total opposition....After them, the caliphs and kings of Islam were faced with two irreconcilable alternatives both necessary for their religion and the state. If they followed the traditions of the Prophet and his mode of life, kingship and government would be impossible for them. On the other hand, it would be necessary to violate the traditions of the Prophet, which are the foundation and the basis of the Faith....Consequently it became necessary for the rulers of Islam to follow the policy of the Iranian Emperors in order to ensure the greatness of the True word, the supremacy of the Muslim religion, the power of Truth, the suppression and overthrow of the opponents and enemies of the Faith, the execution of the orders of religion and the maintenance of their own authority....Nevertheless Islam totally forbids and prohibits the iniquities committed by the Iranian Emperors.... But just as the eating of carrion, though prohibited, is yet permitted in time of dire need, similarly the customs and traditions of the pagan Emperors of Iran...should from the view point of truth and the correct faith, be considered like the eating of carrion in time of dire need....[10]

The passage is from *Fatawa-i-Jahandari*, in which Barani domesticated to Muslim India the Iranian "pious sultan" theory through which the Delhi sultanate resolved the tension between temporal necessities and religious idealism; if the king placed the attributes of kingship at the service of true religion he became the vice-gerent of God on earth.

The need for the existence of human authority amongst men is founded by Muslim jurists on the inherent selfishness and acquisitiveness of mankind.[11] God out of his infinite wisdom selects whomsoever he likes and delegates authority to him "to do justice amongst

[10] Barani's *Fatawa-i-Jahandari*, cited in Muhammad Habib and Afsar Salim, *The Political Theory of the Delhi Sultanate*, Delhi, 1959, pp. 41-42.

[11] "If there had been no Sultan (ruler) people would have devoured each other" (*Tarikh-i-Fakhruddin Mubarak Shah*, Denison Ross (ed.), 1927 p. 13).

men."[12] The king, according to Najmuddin Razi, is like a shepherd and his subjects like a flock. It is incumbent upon the shepherd to protect the flock from the wolf and to strive to repel evil from them; and if there are among the flock some tups with horns and ewes without horns and the former wish to constrain the latter, it is incumbent upon the shepherd to prevent them.[13] Thus the rulers are appointed by God, the supreme sovereign, and are directly responsible to him. The same views are held by Nasiruddin Tusi[14] and Nizamul Mulk. The latter writes:

> In every age and time God (be He exalted) chooses one member of the human race and having adorned and endowed him with kingly virtues entrusts him with the interests of the world and the well-being of His servants; He charges that person to close the doors of corruption, confusion and discord, and He imparts to him such dignity and majesty in the eyes and hearts of men, that under his just rule they may live their lives in constant security and ever wish for his reign to continue.... Great men have said, 'A kingdom may last while there is irreligion, but it will not endure when there is oppression.'[15]

The sultan was regarded as the shadow of God upon earth. The concept of justice and sanctity of trust are basic to the political theory of Islam and "constitute the essentials of political justice and the supreme purpose of public function."[16] The sultan as such offered protection to all oppressed persons without any discrimination between man and man. The prosperity or dissolution of the universe depended on kings.[17]

The Persian scholar and theologian, Al-Ghazali (1058-1111) writes:

> Know that God has exalted two groups of people and distin-

[12] Al-Ghazali, *Nasihat ul-Muluk*, tr. by F.R.C. Bagley, *Book of Counsel for Kings*, 1964, p. 46.

[13] Najmuddin Razi, *Mirsadul Ibad*, Tehran, Solar 1312, p. 248.

[14] *Akhlaq-i-Nasiri*, Litho, Lahore, 1965, p. 100.

[15] Nizum ul-Mulk, *Siyasatnama*, tr. by Hubert Darke, *The Book of Government of Rules for Kings*, 1960, pp. 9, 12.

[16] Ibn-i-Taymiyyah, *Al-Siyasat-i-Shariah*, quoted by Manzuruddin Ahmad, *Pakistan, the Emerging Islamic State*, Karachi, 1966, pp. 26-27.

[17] *Ibid.*

guished them from other human beings,...firstly, the Prophets, and secondly, the rulers. The Prophets were appointed to guide the people in the right path. The welfare of humanity is bound up with the existence of kings, ... as is related in a saying, 'The Sultan is the Shadow of God on earth,' which is a proof of the fact that the Sultan has been exalted by God and placed over men. Therefore, know that it is God who has given a ruler sovereignty and divine light. It is on this account that one should render obedience to them (the kings) and regard them as friends, and be submissive to them. They should not resist the rulers or be inimical to them. Almighty God has ordained 'Obey God, obey the Prophet, and obey those in authority over you....[18]

Nizamul Mulk writes: "God Almighty is the supreme king over kings....A true ruler is one who dispenses justice amongst men."[19] The sultan who does not award justice is ill-starred and shall be punished on the Day of Judgment. Both Nizamul Mulk[20] and Ghazali[21] quote the *hadis* that sovereignty endures even when there is unbelief, but will not endure when there is injustice.

Hamadani writes:

You are to know that conducting the government of the Mussalman is a very serious affair and undertaking the administration is a delicate business. If rulers and kings follow the path of justice and kindness and strive to enforce the punishments of the *shariat* and the rulers of religion they will be His deputies, the chosen people and the *khalifas* of God on this earth. But if they forsake the principles of justice and kindness, if they are not kind to the people of God and follow their desires and passions and are negligent in enforcing the punishments of the *shariat*, then in truth they are the deputies of *Dajjal*, the enemies of God and His Prophet and are the *khalifas* of Satan.[22]

[18]*Tarikh-i-Fakhruddin Mubarak Shah*, p. 13. See *Quran*, IV, 58 59; V, 81.

[19]*Siyasatnama*, Chap. II. See also Abdul Quddus Gangohi, *Maktubat-i-Qudsiya*, Delhi, 1870, Letter No. 34.

[20]*Siyasatnama*, Chap. II.

[21]*Nasihat ul-Muluk*, p. 46.

[22]Shaikh Hamadani, *Zakhirat ul-Muluk*, Lahore, 1905, pp. 115-116. Najmuddin Razi also refuses to recognize the tyrannical ruler as the "shadow of God" (*Mirsad*, p. 5.)

Kings are gifted with divine light (*farr-i-izadi*)[23] and they must be obeyed and loved.[24] Indeed, the obligations of the king's officers to him are virtually religious obligations. The officer's oath of loyalty bound him to accept that disobedience to the king was "tantamount to disobedience to God."[25]

These statements reveal that the most authoritative jurists and writers on Muslim political philosophy were agreed on the following points:

(1) That sovereignty rested with God.
(2) That God delegates his authority to rule over men to whomsoever he likes.
(3) That the need for the creation of such an authority arises out of the viciousness of man.
(4) That the prime duty of a ruler is to do justice amongst men.
(5) That the ruler will be accountable to God for his conduct.
(6) That his duty is to defend and exalt the faith and to enforce what is ordained and prohibit what is prohibited.

THE HINDU THEORY OF KINGSHIP AND MUSLIM RULE IN SOUTH ASIA

Among the early Muslim rulers of South Asia there was no sharp break from the political theory and practice of the kings who preceded them. Hindu sages ascribed the origin of kingship to "human need and military necessity ostensibly to maintain peace under divine sanction." According to Buddhist tradition kingship originated in a contract between the people at large and the one whom they appointed to maintain order. Whether kingship originated by divine dispensation or by contract, the main need of the people was the maintenance of order in the country.[26] In "the pathological dread of anarchy"—the way of the fishes according to the Hindu sages where the larger fishes eat the smaller—was found the origin of the state.[27] The king was not a law-maker but a protector of his people and of *dharma*. Though revolt against a king who was impious and cruel

[23]For *farr-i-izadi*, see *Nasihat ul-Muluk*, pp. 45, 73-74.
[24]*Ibid.*, pp. 45-46.
[25]*Insha-i-Mahru*, Aligarh, 1956, pp. 21-22.
[26]A.L. Basham, *The Wonder That Was India*, 1954, p. 82.
[27]*Arthashastra*, tr. Shamasastry, Mysore, 1929, XIII.1.

was morally justified it was discouraged. The institution of kingship was accepted and respected. The *Mahābhārata*, while accepting the right of revolt by the people, insists on having a king:

> A man should first choose his king, then his wife,
> and only then amass wealth;
> for without a king in the world
> where would wife and property be?[28]

In the various *Pandnamas*, *Wasaua*, Mirrors for Kings and other manuals on statecraft compiled by Muslim writers, kings are advised to desist from acts of wanton cruelty. But if the general welfare demanded it the shedding of blood was justified. Such punishments, cruel and relentless, did not reflect the religious or ethical norms but were considered necessary because of the prevalent insecurity. The apparent inconsistencies between acts and axioms were condoned as acts of political expediency to achieve a higher good.[29] Proper care was to be exercised in the selection of officers, who were to be upright, God-fearing, fair-minded and scrupulously honest. Cultivation was to be extended to secure the prosperity of the realm.[30] The author of *Qabusnama* writes: "Make it your constant endeavour to improve cultivation and govern well."[31]

During the early Muslim period in South Asia the peculiar military and political conditions and the ever-recurring fear of foreign invasions made the development of political institutions halting and uncertain. The government was mild or severe, benevolent or autocratic according to the changing political and economic conditions. These conditions contributed to make the power of the king and the ruling class more autocratic and less responsive to pressure of public opinion. However, the village administration surviving from the time of the Mauryas continued to function, providing an element of continuity in social and economic institutions.

Neither did the Mughal state break away from the kingship system established by its predecessors. Its contribution lay in giving the system a new power, effectiveness and vitality, borrowing liberally

[28] *Mahābhārata*, tr. P.C. Roy, Calcutta, 1919-35, pp. xii, 41, 57.

[29] "Executions prevent executions," *Al-Fakhri*, p. 39.

[30] Dai Kaus ibn Sikander, *Qabus Nama*, composed A.D. 1082, tr. by Reuben Levy, *A Mirror for Princes*, 1951, p. 88.

[31] *Ibid.*

from the Indian tradition, the Turkish and Afghan Sultans' experience extending over more than four centuries, and the institutions which had developed in Central Asian Muslim states.

During the centuries preceding the establishment of the Mughal empire there had been considerable increase in the Muslim population by immigration, conversion and natural increase. But the Indian population was predominantly Hindu and the Mughals had to respect their religion, customs and traditions, secure their loyalty and bring about an integration of different sections of the people. A beginning was made towards establishing a secular state in the modern sense, though the ruling class was predominantly Muslim. The racial, religious, linguistic and cultural differences amongst various groups made the task of integration complex and difficult. The responsibility for maintaining peace and order within the realm, defending the frontiers, dispensing justice and promoting the happiness and prosperity of the people rested traditionally with the ruler. All power was concentrated in the hands of the king, and the officers of the state, from the highest to the lowest, were merely his agents. His absolute power was universally sanctioned, by Indian tradition and by the strictly pragmatic Muslim political theory evolved during centuries of Muslim rule over various lands and peoples. As an historian writes: "Never was the divine right of kings to govern wrong more clearly recognized. It was possible to rebel, but it was not possible to assert that the king was wrong."[32]

THE POLITICAL THEORY OF THE MUGHAL EMPIRE

The best exponent of Mughal political theory is Abul Fazl (1551-1602),the talented wazir, counsellor and friend of Akbar (1556-1605). In his well known works, *Akbarnama* and *Ain-i-Akbari*, and the several official letters written on behalf of the emperor to contemporary rulers, Abul Fazl gives a systematic exposition of the origin of the ruling institution, the need for the existence of a ruler amongst men and the rights and obligations of the rulers and the ruled. The ideas of Abul Fazl reflect certain trends in contemporary political thought and epitomize the accepted political principles of Muslims as well as the Hindus. Abul Fazl stresses the charismatic character of kingship, which required not only military power to build it up

[32]Sir Percival Griffiths, *The British Impact on India*, 1965, p. 124.

but academic propaganda to sustain it.[33] Abul Fazl was eminently fitted by training and temperament to stand forth as the champion of Akbar's claim. But the political philosophy that he propounded was neither original in conception nor novel in exposition. He was only restating, though perhaps with more clarity and logical consistency, what had been said by earlier theorists outside India.

The Mughal conception of kingship represents an important stage in the historical development of the idea of a divinely appointed political authority amongst men—a "charismatic legitimization of political institution." With the magic of great names behind them, an unbroken tradition of kingship in the family, the ability and the dedication to duty of the first six rulers of the dynasty, the Mughal emperors were able to inspire their subjects with personal devotion and confidence in their ability to remedy extraordinary internal and external dangers. The legitimization of their functional competence by jurists helped them make their position secure and stable. Abul Fazl's metaphysical conception of sovereignty is tempered by the Islamic notion of the sovereignty of the Islamic canon law interpreted in the light of reason and political expediency.

In the *Ain-i-Akbari* Abul Fazl gives us his views about the origin of kingship and the rights and obligations of the rulers and the ruled:

> No dignity is higher in the eyes of God than the dignity of kingship. All the wise men of the world drink from its auspicious fountain. Royalty is the only safeguard against the spirit of rebellion and the means of keeping the people on the right path. The very meaning of the word *padshah* strengthens my claim, for *pad* signifies authority and possession. If royalty did not exist the world would not escape the devastating storm of strife, nor would selfishness and self-indulgence be rooted out from the world. If there had been no kings amongst men, mankind would have lost all its grandeur and the whole earth rather than being a flourishing garden would have become a barren waste.
>
> Royalty is the brilliant light emanating from God and a ray from the sun, the illuminator of the universe, a convincing argument of the book of perfection and the receptacle of all virtues. In modern terminology this royal light is spoken of as the divine

[33]See my "The Treatment of History by Muslim Historians in Mughal Official and Biographical Works," C.H. Philips (ed.), *Historians of India, Pakistan and Ceylon*, 1961, p. 147.

> light—*farr-i-izadi*. In old times this auspicious light was termed '*kiyan khurra*' (the divine halo).
>
> The office of a king is bestowed by God on a distinguished person without the intercession of an intermediary. The splendour of this exalted office envelops the recipient and the entire mankind bend their head in submission before the king. Besides this many excellences flow from the possession of this light.[34]

Similarly, Jehangir (1605-27) held that "acts of sovereignty and world rule are not things to be arranged by worthless endeavours of a few defective intellects. The just creator bestows them on him whom He considers fit for this glorious and exalted duty."[35]

Abul Fazl divides the king's subjects into four classes: The warriors are the instruments of quelling rebellions and maintaining law and order. The artisans and merchants provide the necessaries of life and as a result of their labours "the breeze of contentment nourishes the rose-tree of life." The learned people enrich life and "the garden of creation receives from their irrigating powers a peculiar freshness." The peasants and labourers sustain life and "strength and happiness flow from their work."

> It is therefore obligatory for a king to put each of these in its proper place, and by uniting personal ability with due respect for others, to cause the world to flourish. And as the grand political body maintains its equilibrium by the above four ranks of men, so does royalty receive its final tint from a similar fourfold division of nobles, revenue officials, intellectuals or philosophers, and servants.[36]

By the time of the Mughals division into classes was not entirely on the basis of birth, though great store was laid by birth and ancestry, mostly as a result of Persian influences. The geographer Ibn-al-Faqih, writing about 903, quotes the Abbasid courtier al-Fazl b. Yahya as having divided mankind into four classes:

> Firstly, rulers elevated to office by their deserts; secondly, *viziers*, distinguished by their wisdom and understanding; thirdly, the

[34]Abul Fazl, *Ain-i-Akbari*, tr. H. Blochmann, Bib. Indica, Calcutta, Asiatic Society, 1873-1948, Preface, pp. ii, iii.

[35]*Tuzuk-i-Jahangiri*, tr. Rogers, Vol. I, p. 51.

[36]*Ain*, Vol. I, p. 4.

> upper classes, elevated by their wealth; and fourthly, the middle classes, to which belong the men marked by their culture. The remainder are filthy refuse, a torrent of scum, base cattle, none of whom thinks of anything but his food and sleep.[37]

How deeply the pre-Islamic Persian ideas had permeated Muslim society is reflected in the literature of the time. Constant reference was made to the practices and principles of ancient Persian rulers. The often quoted essayist Jahiz of Basra, writing about the middle of the A.D. 9th century, tells us that the Persian king Ardshir (Artaxerxes) divided his subjects into four classes and kept them rigidly in their separate divisions. He claimed that nothing more swiftly led to the destruction of empires than the transfer of one class to another, be it the elevation of the humble into a higher class or the degrading of the noble into a lower one. His classification was: first, knights and princes; second, religious leaders and guardians of the fire-temples; third, physicians, scribes and astrologers; and fourth, cultivators, menials etc.[38]

The structure of society was thus based on acceptance of distinct orders and the prestige of each order is based on its traditional sanctity rather than on its ability.[39]

In spite of the elaborate theory about the king's all-pervading all embracing power, which has led European scholars to speak of Mughal monarchy as "despotic," "absolutist," "a military oligarchy," a "feudal autocracy," the Mughal monarchs were not above law. They were as much subject to it as the meanest of their subjects. Their law-making competence was limited by the existence of religious law which they could not abrogate or modify. Another limitation was that of customs, which, because of their antiquity, had the force of law. There was an intimate relationship between royal duties and the divine right of kings. The Mughal rulers had many responsibilities but limited power.

Abul Fazl, like other political thinkers before him, speaks of the *farr-i-izadi*, the "divine effulgence" or the "divine shadow," "a

[37] *Kitab-ul-Buldan*, Vol. I, quoted by Reuben Levy, *The Sociology of Islam*, Cambridge, 1933, p. 67.

[38] Jahiz, *Kitab-ul-Taj*, quoted by Levy, *op. cit.*, p. 69.

[39] See *Proceedings of the President and Council of the East India Company*, 16 August 1679, quoted by Tara Chand, *Society and State in the Mughul Period*, Faridabad, 1961, p. 23

Persian concept of the sacred element of fire or light in the person of the rightful ruler," as illuminating the heart of a king. With such precedents and forceful academic justification of a ruler's authority, the Mughals were able to place themselves on a pedestal from which they could not be overthrown even when they had lost all power. Badauni was fully conscious of this and wrote:

> Shaikh Taj ud Din looking on the reverence due to a king as an absolute religious command, called the face of the king *Ka'ba-i-Muradat* (sanctum of desires), and *Qiblah-i-Hajat* (goal of necessities). And in support of these matters be brought forward some apocryphal traditions, and the practice of the disciples of some of the Shaikhs of India. And thus after a time the titles 'the only one', 'the absolute', 'the perfect man' came to be commonly applied to the just, majestic and magnanimous emperor."[40]

THE ADMINISTRATIVE STRUCTURE OF THE MUGHAL EMPIRE

The Padshah

The Mughal empire was a highly centralized monarchy in which the monarch, styled as *Padshah,* occupied the pivotal position as the source of all authority, claiming the unquestioned allegiance and absolute loyalty of all his subjects irrespective of religious, tribal or regional affiliations or personal or social status.

The Mughal governmental organization was like a pyramid, with the king at the apex squarely resting on the ruling class, consisting of the near relations of the king—some of them occasionally in opposition—the army, the bureaucracy, the *ulema* and the *mashaikh.* The Mughals, like the Abbasids before them, had "tamed and domesticated" the *ulema* and the *mashaikh,* but there were some amongst them who had the courage of their convictions to express their disapproval of state policy. However, they supplied the moral and religious sanction for the existence of the Mughal state. At the base of the pyramid stood the vast heterogeneous mass of the king's subjects absorbed in their regional, ethnic and sectional loyalties and generally oblivious of and indifferent to both the glamour of

[40]Badauni, *Muntakhab ut-Tawarikh,* tr. G.S.A. Ranking, Bib. Indica, Calcutta, Asiatic Society, 1895-1925, Vol. II, p. 266.

the court life and the shady, sordid and often relentless pursuit of power and pelf by the upper classes. In such a system, without any definite rules about succession to the throne, the stability of the government and the survival of the dynasty depended on the personality of the ruler, his ability to maintain a balance between the different sections of the ruling class, and the contentment of the subjects. The *Padshah* had to choose his own system. If he was unequal either by temperament or training to the task of government his duties fell by default to unsuitable persons.

The Mughal empire was multi-racial, multi-religious and multilinguistic in a country and amongst a people whose separatist and parochial tendencies were deep-rooted. This made the work of unification extremely difficult. Any weakening of the authority of the ruler or any diminution of his prestige always led to disorganization and anarchy. This constant conflict between the emperor as the sole source of all authority and the latent desire of the members of the ruling class to become independent of him continued throughout the history of Mughal rule in the sub-continent.

The early Mughal emperors diligently and conscientiously performed their functions as the chief executive authority, the highest judicial authority, the only law-making authority in the fields where their law-making competence was not limited by religious or customary law, as commanders of the armed forces and above all as the guardians and promotors of the happiness and welfare of their subjects. The schedule of daily work was carefully prepared and meticulously followed.[41] A most remarkable feature of Mughal government was the ruler's accessibility to his subjects. The appearance of the emperor at the *Jharoka*,[42] the *Darbar-i-Aam* (also called *Diwan-i-Khas-o-Aam*), the chain of justice which continued to the time of Mohammad Shah (1718-48), the frequent tours of the emperors in the empire, and an elaborate and efficient system of obtaining information about administration, all combined to bring the Mughals nearer to the people. The splendour of the public darbars of the emperor, and even that of the provincial governors, filled the hearts of their subjects with awe and reverence. These darbars have been rapturously described by European travellers. Dr Qureshi writes:

[41]*Ain*, Vol. I, p. 721; *Tuzuk-i-Jehangiri*, pp. 9, 130, 232; Chandra Bhan, *Qawaid-us-Saltanat*, tr. Gladwin, Sec. 1.

[42]*Ain*, I, 72.

> The splendour which surrounded the monarch in that period was an institution of great importance because of its public appeal and its psychological impact. Apart from other factors, the magnificence of the Mughal court created the halo around the monarch which made the dynasty stable and raised its prestige so high that it became a legend with the people in spite of its inherent military weakness. The Mughal monarchy was an expensive institution but it justified the expenditure by giving peace and good government to the subcontinent which had been a prey to anarchy before the Mughals and which relapsed into anarchy as soon as their authority weakened.[43]

A remarkable feature of this period is the spontaneous and passionate devotion to the ruler, "more symbolic than personal."

The Ruling Class under the Mughals

The predominance of court and crown in the country was well established and generally recognized. The bureaucratization of the state enhanced the power of the nobility and enabled the ruling class to exercise great influence over the governed. The Mughal nobility, or more correctly the civil and military officers of state and the distinguished *ulema* and *mashaikh,* was different in origin, composition and social and political status from the baronial class of contemporary European states. It was an aristocracy of service rather than of birth. The practice of putting to death the sons of the royal family was a method of preventing the rise of an aristocracy of blood. The rules governing the bureaucracy made difficult, if not impossible, the perpetuation of offices, titles or emoluments in a family. Yet in spite of the equality of all Muslims in the eye of law, the privilege of birth played a large part in the evolution of bureaucracy. This was so because of the needs and difficulties of the government over people of diverse characters and traditions. Members of the nobility were constantly trying to transfer their offices, titles and sources of income to their children and adherents and to establish a hereditary ruling class not dependent on the emperor's continued favour. It was only natural that such a class would during the lifetime, covertly, and after the death of a ruler, overtly, form themselves

[43]I.H. Qureshi, *The Administration of the Mughul Empire*, Karachi, 1966 p. 160.

into groups on a regional, tribal or sectarian basis for personal ends. While a strong and capable ruler would keep a strict control over these groups, converting their mutual jealousies and rivalries to his own advantage, a weak ruler would be dominated by one group to the disgust and annoyance of other groups. These inter-group rivalries were endemic in the empire. They came out into the open after the death of Alamgir and constituted the greatest single cause of weakness of the government. These factions were responsible directly and indirectly for the maladministration within the empire in the 18th century, the fall in agricultural production and the fanning of the pent up hostility of the Hindu upper classes to foreign rule. The Hindu subjects had never emotionally reconciled themselves to Muslim rule. Every concession made to them awakened new hopes, particularly amongst the ruling class and the landed aristocracy, to recover their privileged position in society by exploiting the religious-tribal traditions of the masses to their own advantage.

The elaborate administrative machinery devised by Akbar, who had the good fortune of having in his service some very able administrators, statesmen, men of letters and military officers, contributed considerably to the stability of the dynasty and the strength of the empire. As long as the administration was strong and efficient under the able and vigilant care of the emperors, the *zamindars* and the feudatory Indian princes were kept in check. When the administration weakened, parochialism, regionalism, political, tribal and religious factionalism combined to undermine the unity of the empire and expose it to foreign pressure and internal atomization. These factious fights destroyed the political integration which Mughal genius had attempted to bring about.

Akbar's creation of a bureaucracy with carefully prescribed and regulated grades, emoluments, perquisites, privileges and obligations made the nobility entirely dependent on him. The members of the ruling class, on account of the privileges and high salaries enjoyed by them, dominated the politics of the country as well as the social, artistic and economic life of society. It was an aristocracy of service but because of the deeply-rooted Muslim respect for birth and status, the ruling class became an elite in which personal merit came to count less and nobility of birth more than before. Selection of officers for the upper grade services was made by the emperors on the advice and recommendation of leading noblemen for the lifetime and during good behaviour of the incumbents. This prevented the growth of an independent hereditary peerage as a check on royal authority. There was no specialization of services except in the lower grades and this prevented the growth of a professional civil service. The services vastly increased in numbers but declined in efficiency. They became tyrannical, the chosen instrument of the state standing apart from the public.

The Mughals had no cabinet ministers in the modern sense of the word. There was no joint responsibility of ministers, who held office during good behaviour. They had no right to give advice which the ruler was bound to follow. On important occasions they might be summoned collectively or severally but all important decisions were those of the emperor. This system had the merit of making ministers individually responsible for the departments under them. Their salaries, honours and status depended on their worth. The weakness of the system was the difficulty of finding really competent persons and developing an *esprit de corps* amongst the officers. It placed too much responsibility on the emperor himself and the efficiency and effectiveness of the administration depended on the vigilance and sagacity of the ruler. The system of checks and balances devised by Akbar maintained a precarious balance between the different departments and their relations with the emperor. The religious classes were given adequate financial support by the state. Though their claim to interfere with the administrative policy of the emperors was resisted by the latter, they were consulted and treated with respect by most of them. This created and maintained a religious tension in state affairs.

The public services were organized into a single service by Akbar and elaborate rules were prescribed for recruitment, emoluments and conditions of service of all servants of the state. There was no system of public examinations, no fixed salaries for any office, and no specializaion of services. Promotion depended on merit, sometimes on favour, but it was not automatic. The officers of the state therefore depended on the continued favour and good opinion of the king and assiduously worked to retain it. The *mansabdari* system carefully worked out and elaborated by Akbar covered all services civil and military. The recruitment was made from amongst foreign immigrants, noble Indian families, and the upper Hindu classes. If the lists of officers in Mughal service are carefully analyzed one has to agree with Dr Tara Chand that:

> the Mughal rule was based on the support of the higher caste alone. This is forcibly brought out in the organization of the *mansabdari* system. Among the Muslims the *mansabdars* were mainly recruited from the three upper castes i.e., mostly Mughals and Pathans, and some Sayyids. Among the Hindus the Rajputs of Rajasthan and of the upper provinces, and of Maharashtra, almost exclusively contributed the quota.[44]

The emperors maintained a balance between different castes and classes of their subjects. Dr Tara Chand quotes the proceedings of the Council of the East India Company in 1679:

> 'When any man has naturally forfeited his caste, you are to observe that he cannot be restored to it without the sanction of Government, which was a political supremacy reserved to themselves by the Muhammadans.' Apparently jurisdiction in caste matters was exercised by local chiefs and zamindars, from which an appeal lay to the governor of the province.[45]

The aristocracy occupied a considerable place in the contemporary annals. The aristocracy was the centre of social, aesthetic and economic life of the people and constituted the dominant form of life, over-shadowing the life of the common man and creating an illusion of general prosperity.

The Nature of the Mughal State

The Mughal empire has been described variously as a "police state," a "military state," a "theocracy," an "oriental despotism" and lastly, by Muslim writers, as an Islamic state. While all other descriptions are incorrect, it is the last description which deserves careful examination. It was an Islamic state in as much as the religion of the emperors and the Muslim ruling class, which was always in a minority, professed the religion of Islam and directly

[44]Tara Chand, *op. cit.*, p. 68.
[45]*Ibid.*, p. 33.

and indirectly strove to exalt Islam and prevent any attack on it. But for all practical purposes it was a religion-oriented secular state. Abul Fazl says:

> Kingship is a gift of God...and on coming to exalted dignity if he does not inaugurate universal peace (toleration) and if he does not regard all conditions of humanity, and all sects of religion with the single eye of favour—and not bemother some and bestepmother others—he will not become fit for the exalted dignity.[46]

Again, he adds, "differences in religion must not withhold him from his duty of watching, and all classes of men must have repose, so that the shadow of God may confer glory (on him)."[47] "Thus," in the words of Ibn Hasan, "both Islamic law and *Hadis* ceased to be the code of government,"[48] supplemented as the *shariat* was by "*zawabit*" or state law. The tradition of the pious sultan was sustained but emphasis was given to the rational, the secular and the ethical basis of the Mughal government. Still, the ideals which inspired the rulers were purely Islamic and no attempt was made openly to transgress them.

Islamic law, except the criminal law, did not apply to non-Muslims. Converts to Islam did not always follow the Islamic law in matters relating to marriages and inheritance. Customary law was respected and enforced by public opinion. Aurangzeb recognized that the "non-Muslim subjects, that is the *zimmis*, are not subject to the laws of Islam, their affairs should be regulated according to the principles of their own religion."[49] *Zakat* was not officially collected, *jiziya* was not always levied; taking of interest and use of wine were overlooked. The universalism of Islam as symbolized in the institution of the *Khalifat* was ignored. Punishments were arbitrary and in complete disregard of *shariat* law. The main strength of Mughal government lay in its consistent effort to dispense justice without fear or favour and in its religious

[46]Abul Fazl, *Akbar Nama*, tr. Beveridge, Bib. Indica, Calcutta 1912, II, p. 421.

[47]*Ibid.*, p. 680.

[48]Ibn Hasan, *The Central Structure of the Mughul Empire*, 1936, p. 61.

[49]*Fatawa-i-Alamgiri*, quoted by M.B. Ahmad, *Administration of Justice in Medieval India*, Aligarh, 1941, p. 101.

tolerance. Two maxims may be cited in this connection: "A kingdom may last if there is irreligion but it will not endure when there is oppression.[50] And: "The justice of one day is better than sixty years of worship."[51] Justice was regarded as the major responsibility of a monarch. Mughal historians have recorded numerous instances of severe punishments meted out by the emperors. Babur blinded Muhammad Zaman Mirza, who was a very near relation of his, because he had murdered Haji Muhammad Khan Koki's father. Akbar personally administered summary justice in the case of his foster brother, Adham Khan, who had conspired to kill Atka Khan. In the *Ahkam-i-Alamgiri* of Hamid ud din Khan's Nimcha occur the following passages: "What have the worldly affairs to do with religion? And why should bigotry intrude into matters of religion? For you there is your religion, and for me mine." And: "If the law were followed it would have been necessary to annihilate all the Rajas and their subjects."

Though the *ulema* never secured a dominant position in Mughal administrative system and had little say in determining state policy, their influence on the masses and the control of education made them a force to be reckoned with. Akbar's religious eclecticism was curbed by the efforts of the *ulema* led by Hazrat Mujadid Alaf Sani. Earlier, Abdul Nabi and Makhdoom ul Mulk had paid with their lives for not joining the bandwagon of Akbar. Aurangzeb's *sandrus sadur* refused to read the *khutba* in his name as his father Shahjahan was still alive. The attempt of Bahadur Shah I to change the wording of the *khutba* was resisted by the *ulema* of Lahore, Ahmadabad and Kashmir. One Miran Shah had the courage to signify his dissatisfaction with Mohammad Shah's rule by prohibiting the reading of the *khutba* in the name of the emperor who had flouted the *shariat* and had oppressed the people. The Mughal state may not have been an Islamic state where the *shariat* was supreme, but the conduct of the ruler, his officers and his Muslim subjects was directed and controlled more by religion than by state regulations.

Though hereditary kingship, indeed kingship itself, finds no warrant in Muslim law it became an accepted political postulate that the ruler was to be from the family of Babur. There were

[50] *Siyasatnama, loc. cit.*, p. 12.

[51] Mirza Muhammad Baqir, *Mauiza-i-Jahangiri*, Persian MS. No. 1666, I.O.L., London.

numerous palace revolutions, wars of succession and cases of fratricide and regicide but the selection of the candidate for the throne was invariably confined to princes of the royal blood.

Theology and political theory apart, the greatest achievement of the Mughals was to inculcate in their subjects a sentiment of loyalty and devotion to the dynasty. This withstood the troubles and turmoils of the 18th century that reduced the emperors to mere figureheads and playthings of politicians and military adventurers. The emperor was looked upon as the father of the people, the protector of the poor, and the only defence against the "violence of the violent." Amongst the Hindus a sect known as the *Dharshaniya* had grown up who considered the sight of the emperor (*darshan*= to behold) a religious duty before starting the day's work.[52] Members of the *Chishtiya Sufi* order similarly preached reverence for the king in spite of their objection to some of the state regulations. Shaikh Abdul Quddus Gangohi (1828-1905) speaks of the sight of the "Sultan-i-Adil" as tantamount to "*ibadat*" (worship) and the sultan as *Khalifa-i-Rahmani* (vice-regent of God).[53]

The duty of the emperor to dispense justice and that of his officers to look after the interests of the subjects, to promote their prosperity, to extend cultivation and populate the villages is reiterated again and again in the *dastur-ulamals*, letters of appointment of government officials, and *faramin* issued from the court. Tara Chand writes:

> We find emperors and kings issuing instructions to their officials to consider the welfare of the peasant as their primary duty. Akbar regarded that agent of his government upright who protected the husbandman, watched over the subjects, developed the country and improved the revenue.[54]

These were not propaganda stunts but embody the genuine concern of the emperors to stand forth as the champions of justice

[52]Muhammad Hashim, *Muntakhab-ul-Labab*, Bib. Ind., Calcutta, I, p. 213. Saiyid Ashraf Khan, *Roqaim-i-Karaim*, Ethe, 375, fol. 34B.

[53]Abdul Quddus, *Maqtubat-i-Qudusiya*, Delhi, 1870, pp. 44-45: Kingship and Prophethood are two jewels of the same ring (letter No. 34). See also Mohammad Tahir Sabzwari, *Rauza-ul-Tahirin*. B.M. MS. OR. 168, fol. 524B; Fakhr-i-Madabbir, *Kitab Adab-ul-Harb wal Shujaat*, B.M. Ad. MS. 16853, fol. 8B; Fazl-bin-Rozbhan, *Suluk-ul-Muluk*, B.M. MS. OR. 53, fols. 15-18.

[54]Tara Chand, *op. cit.*, p. 49.

and fair play. It is by their conduct that the Mughals captured the imagination of their subjects and mobilized the talents and the resources of the country to the service of the imperial state. Even at a time when the Mughals had lost all political power and lived on the sufference, first of the Marathas and later of the British, the emperor's legal claim to sovereignty was still recognized. In 1794 the Peshwa solicited and received with solemn ceremony the insignia of certain dignities from the emperor of Delhi. In Seringapatam, when the body of Tipu had not yet become cold, the representative of the Nizam had the *khutba* read in the name of the Mughal ruler. The empire by ceasing to be a fact had become an accepted idea. According to Abul Fazl, Akbar held that for rulers, worship consists in the dispensation of justice and the improvement of the realm.[55] Alamgir Aurangzeb's guiding principle of government was "affection and kindness towards the great and the small."[56] According to Akbar kingship was "in fact the understanding of man's worth."[57] In their quest for political unity in the subcontinent many small states were conquered and incorporated in the empire or reduced to vassalage, but the intention of the ruler, in the words of Jahangir, was not to destroy old families.

The enlightened and liberal patronage of the Mughal emperors and the aristocracy encouraged trade, industry and craftmanship. Fine cotton and silk fabrics, carpets and shawls, metalwork, swords and other weapons, jewellery etc., were manufactured and exported. In the 17th century India was probably the largest producer of industrial goods in the world and this was entirely due to the peace and order established by the Mughals. Prices were low and necessaries of life cheap and easily available. Regional languages were patronized. Medicine, mathematics, astronomy, fine arts, painting, architecture and music attained to great excellence.

The Mughal conquest of India re-established the international character of the Indo-Pakistan subcontinent which since the 13th century had been practically isolated from the rest of the world. Once again the subcontinent assumed a position of importance and of honour in the world. The extent of the Mughal empire, its wealth, its armed strength, its trade and commerce, and the

[55]*Ain*, V, p. 244.
[56]Farman to Mohammad Hashim, *Oriental Miscellany*, p. 50.
[57]*Ain*, V, p. 243.

arts and crafts it fostered and the peace and prosperity which reigned there made it the envy of the contemporary European and Asiatic countries.

The Mughal emperors though alien in race, language, religion and cultural traditions, soon after the military occupation of the country, completely identified themselves with the interests of the people whom they had conquered. The rulers stood forth as the living symbol of the growth of a composite culture, rich and varied in content, growing and embracing the splendid cultural heritage of the rulers and the ruled. They gave this culture a new meaning, a new direction and a new content. They enlisted in their service the military, administrative, financial and artistic talent of India. The conferring of high offices on the conquered non-Muslims was a new experience, a new political idea, derived from Mongol tradition, in the history of this country.[58] The institutions of the Hindus, their religious and secular literature with its vast storehouse of learning and the accumulated wisdom of its sages came to be studied with reverent assiduity.

As for their relationship to Hindu ideas of kingship, it could not be said that the Mughals broke with the Hindu *Dharmaśāstra* tradition of pious kingship, which resembled the Muslim concept of the "pious Sultan." And they brought the royal mystique to its apogee in the subcontinent. However, during the palmy days of the empire, before their arm had become numb and their sword dull, the might of the Mughals, the peace that they imposed, the justice that they provided and the arts that they encouraged seemed to provide proofs of their divine right to rule. The practice of pious kingship was made consonant with the theory, and good works rather than conquest became evidence of divine election. The norm of political stablility superseded the norm of turbulence, which in itself gave a fresh emphasis to the duties of the king.

[58]Chingiz Khan's prime minister was a Chinese.

8. The British and the Indian State to 1830

PERCIVAL SPEAR

The relation of the British to Indian political tradition poses the prior question of the meaning of this latter term. For there are, in fact, several political traditions in India, the Hindu, the Buddhist, the Muslim, and sundry variations of them. The Rajputs, for example, accepted Hindu ideology in general but certainly added tribal concepts of their own. If, however, the matter be placed in the setting of time, the question becomes one of the relations of the British with the regime immediately before them. But here again there are difficulties for it must then be asked, which regime? In the north it was the Mughals or their surviving wreckage; in the south it was, at some removes, the Hindu empire of Vijayanagar, itself a highly artificial creation; while in the west it was the Marathas. Nor can it be said, if we proceed chronologically, that the pre-existing regimes were consistent in themselves. The Mughal empire, for example, contained elements other than the Islamic or Turkish, yet every component element appeared impartially to the British observer or administrator as "Indian tradition." With these considerations in mind, we are forced back to a pragmatic approach. For the purposes of British comprehension and action what they found actually existing was "Indian tradition."

Yet here again some qualification must be made. For the British administrators did not depend only on what they saw; they were also influenced by what they read or were told of "the men aforetime." Thus Charles Metcalfe was not content merely to collect revenue through the customary *amils* but also listened to what the *muqaddams* had to say about their proprietary and coparcenary rights. Mountstuart Elphinstone, with his historical sense, went back from the last Peshwa to Sivaji looking for precedents. He was concerned, not only with the existing Indian practice but with the more perfect model of the more distant past. Sir Thomas Munro always had his idea of the ancient Indian village in mind as he surveyed the institutional debris left by the successive waves of Mughals, Marathas and Muslim Mysoreans. When we come to Holt Mackenzie's proposals for the ceded and conquered provinces it becomes almost a question of resurrecting village communities from the *zamindari* overlay of centuries. The view of the British idea of tradition as consisting only in the actually existing institutions and customs which they encountered has therefore to be modified. They included in their purview institutions and customs from which they believed existing ones had derived or descended, perhaps in a degraded form. Those that they found were often regarded as signposts of what had been and ought to be revived.

There is one other aspect of political tradition, its religious overtones. In a theocratic multi-social society such as India every institution had its religious implications, if not in the institutions themselves then in the persons who controlled them. Custom itself was allied to religion, its sanction being asserted on occasion by learned pundits as being equal to that of the Vedas or *śhāstras* themselves. When the British surveyed political tradition, therefore, they had in mind the traditions which they found actually subsisting on their arrival, the model from which they believed that these traditions derived, and the connotations with the great religious systems which they believed they involved. They did not attempt to sort them out or to judge them at first; rather they wished to accommodate themselves to them, so that they could build on firm foundations on the one hand, and avoid the ever present danger of an upheaval on the other.

The earliest British attitudes to the Indian state were frankly hostile. A man like John Mildenhall might be impressed by Akbar and his court or like John Hawkins bemused by the bibulous high court life in which he found himself. But the early factors' letters are full of complaints of official highhandedness while so percipient an observer as Sir Thomas Roe found the Mughal state despotic and cruel, the government harsh and insensitive to the poverty and suffering around them and the official nobles grasping, greedy and corrupt.[1] Thomas Ovington might see some virtue in Hindu society, but I know of no bouquets awarded to any state as such. During the 17th century the East India Company had to do with Hindu as well as Muslim powers. On the west coast there were

[1]*The Embassy of Sir Thomas Roe to India, 1615-19*, Sir W. Foster (ed.), 1926.

the Marathas and further south the trading rajas of Malabar; on the east coast the Madras factory began as a dependency of the *epigoni* successors of the Vijayanagar kings. The factors' reports have little good to say of these governments either, though, being less powerful than the Mughals, they were also less dangerous.

Personally and socially, there was also surprisingly little tendency to borrow from local society. Social intercourse was largely inhibited by the Hindu caste system and Muslim clannishness. The British dislike of learning languages, as evident in the 17th as in the 19th century, heightened this barrier, for it gave them no chance of meeting Indians on their own cultural and intellectual grounds. Gerald Aungier's mastery of Persian at Bombay was quite exceptional. Not, indeed, that they had very much culture to offer, for the average factor, like his Dutch colleagues who decorated the domes of their Mughal style tombs at Surat with wine bowls, was mainly interested in bottles and dining boards. In Surat young factors found that they could collect money from life conscious *banias* by pretending to shoot birds;[2] a more tangible sign was the removal of images from the Company's chapel in Surat in order not to offend the Muslims;[3] but both of these instances only suggest some awareness of others' customs rather than any inclination to borrow. Even hookahs were not much used before the 18th century, for we find "churchwarden" clay pipes commonly listed in the early inventories. The borrowings, such as they were, were superficial and practical. The British adopted the Indian taste for processions with cheerful noises such as "the country music" with a generous ration of gunfire salutes (to the scandal of the economic directors in London) and fireworks.[4] Or perhaps it was the British taste for public ritual given an Indian dress. Indian clothes were often used as "undress" indoors but never official Indian costume outside. Apart from this the main loans were in the sphere of eating and drinking. Indian curries were added to English diet at the main midday dinner, thus laying the foundation of the over-consumption that

[2]Capt. W. Symson, *A New Voyage to the E. Indies*, 2nd edition, 1720, p. 46-47.

[3]T. Ovington, *A Voyage to Surat 1689*, H.G. Rawlinson (ed.), Oxford, 1929, p. 235.

[4]In general see T.G.P. Spear, *The Nabobs*, 1932.

gave body to the later Calcutta saying, "two monsoons are the life of a man." The same held good for drink; the factors added Persian wines (when procurable) to their pipes of Madeira and bottles of port, together with country spirit or arrak before Scotch influence brought in whisky.

It is well to remember at the outset this general condition of separatism or apartness between the three societies, for it is this attitude that the British carried with them when they entered into politics and began to administer territory. Their instinct was to leave Indian life and institutions as much to themselves as possible. It was to need a very strong motive to induce interference, and much hardly-earned experience before they thought of learning rather than commanding or taking. In the mid- and late- 17th century the British found themselves in closest contact with Indian powers in western India, at Bombay and Surat. Here occurred a kind of abortive confrontation, conducted with distinction by Gerald Aungier and ended when Sir John Child was compelled by his London namesake to go to war with the Emperor Aurangzeb.

The first serious confrontation occurred in south India with the Anglo-French wars of the mid-18th century. But it never went much beyond the political sphere because, after the initial clash between the companies, each side tended to use Indian agency. They worked through rather than over the Indian state. Dupleix's invention of the sponsored state, practised with masterly skill by de Bussy for seven years in Hyderabad, was imitated by the British in their dealings with Muhammmad Ali Walajah, Nawab of the Carnatic. The only territorial acquisition south of the Kistna before 1792 was the *jagir* south of Madras given by the nawab for services rendered in the French wars. Until the 1790s this was administered on the traditional system just as if it was still part of the nawab's state. Relations with the nawab were continuous and close, it is true, but they were as between states on a diplomatic level, and as between individual European creditors and a debtor nawab on a financial level. Of loans or impositions by one side or the other there were none.

It is in Bengal that we get the first real confrontation of the British with the Indian state. And here at first the attitude was borrowed from the past and the pattern of procedure from the south. There was no desire to take over the state at Bengal, to impose Western moulds upon it, or to absorb elements of its tradition. The principle of apartness, which may be expressed in the term non-interference, continued. But Bengal had to be controlled in the interest both of the Company's security and its trade. At the time of Plassey (1757) the Mughal empire, as an ecumenical Indian state, was in the throes of dissolution between the marchings of Afghans and Marathas. It was to be virtually extinguished, by proxy as it were, four years later at Panipat. So Clive followed the south Indian precedent of the sponsored state. Like Dupleix in Hyderabad he engineered a successful military take-over which placed his candidate on the Bengal *gaddi*, and, like Dupleix's operating agent de Bussy, he proceeded to sustain him against all rivals for nearly three years. Apartness was to continue; political management would do duty for government.

But the results of Clive's actions were very different from those of Dupleix and de Bussy and from his own intentions. There were other factors in the Bengal scene which distinguished it sharply from Hyderabad. In Hyderabad there were virtually no French merchants and little French trade. De Bussy had a free political hand. In any case Hyderabad was not an important economic unit. In Bengal the Company had a flourishing trade and thought it should have more. Calcutta contained many British merchants who thought their own fortunes were due for expansion too. Bengal was reputed the wealthiest province of the empire, paying an annual tribute to Delhi of fifty-three lakhs, nearly 20 per cent of its average revenue. The merchants had noticed the very large sums donated to the civil and military authorities by the new nawab.[5] This was a normal Indian procedure in such cases but blown up to quite unusual proportions. Their *quid pro quo* was the grant of free *dastaks* or passes for private trade. The British thus involved themselves in internal Bengali affairs for essentially mercenary reasons. Underlying the human avarice of their proceedings lay a big overestimate of the potential resources of Bengal. With Vansittart's failures to restore order in the Company and the defeat of Mir Kasim and Shah Alam in 1763-64 the sponsored state was in ruins.

But neither the directors in London nor the government in Calcutta were yet prepared for a take-over. The problem was envisaged as one of reviving the Bengal goose that laid the golden eggs rather

[5]See P. Spear, *Oxford History of Modern India*, Oxford, 1965, p. 29 and Master of Bengal: Clive and his India, London, 1975, Chapter 9 for details.

than replacing her. The principle of separation still held the field; it was the defects in the working of the system till 1764 which were to be remedied. These defects were conceived by Clive on his return in 1765 to be two: the Nawab's control of finance, which had enabled Mir Kasim to build up an army; and the Company's servants' interference inside Bengal for personal gain. He dealt with the first by obtaining the *diwani* or revenue collecting authority from Shah Alam over the head of the new Nawab Najm-ad-daula. He sought to deal with the second by forbidding the reception of large presents and paying good salaries by means of shares in the salt monopoly. The second of these devices broke down. The first certainly served its purpose, but it must not be supposed that it meant a real deviation from the previous policy of separateness. The system has been known as the Dual system but it should more coriectly be called the Indirect system. Clive now had the revenue of Bengal in his hands, but he collected it through a deputy, Muhammad Reza Khan, who was also the nawab's deputy for the judicial administration. The responsibility for the revenue collection was moved from the nawab of Bengal to the Company, but the system of collection was the same. The Company was still interested in the results of administration rather than tne conduct of the administration itself. From the surplus of the revenue Clive hoped to provide for the Company's annual "investment" and so inspired rosy dreams of wealth in London which led the directors to make rash commitments to the British government.

Clive's second system broke down soon after his departure because a cheeseparing directorate would not agree to his Society of Trade through which substantial salaries were to be paid to its servants. Its virtual end may be said to have been the great Bengal famine of 1770, when a third of the population died and a third of the cultivated lands became waste. Yet the revenue was collected "with cruel severity," only 5 per cent of the demand being remitted.[6] During these years there were two kinds of pressure. One was from London, for order in the administration, which prompted the despatch of the ill-fated supervisors in 1769. The other was from the Company in Bengal. The officials believed that Reza Khan was withholding revenue surpluses which lawfully

[6]See Sir W.W. Hunter, *Annals of Rural Bengal*, 4th edition, 1871, pp. 26' 53-54 (quoting a letter from the Calcutta Council to the Court of Directors, 3 Nov. 1772, par. 6).

belonged to the Company. Therefore he must be corrupt or hostile. Many of the same people in their private capacities believed that much money was passing into Indian hands on its way from the cultivator to the treasury which could more suitably come into theirs. So they accused Reza Khan's officials of being corrupt and demanded interference in the name of clean administration. Reza Khan, as Dr Majed Khan has shown, was in fact fighting a rear-guard action on behalf of the old Mughal system of administration.[7]

It was thus financial pressure which ended the phase of apartness or disinterest in Indian administration. The Company and its servants both believed that more money was to be had in Bengal than they were receiving, and both felt that they needed it. These pressures prepared the way for the next phase, which is associated with Warren Hastings. The key word of his government was direct administration symbolized in the phrase "standing forth as *dewan*." The hollowness of the charges of corruption against the nawabi system is suggested by the fact that after the dismissal of Reza Khan, Hastings, with all the resources of governmental authority and influence behind him, was not able to make good in a court of law his charges of corruption and malversation. The case had to be abandoned. These charges were the pretext but not the reason for the take-over.

The new system involved the direct administration of Bengal by the Company and soon Hastings had his British collectors in the districts, his civil judges and hierarchical network of courts. The big change that this represented was from separateness or apartness to absorption. Warren Hastings took over the nawabi system and controlled it through British agents. His concept was to administer an Indian state on Indian lines as an agent of the Company. We can see this principle working in several directions. His districts were anglicized Mughal *sarkars*, his collectors the equivalent of Mughal *dewans*. From the Bengali point of view, the Governor's authority was as formidable as that of the old *subahdar*. It was not so much the local people, as the British in India or Britain, who resented or were shocked by Hastings' controversial highhanded acts. From the Indian point of view they were convincing displays of the wielding of the sceptre, which increased Hastings' stature in their eyes rather than diminished

[7]See A. Majed Khan, *The Transition in Bengal, 1756-1775*, Cambridge, 1969.

it. The hanging of Nand Kumar, doubtful in law and arguably an executive murder for political purposes, was an act of vigour which confounded his enemies. Its most impressive feature, in Indian eyes, was the failure of the council opposition to prevent it. In the eyes of Indian Calcutta, it convincingly showed that Hastings was master in his own house and so of all Bengal. The financial squeezing of Raja Chaith Singh of Banaras, and his removal when he resisted, was in line with Indian political practice in such cases. In financial duress, there was no limit to the measures a ruler might take except the fear of a general revolt. Hastings' action was thus justified in terms of Indian practice, in view of his admittedly critical position at the time. The same principle covered his dunning of the begams of Oudh, through and over the head of the Nawab Wazir of Oudh. *Raison d'état*, in Indian eyes, covered this exercise also, though it was regarded as in much more doubtful taste. Interference with *zenanas* was an Afghan rather than an Indian Muslim trait. As for the Rohilla war, this was an ordinary political bargain which no-one would think of questioning, let alone conddemning.

In revenue policy the same tendency can be seen. In Mughal terms Hastings was a bad revenue administrator because he did not have a consistent policy beyond that of extracting money from the soil, but he nevertheless came, as it were, within the Mughal terms of reference. While he juggled with the *zamindari* system in the hope of increasing revenue, and so caused much social dislocation, his acts were within the system as a whole. Revenue farming, annual settlements and the sending of special officers to extort more money might be described as deviations from the system, but they assumed the system from which they deviated. The *zamindars* retained their local police and judicial powers. We can also see the continuance of the Mughal tradition in the patronage of learning, the arts and religion. This is a recognized duty of all Indian sovereigns, one which was observed even by the puritan Emperor Aurangzeb. On the Indian side we have Hastings' consorting with the learned in Calcutta, his foundation of the Calcutta Arabic College, his protection of temples; and on the British his encouragement of Sir William Jones and his Asiatic Society of Bengal.

It is true that the system was not an exact replica of the old, for it was not a revival, which has to imitate closely in order to prove its genuineness, but a continuation. All living institutions are modified as they continue. In this light we can view Hastings' civil and revenue courts as an improvement rather than a supersession, for they administered Hindu and Muslim personal law and settled revenue disputes on the old terms. The British judge was "advised" by those who usually in practice decided the cases. So were the British collectors; the argument for them was not that they would collect in a new way, but that they would collect more, and more effectively. Non-interference with religious practice was carried further than by the Mughals, who, for example, discouraged and on occasion prohibited *sati*.[8] But it was the same attitude, if a little more rigorously expressed.

Nor was the system left entirely to itself. It was subject to intrusion from Britain and to attack from within. The chief intrusion came with the Regulating Act. In the end the governor-general's position was enhanced rather than reduced by the Act. But the Supreme Court was an intrusion which could not be explained away. Hastings could set limits to its authority but not get rid of it. It was a legal foreign body in the post-Mughal body politic. The attack from within came from Sir Philip Francis, not on the score of Hastings' authority, but in the vital realm of revenue policy. Francis, as Mr Ranajit Guha has so elegantly shown,[9] was influenced by the French Physiocrats in his thinking. Wealth came from the land; the *zamindars* controlled the produce of the land; therefore the *zamindars* should be sustained and strengthened, not bypassed or depressed. Francis advocated their treatment as landlords, the making of a permanent settlement which would enable them to amass surplus capital for future development. Hastings' counter-arguments were pragmatic, the arguments of a man who did not want the existing traditional system tampered with.

Philip Francis' proposals went down along with the wreck of his political ambitions. But they pointed to the future and formed a connecting link between the Hastings era of Mughal absorption and the Cornwallis period of British lending. Cornwallis came to India instructed to place the land administration on a stable basis, to reform the company's administration and to refrain from wars

[8] V. Smith, *Akbar, the Great Mogul*, 2nd edition, Oxford, 1927, pp. 226 and 382.

[9] R. Guha, *A Rule of Property for Bengal*, Paris, 1963.

of annexation. Before noticing his innovations, ideological and practical, it is well to observe that in certain respects he left the post-Mughal system as it was. It was in intention a benevolent as well as an irresponsible government. Its organization was hierarchical and the supreme authority was if anything enhanced. The foreign character of the upper government cadres was much more pronounced, but was an over-emphasis, not a denial of recognized Mughal practice. The authoritarian structure of the government, and its paternal character, remained unimpaired. But this said, there has to be noted a large intrusion of British concepts embodied in institutions. First came the vital land question. Though Cornwallis deferred to John Shore's plea for greater knowledge of Indian practice, in the end he acted without regard to it. He brought with him the mental stock-in-trade of a cultivated Whig landed aristocrat, and it was this that he passed on to Bengal. In the vital question of land he thought it obvious that you should have property rather than bundles of rights in land. So he turned the diminished *zamindars* into landlords, often of large proportions. Their land tax became virtual rents to government of hereditary occupiers, and all the lesser grades of landholders down to the actual cultivators themselves became their virtual tenants. Cornwallis enjoined on the *zamindars* good treatment of their subordinates, and on the collectors and judges, the protection of the cultivators' rights. But, since these were mostly unwritten and traditional, accepted by folk memory and group affirmation, they could not be accepted in a court of law and all cultivators with unwritten rights became tenants-at-will.

A cardinal Whig principle was the division of power for the curbing of its arbitrary exercise. Cornwallis himself disregarded this principle on practical grounds when he insisted on receiving, as governor-general, the power of overriding his council. But he enforced the separation between the judicial and executive power in the districts, when he added the magistracy to the district judges and confined the collectors to revenue duties. It might be argued that this resembled Akbar's division of authority in the *subah* between the *dewan* and the *nazim*. But this was, in effect, a device for tighter financial control by the centre rather than an equal division of authority. The *nazim* or *subahdar* was, in fact, always the senior. In the *sarkar* and the *pargana*, on the other hand, corresponding to the British district and sub-district or *tahsil*, there was only one responsible officer, the *faujdar* and the *amil*.[10] In effect, these officers were collector-magistrates. Then there was the rule of law, which enabled the citizen to sue the government or its officers in the courts of law. The only traditional equivalent was the theoretical check of Islamic law for Muslims or the *śāstras* for Hindu rulers. But in most Muslim regimes the judges were "lions under the throne" who could be appointed or dismissed at pleasure. Akbar did not shrink from dismissing his *sadr sadur* or chief justice, Sheikh Abdu'l Nabi, as well as his opponent the obstinate Maulana Makdumu'l Mulk.[11] And while the law held good as a standard with divine backing not to be tampered with, or altered except in details, its administration could be arbitrary to a degree. The elements of personal discretion and of official pressure were such that a rule of law could not be said to exist. The ruler not the judge learned in Muslim law, was the individual's "father and mother," and the very use of such a phrase suggests the gulf which separated the mental attitudes of contemporary India and Britain towards authority.

Under Cornwallis it can therefore be said that there was an Indian framework of government subjected to a number of quite radical British innovations. These, it was fondly imagined by its sponsors in India and Britain, had converted a corrupt post-Mughal regime into an oriental version of 18th century England, a garden of benevolent and improving landlords. The period of Wellesley's governor-generalship (1798-1805) was the high noon of these hopes, when the *zamindari* system was extended to the Madras presidency and planned for the newly acquired conquered and ceded territories as far as the banks of the Yamuna. But then a reaction began. The pendulum of change, which had swung far in the direction of European innovation, now began to move back towards a study of Indian society. There was a world, it was increasingly suspected, beneath that of the *zamindar* who paid his annual fixed dues or was sold up, and beyond that of the courts, overwhelmed with people clamouring for rights alleged to exist but not recorded. It began to be recognized that the *zamindari* Eden had its serpent after all, and people began to ask what social thickets had bred and concealed it.

As Philip Francis was the connecting link between the Warren

[10] See I.H. Qureshi, *The Administration of the Mughal Empire*, Karachi, 1966.
[11] V. Smith, *Akbar the Great Mogul*, 2nd edition, Oxford, 1927, pp. 161, 163.

Hastings world of the Indian take-over and the Cornwallis period of European influence, Sir John Shore linked the Cornwallis Eurocentric world with the Indian questionings which followed it. He had studied local conditions and had advocated fuller knowledge, only to be overruled in the end. This phase, like those which had preceded it, arose from administrative problems which pressed on the government. Warren Hastings' take-over was a reply to the breakdown of separatism, the attempt to divorce the Company's paramount authority from the administration of its territories. The Cornwallis innovations arose out of the shortcomings of the take-over administration, of which the Hastings' impeachment was the symbol if not an accurate description. The new movement arose from the challenge of newly acquired territories, where authority had broken down and the administration had to be constructed afresh. In the south there were the extensive lands taken at first or second hand from Tipu Sultan, himself the son of the usurper Haidar Ali. In the north there were the lands acquired from the nawab of Oudh, and conquered from the Marathas, themselves usurpers of former Mughal lands. There were no established regimes on to which responsibility could be shuffled, and no ready-made framework which could be taken over. The superstructure of society had been knocked away, leaving society bare and raw beneath. To settle with the local chiefs in possession was only to deal with another set of usurpers who had seized power with a strong arm in troubled times. The *polygars* of Munro or the "Plunderers" of Metcalfe illustrated Augustine's dictum of a state without justice: "For what are robber bands but little states?"

It was in these circumstances that Thomas Munro, in the course of some fifteen years laborious work under canvas in the countryside, discovered the peasant proprietor with whom, scorning synthetic *zamindars*, village revenue farmers or the joint-holding *mirasdars*, he determined to settle on his *ryotwari* plan.[12] It was in these circumstances that Charles Metcalfe, at first collecting revenue from fortified villages at the point of the bayonet and to the sound of grapeshot, discovered the village community of cultivating *zamindars* and controlling *muqaddams*.[13] In both cases they had uncovered the Indian underworld, or rather it should be said

[12]See A.J. Arbuthnot, *Sir Thomas Munro. Selections etc.*, 2 vols., 1881.

[13]See T.G.P. Spear, *Twilight of the Mughals*, Cambridge, 1951, Chaps. V & VI; and J.W. Kaye, *Papers of Lord Metcalfe*, 1855, pp. 34-65.

real world, with its labyrinth of tenures, interlocking rights, duties and obligations. The experience bred in both men a passion to understand and to conserve. "Innovation is the ruling vice of our government,"[14] wrote Munro in his famous Minute of 31 December 1824. "The village communities," said Metcalfe, "are little republics," which "seem to last where nothing else lasts."[15] This knowledge was obtained by long residence in their areas and by close contact with the people. It was made fruitful by striking ability, which made their administrations a success, and by forceful pens, which enabled them to get their views across to authority in Calcutta and London. Rights must be respected, tenures and customs must be understood, was their battle cry. By convincing the court and board of his case Munro secured the adoption of their viewpoint in India.[16] He was, in fact, specifically sent to Madras to implement it. This attitude received powerful support from two other sources. The first was Mountstuart Elphinstone, whose administration of the Peshwa's Maratha territories from 1818 was a conscious attempt to conserve as much as possible based on a close study of local conditions. "Above all," he said, his rule was "to make no innovations."[17] An unexpected ally came from Bengal in the person of Holt Mackenzie, the talented young territorial department secretary in Calcutta. His great memorandum of 1 July 1819 insisted, in language which the Calcutta secretariat could understand, on the necessity of a full knowledge and record of rural rights before any settlement was made which would affect them.[18] All these men together ended the age when a district officer could gallop through the countryside, settling estates, as it were from the stirrup.[19] It ushered in the period of respect for rights, customs and traditions, when the district officer was as much a learner as a teacher. It amounted, in fact, to a return to the outlook and methods of Akbar's revenue minister, Raja Todar Mal and his *bandobast*.

[14]A.J. Arbuthnot, *op. cit.*, Vol. I, p. 273.

[15]T.G.P. Spear, *op. cit.*, p. 17 (minute by Metcalfe, 1 November 1830).

[16]See T.H. Beaglehole, *Thomas Munro and the Development of Administrative Policy in Madras, 1792-1828*, Cambridge, 1966.

[17]M. Elphinstone, *Report on the Territories Conquered from the Paishwa*, Calcutta, 1821.

[18]*Selections from the Revenue Records of the N.W. Provinces, 1818-20*, Calcutta, 1866, pp. 9-193.

[19] E.I. Brodkin, "Rohilkhund from Conquest to Revolt, 1774-1858," Ph. D. thesis, Cambridge, 1968.

The revenue system, like the crops, was to spring from the local soil. Only it would have more administrative fertilizer.

This phase led on to a further one when the advice of Polonius was reversed to read, "Both a borrower and a lender be." In this case again there was a bridge builder to connect the two periods. This was Holt Mackenzie. He is generally regarded, and particularly by Professor Stokes, as a stern and unbending Benthamite theoretician who had to be restrained by Bentinck from using the holy name too frequently in his state papers.[20] It is true that he tried to apply Ricardian ideas of rent in fixing the revenue demand for the North-West Provinces, a potentially explosive innovation; that he prompted both administrative and judicial reforms on the utilitarian principle of a "determinate human authority"; that he advocated centralizaton both legislative and executive, both in Calcutta and as an assistant-commissioner at the Board of Control. But this is only one side of the picture. His Memorandum of 1 July 1819 contained not only utilitarian principles but a knowledge of conditions in the countryside surpassing that of most district officers, which for a young Calcutta secretary, was phenomenal. Not only this, it showed a concern for individual justice and rights, an insistence on their record and preservation, which put him in the company of Munro and Metcalfe. Writing barely three years after Metcalfe's report on the Delhi administration, and without Metcalfe's first hand knowledge, he put the village community with its traditional rights and intricate patterns of relationships, as it were on the administrative map of Calcutta.[21] This memorandum was accepted *en bloc* by those who had not the energy or interest to work things out for themselves. It was translated into Regulation VII of 1822. A second memorandum in 1826 surveyed the obstacles to putting this Regulation into practice; again, it is full of concern for the people's rights and of practicable means of both preserving them and levying an equitable revenue.[22] In its turn it laid a foundation for Regulation IX of 1833, by which Bentinck and Bird firmly anchored the revenue system of the north-west to a recognition and

[20]E. Stokes, *The English Utilitarians and India*, Oxford, 1959, p. 95. T.G.P. Spear, "Holt Mackenzie: Forgotten Man of Bengal," *Bengal Past & Present*, Diamond Jubilee Number 1967, pp. 26-37.

[21]*Selections from the Revenue Records of the N.W. Provinces, 1818-20*, Calcutta, 1866, pp. 9-193.

[22]*Parliamentary Papers*, 1831-32, Vol. XI, Appendix 81, pp. 243-298.

record of local rights, a recognition and respect for local conditions in settling the revenue demand. Bentinck and Bird watered, but it was Holt Mackenzie that planted.

This dual approach of basic acceptance of the Indian state structure and the addition of improvements based on Western ideas was the dominant feature of the latter part of the early British period, whose end date may be put at 1835. In different people one approach or the other was emphasized, but the overall result was the same. Thus Charles Metcalfe professed liberalism, but his actual theme was the inviolability of the village community as the foundation of all Indian society and revenue administration. Munro was biased in the same direction, firmly believing that his *ryotwari* system, properly administered, was a return to the soil and tradition. "We proceed," he wrote, "in a country of which we know little or nothing, as if we knew everything.... We must not be led away by fanciful theories founded on European models, which will inevitably end in disappointment."[23] Elphinstone was equally solicitous of the past with his motto for the Deccan, "no innovations." But he was also well aware that change must come and studied how it could be managed without unbalancing society. His young revenue officer, Robert Pringle, had no such qualms and sought to settle the district of Indapur according to the pure milk of the Benthamite word.[24] His failure may perhaps be equated with that of Sir John Malcolm in the opposite direction, whose love of rajas, *jagirdars* and chiefs of all kinds even led him to take Munro to task for being hard on the south Indian *polygars*.[25]

We may note the same tendencies at work in two other directions, the religious and the educational. Charles Grant, William Wilberforce[26] and their friends wished to loan Christianity to India. When they were repulsed on the official front they promoted a missionary society and succeeded (1813) in securing entry for missionaries into British India. They further attacked the Company's connection with the Indian religions as well as particular abuses like *sati*.[27] On the whole it can be said that they did not

[23]A.J. Arbuthnot, *op. cit.*, Vol. I, p. 237.

[24]Ravindar Kumar, *Western India in the Nineteenth Century*, 1968, Chaps. II and III.

[25]G.R. Gleig, *Life of Sir T. Munro*, 1830.

[26]R. Coupland, *Wilberforce*, 1923 and 1942.

[27]See J. Kaye, *Christianity and India*, 2nd edition, 1859.

succeed in breaching the governmental policy of toleration, but they did make it more bleak and forbidding. Their greatest achievement in this sphere was the admission of missionaries, the results of whose work, unsponsored by government, were incalculable. In education also Charles Grant and the Evangelicals were active. English education was to be the prelude to conversion, and English education meant Western science and knowledge as well as the English language. In cooperation with rationalists like Macaulay they succeeded in 1835, but they did not overthrow the indigenous system or even prevent the continued patronage of higher oriental learning. What they did succeed in doing was to reinforce the age old principle of Indian government that the patronage of learning and education was a duty of the ruler of the day.

In the period from 1835 to 1857 these tendencies continued with some accentuation. The organization of the land systems continued to observe Indian traditional forms. If there was some bias towards village communities and against large *zamindars*, this was seen as the correction of a more recent tradition by an older one. The full-blown Utilitarianism of Pringle in western India was firmly put down. Religious toleration continued unimpaired and so did the government patronage of learning. As with the Mughals, the alien character of the higher services began to be diluted by the admission of Indians in a subordinate capacity. Bentinck's moves in this respect, as testified in the contemporary parliamentary papers, were the result of many years of discussion and in response to a long felt need. What remained outside the ken of the British was any notion of partnership with the princes or any other Indians.

The accentuation was in respect of the loans from Europe. Governmental patronage of education was an Indian tradition but its form was now to be Western. While the support of indigenous learning did not cease after Bentinck's frontal attack, all new developments were along Western lines. Missionary propaganda notably increased, with some dramatic results in Bengal. Though the government was strictly neutral, this was generally assumed to have its countenance. The critical attitude towards certain religious and moral aspects of Indian society increased steadily, spilling over into a demand for interference. The question of *sati* exposed the clash of standards in an acute form. The clash over female infanticide was scarcely less sharp though the method of dealing with it was less minatory and more persuasive. The opening of inheritance to Christian converts,[28] the insistence of liability to service overseas for new military recruits,[29] the increasing disregard of the rights and privileges of displaced dynasties, all were examples of the increasingly sharp intrusion of the West. Yet it did not amount to a denial of Indian tradition as such. It was rather an increasing bias towards the lending side of the double account. In the army caste distinctions continued to be meticulously maintained. The case of the greased cartridges, which might well appear to have been the final provocation, was not, in fact, anything of the kind. It was an unusually obtuse bureaucratic blunder. What this accentuation did in fact achieve was a rising tension between the traditional forces in Indian society and the government. Some such tension was inevitable in the circumstances. It was its "management" by the government leading to the Mutiny explosion which is debatable.

The Indian states were the exception to the general rule of British acceptance of the Indian state and its subsequent modification. They were included in the British attitude of non-involvement with Indian government before Cornwallis' war with Tipu Sultan in 1791 in south India and the days of Warren Hastings in the north. But whereas the British took over, as it were, the Indian state in its own dominions, they continued to leave the diminishing number of Indian states severely alone. They fettered them with subsidiary treaties, beginning with Clive's treaty with Shuja-ad-daula in 1765, and brought to a fine art by Lord Wellesley between 1798 and 1805; they tethered them to the British power by the stationing of subsidiary forces near their capitals; they ensured the poverty of the states by making them pay for the subsidiary forces as well as their own armies. But they not only left them with internal autonomy, they kept them at arm's length from the central government. There was interference in the case of gross misgovernment, towards which the whole system tended, as in the cases of Hyderabad and Mysore. Europeans might exploit the resources of an Indian state, like Palmer and Co. in Hyderabad and many individuals in Oudh, or earlier, in the Carnatic. But there was no

[28] Regulation VII, 1832, Clauses VIII & IX, and Act XXI of 1850. See M. Mohar Ali, *The Bengali Reaction to Christian Missionary Activities, 1833-1857*, Chittagong, 1965, Chap. VI, pp. 117-136.

[29] General Service Enlistment Act, 1856.

collaboration, no cooperation. The only guises under which Indian princes appeared in British India were as the givers of loans, like that arranged by Lord Hastings from Oudh at the time of the Nepal war, or as contributors to British enterprises such as Lord Hastings' projected donation from the nizam towards the building of Calcutta cathedral. After the British had taken over the main structure of the Indian state in their own dominions, the princes remained segregated, decaying hulks moored in a stagnant political backwater. The general opinion was that one by one, as they grew too leaky to keep afloat, they would be removed to the company's capacious boatyard for breaking up.[30] In all this there was not a trace of either the Mughal or pre-Mughal attitude stretching back to the immemorial past. Dependent states have always been an integral part of traditional Indian empires. They were subordinate, but they were also organically connected with the paramount power. The badge of the dependence was the payment of *peshkash* or tribute. But they supplied troops to their superior and often high officers as well. We know most of this system in its developed form from Mughal practice. They turned Rajasthan into a *subah* or province, the princes governing their states as Mughal approved rulers, a Mughal governor and troops only holding a watching brief at Ajmir. Rajput contingents served with the Mughal forces, Rajput chiefs sat on Akbar's inner council, commanded armies and governed provinces throughout the Mughal period. It was a Rajput who defeated Sivaji and brought him to Agra for a settlement with Aurangzeb. Politically, they formed a makeweight to rebelliously inclined Muslims; religiously and culturally, they gave the empire a Hindu as well as a Muslim flavour. Instead of weakening or being a drag on the Mughal power, they strengthened it. They were an integral part of it, sharing in its fortunes. Not till very much later did the British think of anything remotely resembling this, and then they did too little too late. Princely *apartheid* prevailed in the British imperial system.

To the question, what was the attitude of the early British to the traditional or contemporary Indian state system, it is now possible to supply some sort of answer. The British didn't borrow this and that from India for their own political structure. They

[30]For a general review, see *Parliamentary Papers, 1831-32*, Vol. XIV, pp. 176-335.

took over the Indian state and then made additions and adjustments according to their own ideas. They never intended to precipitate social revolution or disrupt society, though some of their imported adjustments or additions had just that effect. They started by trying to contract out of administrative responsibility altogether through the device of the sponsored state in the Carnatic and Bengal. It was only when this experiment broke down in Bengal that they decided on a take-over, and then from by no means unmixed motives of public good. With the increasing pressures from Britain in Hastings' time came the beginning ɹo Western innovations. The threat of radical Europeanization in the state structure of Cornwallis' time was beaten off by the great administrators of the early 19th century who dicovered some of the true springs of Indian life and insisted on leading their waters to work the wheel of Indian state power. Then came the period of simultaneous borrowing and lending, a system which sometimes produced bizarre results. But it never affected the fundamental fact that the system as a whole was in line with and a continuation of Indian tradition. For this reason the British power was rightly named the Indian empire as distinguishing it from colonies and self-governing Anglo-Saxon communities. The title expressed the distinct nature of the Indian state structure.

In what then, did this "Indianness" fo the British Indian state consist? A glance at the early British system alongside that of the Mughals reveals the large degree of resemblance and continuity. Indeed, it might be asked what had changed in essentials beyond the substitution of the white skins of the Europeans for the copper-coloured and bronze faces of the Central Asians? On the executive side there is the same principle of authority, the governor-general being, to the Indian observer, even more powerful than the emperor. For if a governor-general could be recalled an emperor could be overthrown, and frequently suffered that fate during the 18th century. His councillors corresponded to the *lal purdahris* or confidential advisers of the emperor. If they were occasionally obstreperous, as for a time under Warren Hastings, they only recalled the factions which rent the imperial entourage in times of crisis (as in 1580) or under a weak ruler. The governors and lieutenant-governors tallied with the *subahdars*, both in the dependence on the Supreme Power and their occasional insubordination and evasions. Beneath these great figures came the local administration, where the district corresponded with the *sarkar* and the sub-district or *tahsil* with the *pargana*. The division between judge-magistrate and collector was altered by Bentinck who returned to the collector his magisterial powers. The institution of commissioners only strengthened the chain of authority and so did the centralization of legislative authority in Calcutta in 1834. The Mughals enforced their authority through the imperial service of the *mansabdars*. They were a civil-cum-military order, highly paid, but dependent on the emperor. Their British counterparts were the civil service, highly paid and disciplined from the time of Cornwallis. The methods of payment and organization differed, but the principle was the same. In revenue matters the same principles held good, for after false starts under Hastings and allowing for the big exception of Bengal with its new landlords, the essence of the system in the north was a return to the attitudes of Raja Todar Mal and his *bandobast*. The cultivator must be cherished, his rights respected, his assessment moderately fixed on scientific principles. There were big changes, of course, but these (again apart from Bengal) were within the system rather than outside it—more exact measurement, better records, more precise collection and severer penalties for defaulting. In law the case was much the same. The Cornwallis criminal code may be described as the Islamic code minus the amputation of limbs. Hindu and Muslim personal law were retained as before. Apart from the intrusion of the Supreme Court, only in public law did English legal ideas penetrate. In time, no doubt, these and English legal procedures had a great effect, but their implications were not at first realized, and even the import of Cornwallis' declaration of the rule of law was not grasped.[31] The personnel of the government was indeed more foreign than before, but this was only an extension of a recognized Mughal principle. Seventy per cent of the Mughal *mansabdars* in the 16th and early 17th centuries were of foreign extraction.[32] The same was the case with language. Persian was actually retained as the official language until 1835, and when English took its place, it was only a case of the substitution of one foreign conqueror's languge for another. The attitude to religious toleration was much the same, the British being more punctilious and aloof. So was the general attitude of

[31]See *Oxford History of India*, 3rd edition, 1958, p. 537, and C. Ross (ed.), *Correspondence of Charles 1st Marquis Cornwallis*, 3 vols., 1859, Vol. II, p. 558.

[32]W.E. Moreland, *India at the death of Akbar*, 1920, pp. 69-70.

paternalism and with it, the patronage of learning and culture. Here again the British were less generous and more remote, but they recognized the obligation until the controversies which arose after the formation of the Committee of Public Instruction in 1823.

It can therefore be argued that early British India, until about 1830, was really Mughal India writ large. It was the conformity to Indian attitudes and practices which were dominant, the innovations which were or seemed at the time, to be peripheral. It was the Indian states which were out in the cold, being neither full states nor participating in the life of the all-India empire. Like decapitated bodies, their trunks lay festering in the sun of History until Dalhousie essayed to bury them. Canning did not resurrect the survivors, but embalmed them until the more thorough Vallabhbhai Patel took them all to the burning *ghat* of oblivion. In the first period of British rule down to 1830, British India was Indian India continued, and princely India was politically outcaste India.

9. Rabindranath Tagore's Political Writings and Indian Tradition

T.P. MUKHERJEE

In one of his letters to C.F. Andrews Tagore wrote: "Politics are so wholly against my nature; and yet, belonging to an unfortunate country, born to an abnormal situation, we find it so difficult to avoid their outbursts." By "politics" Tagore meant Indian nationalism. Tagore was not a political leader. He did not form a party, nor did he belong to one. But during the period in which he lived the Indian national movement passed through a series of severe tests, and Tagore could hardly turn his mind away from it. It is unfortunate that his reputation as a poet should have obscured his contribution to Indian nationalism. It is perhaps not widely known that at one stage he was actively involved in the national movement, although not fully agreeing with its policy. Tagore's numerous speeches and essays, written mostly in Bengali, bear testimony that he had a clearer understanding of the situation and more positive answers to the fundamental problems than many of the professional politicians. This essay is an attempt to give a brief exposition, quoting as freely as possible from the original, of Rabindranath Tagore's political writing during the Bengal anti-partition movement (1905-11).

However, before we come to Tagore, it is desirable to set the scene for him by a quick review of the intellectual climate of thought of 19th century Bengal, particularly of Rammohan Ray and Debendranath Tagore, the two great men for whom Rabindranath had the highest respect and to whom he owed much.

I

The first half of the 19th century in Bengal is ordinarily referred to as the period of the "Renaissance." It was a period of intense national vitality, bursting out in the arts, literature, journalism, political activity, social reorganization, religious reforms and educational ideas. At the root of this national exuberance was India's close contact, through the servants of the East India Company in Bengal, with the free thought and positivist knowledge of the West, on the one hand, and with the cultural wealth of ancient India, on the other. The two primary factors contributing to the "Bengali Renaissance" were the reception and assimilation of Western thought by the Bengali mind and the profound sense of national dignity aroused by the discovery of India's cultural heritage. The foundation of the Royal Asiatic Society of Bengal (1784) and Hindu College of Calcutta (1817) were the most significant events in the emergence of the Bengal renaissance.

In the 19th century contact between Bengal and Europe there were religious, cultural and political strands.The religious contact, that is, the propagation of the Christian faith in India, tended to lead to conflict and hostility. The cultural contact, on the other hand, resulted in assimilation and absorption. The political contact, in the early years at any rate, was marked by acceptance, gradually turning to repudiation. The response of the Bengali society to this threefold impact of the West was seen first in social and religious reform and later in the evolution of political ideas.

In spite of the conversion of a large number of Hindus, mostly from the lower castes, the evangelical attempts of the Christian missionaries by and large were a failure. Duff's description of the commotion roused by the baptism of K.M. Banerji, a prominent Brahmin of Calcutta and one of the earliest converts, clearly illustrates the Hindu attitude towards conversion:

> ...his [Banerji's] baptism, in particular, became the theme of conversation and discussion with every group that met on the street or in the bazar; in every snug coterie reposing under shade from the mid-day sun; in every school; and in every family circle. Hundreds, or even thousands of baptisms among the low caste, or no caste, or illiterate grades, generally would not have excited a tithe of the mental stir and inquiry then exhibited among all classes.

This description stands in sharp contrast with another of Duff's, in which he describes the eagerness of 19th century Bengal for Western education:

> The excitement for western education continued unabated. They pursued us along the streets, they threw open the doors of our palankeens, they poured in their supplications with a pitiful earnestness of countenance which might have softened the heart of a stone.

The rejection of Christianity and the adoption of Western education, anomalous though it may appear, is the expression of a social attitude which is traditional and at the same time rational, conservative as well as radical. By resisting the penetration of Christianity Hindu society demonstrated its allegiance to its own tradition. However, the allegiance was not uncritical; nor was it a pledge of acceptance of the authority of the priesthood or its interpretation of the scriptures. The validity of tradition was subjected to severe criticism by the missionaries. Their attack on Hinduism exposed certain areas of Hindu society, those that had hitherto been guarded by convention and thus established the need for a reinterpretation of the old tradition in the spirit of rationalism. In the early 19th century the spirit of individualism dominated European thought, and the excitement of the Bengalis by Western education was therefore excitement about the replacement of convention by rationalism and blind faith by individual conscience. Rammohan Ray was the first Indian to combine the old tradition with individual conscience. B.C. Pal brings out this point in summing up Rammohan's work:

> The raja's movement could hardly be called a movement of religion and social revolt. While claiming the right of private judgment in the interpretation of ancient scriptures, the raja never repudiated their authority; nor did he, while seeking to assert the right of the individual conscience to determine for itself what was right or wrong, ever repudiate the authority of that social conscience which spoke through ancient social laws and sanctified social traditions. He tried really to reconcile individual reason with the ancient scriptures and individual conscience with social authority.

The compromise between "social authority" and "individual reason," between "tradition" and "experiment," envisaged by Rammohan Ray, became a guiding force in 19th century Bengal in the form of the Brahma Samaj. There were indeed strong traditionalists, such as Radhakanta Deb, and extreme radicals, such as the young Bengal group. But in the mid-19th century the Brahma movement, under the leadership of Rabindranath's father, Debendranath Tagore, upon whom the mantle of reform fell after Rammohan's death in 1833, was the most powerful force in the country. Debendranath's religious character illuminated the age with a moral grandeur of its own. The *Maharshi*, as he was called by common consent, gave the Brahma Samaj a definite Hindu character by codifying the first ever Brahma scripture, *Brahma Dharma*, a selection with slight modifications from the non-idolatrous scriptures of the Hindus. By abolishing idolatry, which had in theory been done by Rammohan, and rejecting the infallibility of the scriptures, the *Maharshi* emancipated the Hindu mind from the bondage of the scriptures without repudiating the national tradition. The new interpretation of the ancient tradition, which was Brahmaism, became the national religion of many educated Hindus; and it brought the blind imitators of the West back within a culture which was national in form and universal in spirit.

The Brahma movement was an important phase of Indian nationalism. It was a movement of religious and social reform calculated to weld scattered forces together and direct them with the purpose of achieving a common goal: to absorb, assimilate and, to an extent, sustain the Western impact at all levels of society while at the same time maintaining the continuity of tradition. The political significance of the movement was contemplated by Rammohan even from the beginning of the movement. In January 1818, Rammohan wrote to his friend James Silk Buckingham:

> I regret to say that the present system of religion adhered to by the Hindus is not well calculated to promote their political interests. The distinction of castes, introducing innumerable divisions and subdivisions among them, has entirely deprived them of patriotic feeling and the multitude of religious rites and ceremonies and the laws of purification have totally disqualified them from undertaking any difficult enterprises.... It is necessary that some change should take place in their religion, at least for the sake of their political advantage and social comfort.

Rammohan, Debendranath and the leaders of the Brahma movement were not merely religious and social reformers; they were the leaders of the national movement. In his reminiscences Rabindranath said of his father: "The genuine regard which my father had for his country never forsook him through all the revolutionary vicissitudes of his life, and this in his descendants has taken shape as a strong patriotic feeling."

II

Though politics aroused little interest in the first half of the 19th century, political consciousness can be seen to be emerging as a result of the spread of Western education. While recognizing the importance of civil liberty, Rammohan's policy in political matters was that of acceptance of British rule in India. He had unflinching faith in the British government, a faith which was shared by many of his contemporaries. The founder of the Zamindary Association (1837), Prasanna Kumar Tagore, wrote: "If we were to be asked what Government we would prefer, English and any other, we would one and all reply, English by all means, ay, even in preference to a Hindu Government." Debendranath's father, Dwarakanath, also expressed his conviction that "the happiness of India is best secured by her connection with England." The editor of the *Hindoo Patriot* and the *Bengalee* gave it as his opinion that "By subverting the British rule—even if it were in their power to do so—they [the Indians] would only prepare their necks for another and, perhaps, a heavier foreign yoke." Rammohan himself in his *Final Appeal to the Christian Public* expressed his deep gratitude to "the Supreme Disposer of the Universe for having unexpectedly delivered this country from the long continued tyranny of its former rulers, and placed it under the Government of the English." The political ideology of the students of the Hindu College, however, began in time to change. During the period 1828-43 they published several periodicals and established various associations (e.g., Academic Association (1828), Society for the Acquisition of General Knowledge (1838) etc.) for the discussion and propagation of their social and political views. They published articles on the condition of the country, the science of politics, the science of government, European colonization in India, female education, freedom, India under foreigners, etc. The following extract from the *Hindu Pioneer* shows the political thinking of some of the Hindu College students:

> The Government of India [under the English] is purely aristocratical; the people have no voice in the council of legislature; they have no hand in framing the laws which regulate their civil conduct. We need not expatiate on the monopoly of the State Service, the laws' delay, the insolence of office, the heavy expenses of Government, the retirement from India of all those who acquire wealth, and the enormous taxation to which the country is subjected—evils too well known in India. The Muhammedans patronised merit wherever it was to be found; the English, like the primitive Hindus, have one caste of men to govern the general body. The violent means by which foreign supremacy has been established, and the entire alienation of the people of the soil from any share of the Government, nay, even from all offices of trust and power, are circumstances which no commercial, no political benefits can authorise or justify.

Although in political matters there was a difference of opinion between the followers of Rammohan and the Hindu College students, it never became unbridgeable. Political activity in the 19th and early 20th centuries was no more than the submission of petitions on public grievances to the government and to the British Parliament. It was a policy of constitutional appeal and pleading based on the conviction that "when the real state of things is understood, the British Parliament will not long delay justice to India."

Political associations submitted memoranda to the British parliament. Debendranath Tagore patronized and financed the foundation in 1867 of an institution named *Hindu Mela*, the aim of which was to launch a movement of self-reliance and self-respect. The chief organizer of the *Hindu Mela* was Rajnarain Basu. On the ninth anniversary of the *Hindu Mela*, "Rabindranath Tagore, the youngest son of Babu Debendranath Tagore, a handsome lad of some 15, had composed a Bengali poem on *Bharat* (India) which he delivered from memory." This was the first of many of Rabindranath's national songs that breathed inspiration in the National Movement of India. The *Hindu Mela* did not last long but the ideology of self-reliance that it preached among its members left a permanent impression in Rabindranath's mind; and it was the dominant theme of his political writings.

III

Rabindranath's mind and personality developed under the influence of Rammohan's ideology and Debendranath's moral grandeur. His family had a cultural tradition of its own. Being outside the pale of orthodox Brahmanism it developed a tradition which was humanistic, tolerant and non-sectarian. Rabindranath wrote of his family:

> When I was born, our family had already cut loose its social moorings and floated away from the common harbour and the common Hindu tradition of numerous rituals and ceremonials, and the worship of gods and goddesses had left only faint traces in our house.... We were on the threshold of a new age, but we could not see its features yet. Besides, we were utterly unlike the other Bengali families and had our own peculiar spirit and tradition.

Rabindranath was brought up with the belief that *upanishadic* humanism was the most sacred truth of the world. He wrote in the preface of his book *Sadhana:*

> The writer has been brought up in a family where texts of the Upanishads are used in daily worship; and he has had before him the example of his father, who lived his life in the closed communion with God, while not neglecting his duties to the world, or allowing his keen interest in all human affairs to suffer any abatement.... To me the verses of the Upanishads and the teachings of Buddha have ever been things of the spirit, and therefore endowed with boundless vital growth.

The ideals of *upanishadic* and Buddhistic humanism were strengthened by his assimilation of what was the best in European culture. In his reminiscences Rabindranath says:

> When I was young we were all full of admiration for Europe, with its high civilization and its vast scientific progress, and especially for England which had brought this knowledge to our own doors. We had come to know England through her glorious literature, which had brought a new inspiration into

our young lives. The English authors, whose books and poems we studied, were full of love for humanity, justice and freedom. The great literary tradition had come down to us from the revolution period. We felt its power in Wordsworth's sonnets about human liberty. We glorified in it even in the immature productions of Shelley, written in the enthusiasm of his youth, when he declared against the tyranny of priestcrafts and preached the overthrow of all despotisms through the power of suffering bravely endured. All this fired our youthful imaginations. We believed with all our simple faith that even if we rebelled against foreign rule, we should have the sympathy of the west. We felt that England was on our side in wishing us to gain our freedom.

As an embodiment of the perfect harmony of East and West Rabindranath had one ideal in life, the ideal of the universal man. In expressing his deep concern about the people of his own nation, he has given expression to his love for all humanity. His political philosophy is not based on a political theory but on the principles of humanism. Andrews writes:

> The poet's belief in soul-force has always been fundamental. It colours all his poems and his personal outlook upon human life. But whenever the popular methods appeared to him to diverge from that high standard, he became pained and immediately expressed himself in writing.

Rabindranath's active participation in politics was not directed towards achieving a political gain but towards the installation in the national movement of that high moral standard in which he himself believed.

IV

The partition of Bengal was the issue that brought Rabindranath into politics. He wrote in the journal, *Bangadarsan*, which he edited: "On the 16 October 1905, a law will be passed to partition Bengal. We shall observe this day as the day of *Rakhi Bandhan* to show the inherent unity of the Bengalees, the unity which is indestructible by law." On the appointed day the *Rakhi Bandhan* ritual was observed and a procession went out with Rabindranath as its leader. In the ceremony a band of coloured thread was tied around the wrists of compatriots as a symbol of brotherhood in the national struggle against partition. The country was, however, far too agitated to register its dissension merely in a symbolic ceremony; it wanted strong actions. The boycott of British products was proposed and students came out in batches to help with it. This was the first participation of students in the national movement. The government soon passed an order forbidding students to take part in the boycott, an action which led to non-cooperation and to the foundation of the National Council of Education.

Rabindranath was deeply disturbed by the partition of Bengal, but he was equally distressed by the excitement and emotion stirred by the anti-partition movement. As early as 1904 he wrote in the *Bangadarsan* that patriotism was not the ultimate aim of human life. In his famous essay *Svadesi Samaj*, written in 1904, Rabindranath asked his countrymen to win back the country, not from others, but from the overpowering force of inactivity and indifference:

> The timid feminine forces of society which hoard and protect have foiled our manly adventure. Even in the field of knowledge we are convention bound, emasculated.... The truest way of protecting one-self is to rouse one's inherent powers.... The only way to stop this cheapening of our intelligence, feelings and tastes is to become our true selves, consciously, actively and with our full strength.

In this essay Rabindranath not only asked his fellow countrymen "to rouse their inherent powers," he also put forward several schemes of action. The first and most important one was to establish contact between the masses and the educated class. Impregnable barriers existed between the masses and the educated people. Rabindranath wanted them to be removed:

> All over Bengal fairs are held at different times of the year. We must make a list of these fairs and get to know our countrymen through that open door. If the educated classes make it their business to give the fairs in their own localities a new life and objective, if through these fairs they bring together the Hindu and the Muslim, and avoiding empty politics, ascertain the real needs of the eople—schools, roads, water reservoirs, pasture-

> land and the like—then the country will indeed be filled with new stirrings.

Rabindranath's message did not appeal to his countrymen. During the partition movement Bengal was far too shaken emotionally to lend its ears to Rabindranath.

In 1906 Rabindranath was nominated president of the Bengal Provincial Conference. As a branch of the Indian National Congress, the conference had held its first session in 1888 and met annually thereafter, mostly in district towns, to form policies on political and cultural matters related to Bengal. Rabindranath accepted the nomination but with reluctance, mainly because he knew that what he had to say about the Congress or the conference would be neither pleasant nor acceptable.

In his presidential address, the first ever to be delivered in Bengali, Rabindranath criticized the policy of the extremists and expressed disappointment at the conflict within the Congress. He did not rule out the possibility or the necessity of different political views in a free government. He referred to the policy of the labour and socialist party in the British parliament as involving nothing short of revolution in the existing social order of Europe; still it had a place in the parliament. The parliament of a free country could contain parties of different political views. The Indian National Congress was neither a parliament nor an assembly of a free country. The role of Congress in Indian national life, as Rabindranath saw it, was that of an instrument for awakening the national consciousness and strengthening the national will. An assembly convened for this great purpose could not tolerate different ideals. In the past when the people were indifferent about the nation, there was unanimity in the Congress. "But now," says Rabindranath, "that the mind of the country has been awakened, let it be directed towards national service.... The time has come to frame regulations not merely for the election of the representatives but also for the conduct of business of the Congress...."

It is in this address that Rabindranath says for the first time that freedom, by which he means political freedom, is the ultimate aim. "For the individual as for the nation, freedom is the ultimate goal." He does not, however, believe that collective freedom, which is national freedom, can be achieved without individual freedom. Individual freedom is to be attained by individual strength, sacrifice and work. Rabindranath warns the delegates of the conference that "the object of our action is not the attainment of any immediate goal. Action is needed to harness our latent powers." To the extremists his advice is not to waste the national energy by pursuing policies which have no direction. To the moderates he says: "Every conflict involves the expenditure of energy. All unnecessary conflict is therefore waste."

In his essay *Svadesi Samaj* Rabindranath had mentioned that the real work of the nation was not in the political battle but in the villages, where lay the heart of the country. He also mentioned the barriers that separated the nation into the educated classes and the general mass of the rural population. As president of the conference Rabindranath repeated his appeal, to people whose business was nation-building:

> We should combine a number of villages to form a regional unit. Self-government will become real only if the leaders of these units can make them self-reliant and capable of coping with the needs of their component villages. They must have their own schools, workshops and granaries, their own cooperative stores and banks which they should be assisted to found and taught to maintain. Each community unit should have its common meeting place for work and play where its appointed headmen may hear and settle local disputes and differences.

The scheme may appear to be idealistic and impracticable. It must therefore be pointed out that even minute details of the scheme had already been put to a practical test by Rabindranath, whose knowledge and experience of the Bengali village community were perhaps greater than that of any of the members of the conference. Rabindranath had lived a considerable period of his life in north-east Bengal, supervising the family property. This contact with rural Bengal made him aware of the real needs of the country. To Rabindranath national service could only mean village reconstruction, work which he himself began on a modest scale. His *zamindari* was a local self-government in miniature. When he proposed to combine a number of villages to form a regional unit, it was the self-government of his *zamindari* that he had in mind. But the presidential address did not please the moderates nor the extremists.

Although regional in character, the Bengal anti-partition movement raised or exacerbated three major socio-political problems of national importance: the deterioration of the Indo-British relationship, the outbreak of revolutionary terrorism and the Hindu-Muslim conflict.

The genuine admiration of Indians for British culture turned into contempt and hatred in this period. Everything British became despicable. The boycott of British products, government schools and colleges, the law courts and executive authority helped the anti-British feeling spread quickly and successfully throughout the country. During the boycott movement there was a sudden outbreak of revolutionary terrorism. A bomb episode at Muzaffarpur was followed by the discovery of the Maniktala bomb factory and the arrest of a large group of terrorists. The government's response was ruthlessly repressive. The Hindu-Muslim conflict broke out into riots in east Bengal when the Muslims refused to cooperate in the boycott movement. The official report stated that Hindus had interfered with the freedom of the Muslim community by compelling them to buy home products instead of British textiles, sugar and salt. Although this allegation was disputed, it was becoming abundantly clear that a sense of Muslim nationalism was growing, even among the uneducated peasants of east Bengal.

These were the dominant themes in Rabindranath's essays of 1905-11. Rabindranath himself was against partition. Having welcomed the partition movement as a symbol of national awakening, he advocated the engagement of the new national consciousness in constructive work. However he failed to see how the boycott of British products could be constructive and he condemned it:

> This is not the right way. This is too cheap. All your feelings are directed towards the aliens, and your countrymen are just incidental. Anger gives you all the stimulus, anger against the foreigner, and not love for your own people.

During the days of the boycott agitation, when the Indo-British relationship was under severe strain, Rabindranath wrote his essay *Purba O Pascim* (1908), not to defend the British but to evaluate the contribution of the British in the emergence of modern India. Unlike his other political essays, *Purba O Pascim* is charged with high emotional feeling, possibly to counteract the emotion which ran high against the British. When British products were being burnt in the villages and towns and the life of an Englishman was not safe on the street, Rabindranath wrote:

> Like messengers from heaven the British have come through our crumbling walls and entered our homes to inspire in us the faith that the world needs us too....Europe has lighted her lamp, we have to light ours from that flame.

This was the task in front of the noblest men of modern India: a perfect union of East and West; not a union for political purposes but a union on the basis of humanity.

Rabindranath goes on to enumerate the causes of the present Indo-British conflict. In the initial years of the Indo-British contact the Indians were overwhelmed by Western ideals:

> The continued passive acquiescence in the superior knowledge and strength of the British was making our souls sick. That sickness was growing by imperceptible degrees. Today it has come to a stage when the spirit of the country is in the grip of a violent revulsion.

However, Indians alone are not responsible for the present revulsion. In the past Englishmen in India broke down the barriers that separated them from the Indians. They came close to the hearts of the Indians, who saw the nobility of the British character. The noble ideals of the Englishmen inspired the Indians and gave a new dimension to their thought and action. However, the present generation of Englishmen in India is not "capable of representing English culture at its best." They are law-makers and administrators:

> Good laws and efficient administration do not meet all human needs. What is lacking is the human touch....To be near each other and yet never to meet is intolerable and hurtful, and sooner or later the desire to revolt against such a state of things becomes irresistible....Yet it is also true that such revulsions are no more than a temporary phase. In spite of all retarding factors our contact with the west must bring about a complete union.

Rabindranath discussed the Hindu-Muslim conflict in a number of essays written during and after the Bengal partition movement. In *Hindu Bisvabidyalay* (1911), he says that there is a very real difference between Hindu and Muslim in India, and that society is allowing it to become permanent. Orthodox Hindu society, guarded by innumerable social prohibitions, created irreconcilable divisions between Hindus and Muslims. They lived like separate islands without being aware of the gap that separated them. Now it is necessary that the two communities should be united to serve a political purpose. How can the two, Rabindranath asks, be united in the political field when they are so widely separated in society? "We have called the Muslims not as one of our own but as an aid to the accomplishment of our ends." The Hindus are now aware of the glory of Hinduhood and want the Muslims to acknowledge the glory and keep quiet; but an awareness of Muslimhood has grown among the Muslims for the same reason as the Hinduhood of the Hindus. It is advantageous, the politicians say, if Hindu nationalism and Muslim nationalism merge together for a common political aim, but it is natural for the Muslim to pause and think whether he would gain more by remaining separate. The problem, as Rabindranath sees it, "is not how to unite by wiping out all differences, but how to unite with all differences intact."

V

We shall now attempt to summarize the main points of Rabindranath's stand on Indian nationalism as expressed in his literary works during the period 1904-11. The reason for selecting this particular period is that Tagore's later writings represent, by and large, developments and ramifications of the ideas that he then expressed.

1. Political Nationalism Versus Social Nationalism

In its initial years Indian nationalism was more social and religious than political. Rammohan envisaged social and religious reform as the first stage towards the development of political consciousness. While political activity was not unknown, and Rammohan himself was involved in bringing the pressure of public opinion and the press to bear upon the government, the main channel of activity was social. In the first instance, Indian nationalism grew not from the sense of nationhood, nor from the desire for national freedom, but from the endeavour to contain and resist the impact of Christianity upon Hinduism and Hindu society. The word "nation" does not exist in Indian vocabulary. Religion and society were the substitutes for politics in the beginning of Indian nationalism. Debendranath was able to combine politics with religious and social reform. As the leader of the vigorous Brahma movement he brought about a reformation that was perhaps beyond Rammohan's contemplation and as the secretary of the British Indian Association he submitted to the British Parliament a memorandum which is regarded as "the first political document of constructive statesmanship emanating from an Indian Public Body."

The position is reversed in the second half of the 19th century when nationalism became more political than social. During Debendranath's lifetime ideological conflict not only broke the Brahma Samaj into several groups; it pushed one group towards Hinduism, another towards Christianity. As a reaction against Keshabchandra's Brahmaism, which was broadly based on Christian doctrine, a prominent Brahma member Rajnarain Basu delivered a public lecture on the superiority of the Hindu religion. This heralded the end of the reform movement and the beginning of the revival of Hinduism. Political agitation became the main characteristic of Indian nationalism.

For Rabindranath Indian nationalism was not primarily a political cause but a movement for social freedom. When nationalism became concerned solely with political activity he made an attempt to shift its attention back to society. Rabindranath believed that political freedom was not real freedom without the liberation of the individual mind, which contemporary Hindu society did not allow:

> What we take for Hindu society is an inert lump. We do not acknowledge the law of life to be the law of Hindu society, for the law of life is the law of evolution, of change, of ceaseless acceptance and rejection. . . . Reason and judgment have no place in our social customs. . . ; it is simply not the form to ask why we do, or fail to do, this or that. In the entire universe India

alone is exempt from the law of cause and effect—her causes are latent in the scriptures. It is the scriptures that must determine whether sea voyages are good or bad, and the pundits must decide whether the entry of a person into your room would contaminate the water in your *hookah.* Why it should be a transgression to drink water touched by a low-caste hand but not milk, date juice or treacle; why one should lose caste if one eats rice prepared by a non-Hindu but not if it is wine —you ask these questions and you will be forced into silence by threats of social ostracism.

The conviction on which Rabindranath's arguments are based is this. A political movement, whatever may be its worth, is a movement against an external condition; whereas the real thrust of Indian nationalism should be against the internal bondage of the individual mind. Rabindranath further developed this idea in his article *Nationalism in India* (1918), which begins with the emphatic statement: "Our problem in India is not political. It is social." Rabindranath disagrees with the politicians who believe that removal of external bondage will immediately be followed by internal harmony and freedom. In an essay of 1906 he addresses the politicians:

> Those who seek liberty on a purely political plane must constantly curtail it and reduce their freedom of thought and action to that narrow limit which is necessary for making political liberty secure, often at the cost of liberty of conscience.

In 1918 he wrote in *Nationalism in India* ;

> What should we do if, for any reason, England was driven away? We should simply be victims for other nations. The same social weaknesses would prevail. The thing we in India have to think of is this — to remove those social customs and ideals which have generated a want of self-respect and a complete dependence on those above us—a state of affairs which has been brought about entirely by the domination in India of the caste system, and the blind and lazy habit of relying upon the authority of traditions that are incongruous anachronisms in the present age.

Rabindranath's message was, "Let the mind be free, and it will go on moving."

2. HINDU NATIONALISM VERSUS SECULAR NATIONALISM

The disintegration of the Brahma movement and the revival of Hinduism brought a significant change in Indian nationalism in the second half of the 19th century. The first important change is that whereas earlier nationalism was based on the humanistic principle of the *Upanishads* (Rammohan and Debendranath, the commentators of the *Upanishads*, were guided by the philosophy of that scripture), the later nationalism derived its inspiration from the *Bhagvat Gita*. The philosophy of *niskama dharama*, "selfless service," as preached in the *Bhagvat Gita* was brought into the nationalist movement by Bankimchandra Chatterji, Aravinda Ghose and Lokamanya Tilak, the three commentators on the *Gita*. The second important change is that nationalism was raised to a religious level. In Bankim's *Anandamath* (1888) the motherland was identified with the mother goddess Durga, the source of energy and power, *sakti*. The deification of nationalism was taken a stage further by Svami Vivekananda, who identified the nation with God and service to the nation with religion. Asking every Indian to realize God in the nation, Vivekananda said:

> For the next fifty years this alone shall be our keynote—this, our great Mother India. Let all other vain Gods disappear for that time from our minds. This is the only God that is awake, our own race, everywhere His hands, everywhere His feet, everywhere His ears, He covers everything.

Vivekananda's disciple, Aravinda, declared that politics was his religion: "It is a religion by which we are trying to realize Him in the three hundred millions of our people."

Condemning Hindu nationalism and showing its weakness, Rabindranath wrote his novel *Gora* in 1909. He wrote of it again in 1918: "Nationalism is a great menace. It is the particular thing which for years has been at the bottom of India's troubles."

3. Conclusion

Rabindranath condemned mob activity and violence in any form. He said:

> The individual thinks, even feels, but the same individual, when he feels with the crowd, does not reason at all. His moral sense becomes blurred. This supersession of higher humanity in crowd minds is productive of enormous strength. For the crowd mind is essentially primitive; its forces are elemental. The Nation is forever watching to take advantage of this enormous power of darkness.

According to Rabindranath, "nations are organizations of power." As early as 1901 he wrote:

> The word Nation does not occur in our language, nor does it exist in the country. We have learnt of late to prize national greatness by virtue of European education. But its ideals cannot be found in our mind. Our history, our religion, our society, our family, none have recognised the ascendancy of the cult of the Nation. Europe prizes political independence; we set store by spiritual liberation. The basis of Hindu civilization is society; the basis of European civilization is the State. But if we ever think that to build up the Nation after European pattern is the only way open and the only aim of humanity, we shall be wrong.

He developed this idea further in *Nationalism:*

> When this organization of politics and commerce, whose other name is the Nation, becomes all-powerful at the cost of the harmony of the higher social life, then it is an evil day for humanity.

He pointed out that nation states had hindered the development of higher humanity and made the nations powerful but not free. He characterized the European war of nations as a "war of retribution."

Rabindranath was alarmed by the growth of the cult of nationalism in India. He condemned Hindu nationalism in his novel *Gora*, and he wrote *Ghane Baire* (1916) to condemn militant nationalism.

Rabindranath's own ideas about militant nationalism are recorded in the diary of Nikhil, the hero of the novel:

> What I feel is this, those who cannot find food for this enthusiasm in a knowledge of their own country as it actually is, or those who cannot love men just because they are men,—who must shout and defy their country in order to keep up their excitement,—they love excitement more than their country. They accuse me of being unimaginative,—that is, according to them, I have oil in my lamp, but no flame. Now this is exactly the accusation which I bring against them: you are dark, as the flints are. You must come to violent conflicts and make a noise in order to produce your sparks. But their disconnected flashes merely assist your pride, and not your clear vision."

Finally, all Rabindranath's political writings were prompted by one idea: the protection of human dignity and human right. Whenever human dignity was ignored and human right was violated he raised his voice to protect them. Many of his bitter criticisms of the British government in India were written as a protest against the encroachment on human right. He said of himself: "I love India, but my India is an Idea and not a geographical expression. Therefore I am ɔt a patriot—I shall ever seek my compatriots all over the world." Patriotism is a great virtue, but Rabindranath knew that "in small minds, patriotism dissociates itself from the higher ideal of humanity." Rabindranath never forsook "the higher ideal of humanity" for the sake of patriotism.

10 Traditionalism and National Solidarity in India

DIETMAR ROTHERMUND

Tradition and Solidarity

Tradition encompasses the whole spectrum of inherited customs, practices, and beliefs of a people. It may be "great" or "little," widely shared or regionally limited, and it very often contains contradictory elements. A traditionalist is generally thought of as a person who is particularly attached to such a tradition and who demonstrates this by practising it or by asserting its values. Traditionalism, then, would be the common denominator of the thought and action of traditionalists. Traditionalism in this way is seen as an attitude opposed to progress, innovation, and social change. However, this interpretation of traditionalism does not account for the thought and action of those who draw upon tradition in order to justify or induce social and political change, who look for the roots of the future by searching for a useful past. Their traditionalism is a deliberate quest for those elements of tradition which fit into their vision of destiny. They reconstruct tradition by eliminating accretions and impurities. If they are interested in the destiny of a nation their main aim will be to trace such elements of tradition as contribute to national solidarity, because solidarity is the foundation of national consciousness. This solidarity has to be based on cultural and religious traditions if there is no specific tradition of a common territorial state or if this state is a colonial one imposed by foreign rulers. Solidarity-traditionalism is, therefore, a frequent feature of the nationalism of subject nations or such nations whose territorial integrity is problematic either because of external challenges or a lack of internal cohesion. The functions of this solidarity traditionalism are the same everywhere but its formal substance may differ according to the kind of tradition on which it is based. Even the respective traditionalists in one nation may disagree as they focus on different elements of tradition.

But they all have the same aim. They want to build the national solidarity of the present and of the future on the implied solidarity of the past.

THE TECHNIQUES OF THE TRADITIONALISTS

In order to achieve his aim the traditionalist must be both flexible and discriminating. He must filter the elements of tradition, distinguish the main theme from accretions and impurities and present a reconstructed tradition which will nevertheless fit into the cultural context from which he has derived it.

In the Indian context a rich heritage of cultural and religious traditions provides the traditionalist with a storehouse of excellent material to draw upon. The very antiquity of many parts of the Indian tradition can be adduced as a good argument for their sanctity. Swami Vivekananda gave a good example of the traditionalist techniques when he said:

> In matters of religious duty the Vedas are the only capable authority, all other scriptures are only valuable as far as they follow the Vedas. The authority extends to all ages, climes, and persons....The Vedas are divided into Jnanakanda (knowledge portion) and Karmakanda (ritual portion). Social laws and customs being based on this Karmakanda have been changing and will continue to change. There has been a corruption of usage, and a degradation of Hinduism—split into sects....[1]

The typical division of the elements of tradition into important ones which are the bedrock of all values and subsidiary ones which may change, the implication that change may lead to corruption, and finally the assertion that this corruption has caused a lack of solidarity by promoting schisms, these are essential parts of the traditionalist argument.

In addition to being discriminating the traditionalist must also be permissive and accommodating, he must convince his audience that he does not demand anything new but that he has only rediscovered the old truth which his audience knows as well as he does.

[1]Swami Vivekananda, *The Complete Works of Vivekananda*, Calcutta, 1958, Vol. VI, p. 183 f.

Again Vivekananda provides a good example of this type of pleading: "This is my method—to show the Hindus that they have to give up nothing but only to move on in the line laid down by the sages and shake off their inertia, the result of centuries of servitude. . . ."[2]

However, this permissive traditionalism was challenged even at that time by other nationalists, who felt that a radical return to the main tradition required a firm attitude. M.G. Ranade expressed these views in a letter to his disciple, G.K. Gokhale:

> It is the Non-Hindu elements of barbarous races. . .which are very difficult to eradicate till puritanism, white burning puritanism, takes hold of our thoughts. It will then burn up all impurities. Even among our better people, the little support that Theosophy and Vedantism as practically realized get, has an influence for blunting this puritanic feeling. . . .The so-called reactionists including even theosophists...make people believe in everything and doubt in everything. . . .This lends great force to the unstable element in our character and our educational institutions and our churches and our press and politics also.[3]

Ranade's approach to "accretions" resembles Vivekananda's but he criticizes the contemporary traditionalists for making people "believe in everything and doubt everything." In this way he implicitly attacks the techniques of the traditionalists, who will do everything in order to impute solidarity and are afraid of taking a firm stand on anything as they do not want to disrupt the consensus of their audience.

Harmony and Conflict: The Fundamental Dilemma

Traditionalists as solidarity makers find it difficult to face the issue of conflict. Solidarity traditionalism implies a belief in social harmony. The traditionalist will refrain from antagonizing his

[2]Swami Vivekananda, *op. cit.*, Vol. IV, p. 373. See also Dietmar Rothermund, *The Phases of Indian Nationalism, and Other Essays on Modern Indian History*, Bombay, 1970, esp. Chap. III, "Traditionalism and Socialism in Vivekananda's Thought."

[3]M.G. Ranade to G.K. Gokhale, Gokhale Papers, National Archives of India, quoted in Dietmar Rothermund, *Die Politische Willensbildung in Indien, 1900-1960*, Wiesbaden, 1965, p. 38.

audience both for tactical and substantive reasons. He must maintain that his views are basically the same as those of his audience, for they are derived from a common heritage, and he must select such elements of tradition as reflect the inherent solidarity of all those to whom his message is addressed. This approach affects his perception and interpretation of social reality. In describing the social order Indian traditionalists tried to emphasize its harmonious features. Even the caste system was seen as contributory to social harmony by instituting a reasonable division of labour. But untouchability and other iniquitous aspects of the caste system could not be easily explained in harmonious terms and they were therefore condemned as accretions. In this way traditionalists became inevitably involved in contradictions and ambiguities when commenting on the caste system. They were bound to explain and defend it as an element of tradition without being able to prove its usefulness for national solidarity. The best escape from these problems was provided by Vedanta monism, which could be used to overcome all temporal contradictions by emphasizing the fundamental unity of all life and pointing out the transient and illusory character of social divisions and conflicts. Anybody who saw conflict where the traditionalists wanted to see harmony could be treated as an ignorant trouble-maker who refused to see the light. This emphasis on harmony, solidarity and the identity of interests proved to be particularly deceptive in the case of Hindu-Muslim tensions. India's national solidarity was destroyed by Muslim separatism because Hindu traditionalists tended to view this solidarity as an immanent quality of India's cultural heritage rather than as a goal which had to be achieved in terms of practical politics. By equating solidarity and identity the traditionalists created their own dilemma. They could not conceive of solidarity as a task of the present and the future without denying the national identity which they believed to be a heritage of the past.

This, then, is the basic dilemma of the solidarity traditionalist: he aims at the problems of the present and of the future but he must restrict himself to an interpretation of the past; he is interested in social harmony here and now but he must derive this harmony from the stability of a traditional order; he cannot account for conflict and he must, therefore, deny its existence; accordingly he does not envisage methods and institutions for conflict resolution, including the constitutional structure of the state.

Gandhi and Nehru as Traditionalists

The two most important political leaders of modern India differed in many respects from their traditionalist predecessors and contemporaries, but nevertheless there were many traditionalist elements in their thought. Gandhi was the most creative innovator in the field of conflict management, but his approach to conflict resolution was based on the belief in the basic unity of all life and in the immanent social harmony of small communities, such as the Indian village as he saw it. He avidly read and quoted the critics of Western civilization so as to emphasize the value of the purity and simplicity of India's traditional culture.[4] The articulation of political conflicts was to him only a means to conflict resolution and conflicts could be resolved because they were only peripheral disturbances of an underlying harmony which the *satyagrahi* was bound to discover. Gandhi's traditionalism was not as self-conscious as that of Vivekananda, and his "experiments with truth," though they were deeply related to traditional Hindu ideas,[5] were not motivated by a traditionalist ideology; but in his quest for social harmony, his attitude to the caste system and his approach to the Hindu-Muslim problem he was very close to the traditionalists. In fact, his implicit faith in the ability of the individual soul to establish an identity of interest with all other souls was even stronger than the intellectual convictions of the solidarity traditionalists. His concept of a *sarvodaya* (the rise of all) epitomized the idea of national solidarity and social harmony.

Nehru differed from Gandhi as well as from the traditionalists due to his Marxist orientation. But his *Discovery of India*[6] contains many passages which echo the traditionalist message. Many passages in his other writings, too, for example, those in his *Autobiography* where he advocates the Brahmanization of Indian culture and praises the Brahminical practice of service and renunciation, are almost identical with those of Vivekananda, whom he greatly admired.[7] Nehru's Marxism passed through the filter of tradi-

[4]M.K. Gandhi, *Hind Swaraj*, Madras, 1908.

[53]See Indira Rothermund, *The Philosophy of Restraint—Mahatma Gandhi's Strategy and Indian Politics*, Bombay, 1963.

[6]Jawaharlal Nehru, *Discovery of India*, Bombay, 1961 edition. See esp. references to Vivekananda, pp. 95, 194, 195, 356-359, 363, 593.

[7]Jawaharlal Nehru, *An Autobiography*, London 1958 edition, pp. 431-432.

tionalism and re-emerged as Indian socialism, an ascriptive socialism which emanates from the genius of the people. This type of socialism is solidarity traditionalism in a different garb. In keeping with his Vedantic inclinations Nehru adopted a kind of Marxist quietism which assumes that revolutionary efforts are unnecessary, for the forces of history progress anyhow.[8] The synthesis of Marxism and traditionalism in Nehru's thought is amazing. But, of course, traditionalism had become a universe of discourse for Indian nationalists of the 20th century, and Nehru could hardly escape its pervasive influence.

CONSENSUS AS AN ASPECT OF TRADITIONALISM

Solidarity—traditionalism and the agitational conditions of the freedom movement coincided so as to foster a general emphasis on consensus. The organizational embodiment of this consensus was the Indian National Congress, which became the state supporting and the state supported party after Independence. Opposition to the Congress was feeble and scattered, and Congress politicians considered it to be a nuisance, distracting the national urge to build up the country. Nehru even called the opposition counter-revolutionary, using a Marxist term to express a concern for national solidarity.[9] Decisions emerging from a consensus were considered to be inherently more virtuous than those arrived at by a majority vote. In spite of an awareness of factional disputes in Indian villages unanimity was put at a premium as it was thought to be an expression of the true spirit of harmony prevailing in rural India. It would be easy to condemn such an attitude as hypocritical but the problem is much more complicated: consensus is indeed appreciated even by those who indulge in factional fighting, just as renunciation is often held in high esteem by those who strive to enrich themselves.

The heritage of the freedom movement, with its record of sacrifice and common endeavour, has become the source of a new traditionalism which reinforces the equation of national solidarity and

[8]Dietmar Rothermund, "Nehru and Early Indian Socialism," S.N. Mukherjee (ed.), *The Movement for National Freedom in India*, St. Antony's Papers No. 18, 1966.

[9]Jawaharlal Nehru in *Lok Sabha Debates*, New Delhi, 17 Sept. 1955.

identity and legitimized the ruling Congress party, the party of Gandhi and Nehru, as the guardian of the nation. However, a large part of the Indian electorate has shown that it is no longer impressed with this traditionalism and is willing to disturb the dominant consensus by precipitating an open conflict. The Congress cannot count on its unchallenged position as the keeper of the national conscience. This change implies that a new concept of national solidarity has to emerge which is bound up with traditionalism and social harmony but provides ample room for political conflict within the nation. This new concept must be based on a greater appreciation of the institutional heritage of the state. This heritage is to a great extent a colonial one and has, therefore, been emphasized much less than the social and cultural heritage of India which fired the imagination of the traditionalists. In fact, the Congress consensus helped both to salvage this colonial heritage and to protect it from immediate exposure to the forces of political conflict.[10] This had the advantage of giving the machinery of the state enough time to adjust to the change of management and to develop its own momentum but it also had the disadvantage of not putting it to any serious test. The time for the test has come and we shall see the results. It is to be hoped that India's national solidarity is strong enough to survive the eclipse of the consensus which was maintained by the traditionalists and the leaders of the freedom movement, and that the state which is supported by this solidarity will emerge from the tests of political conflict in a better shape, so as to be able to cope with conflicts without suppressing them.

[10]Editor's note: G. Austin has argued that the Indian constitution, while inspired by Western liberal and socialist ideas and owing much to the colonial institutional heritage, was created by Indians themselves using the traditional techniques of consensus and accommodation (*The Indian Constitution: Cornerstone of a Nation*, O.U.P. 1966).

11. The Theory of Anarchism in Modern India—An Analysis of the Political Thought of Vivekananda, Aurobindo and Gandhi

DENNIS DALTON

1. The Theoretical Bases of Anarchism

One of the most fascinating aspects of the study of ideas is the respect in which certain conceptions tend to form distinct patterns of thought. As Burke said, ideas sometimes come in "clusters," and then recur as such in various historical contexts. Perhaps these intellectual affinities may be explained in terms of an internal logic of ideas which finds expression within a variety of ideological systems. One striking example of this aspect of intellectual history occurs in the pattern of beliefs and concepts which have long been associated with the idea of anarchism.[1] If we consider the whole historical range of anarchist thought and attitudes, extending from classical Greece to 20th century India, then it would seem that few philosophies can have owed so much to philosophers who, in nationality, personality, and circumstance, appear to have had so little in common. Yet their set of attitudes, presuppositions and theories about the nature of man and society, freedom and authority, government and revolution, form an unmistakable "cluster."

Like many ideologies, anarchism's cluster of ideas has a magnetic

[1]Anarchism, "the principles or practice of anarchy," derives from the Greek *anarchia*, which means "lack of a leader, the state of a people without lawful government." The English usage emerged in the 16th century, then defined as "unlawful liberty or license of the multitude." It is currently defined as "absence of government; state of lawlessness due to the inefficiency of the supreme power; political disorder; non-recognition of authority" (OED). While this definition is suggestive of the common understanding of anarchist practice, it says nothing about the historical concerns of anarchist theory, namely, its concern for social harmony as well as for individual freedom.

centre, a core concept which seems both to attract and repel other ideas. This is its peculiar view of human nature. Man has always been regarded by anarchist thinkers as naturally good, inherently moral, and thus with infinite potentiality for improvement. The fact that human nature has not fulfilled its potentiality is attributed to the oppressiveness of authority, to habits and institutions of an unnecessarily restrictive economic, political, and religious order. Parallel to this view of the natural man suppressed by authority runs that of the natural society repressed by an unnatural and undesirable state. The anarchists' ideal has always been a harmonious community which is freely responsive to man's social instinct. This may arise only when society is liberated from artificial institutions such as private property and the state. The anarchists' dislike of machines, along with much else of the modern industrial and modern technological complex, is associated with their abhorrence of authority and institutions. However, it should be noted that while anarchism became systematized only with Godwin, as a distinct set of attitudes and ideas it nevertheless predates by many centuries the industrial revolution. Thus anarchism cannot be seen simply as an ideological reflection of the machine age.

Finally, in the anarchists' cluster of ideas there occurs a special view of social change, which rests like their other presuppositions on their view of human nature. Right social change must begin with a moral transformation of the individual by drawing out the good qualities which are intrinsic to his nature. The anarchists emphasized the value of education. For them, though, the conventional forms of education too often yield to oppressive discipline and indoctrination, which can only stifle the individual's discovery of his real potential. Change that is imposed from above by institutions of authority, whether churches, political parties, or unenlightened school systems, will be wrong in purpose and effect. Only when change expresses the natural goodness of the individual will the harmonious social order come to fruition. If the essence of the anarchist idea is ever to be grasped, it is necessary to realize its intense moral purpose: the desire to give the process of political and social change a moral orientation, to ground it in the nature of man. The implication is that change will be total, and this is precisely why the idea cannot be considered in a narrow political sense. The effect on the political structure will be revolutionary. But the ultimate aim can be seen only as trans-political, for it is the spirit and vision of the good life, of a moral society of new men, that dynamize the idea and give it a sense of mission.[2]

This nexus of ideas has formed the basis of anarchist theory over the centuries. It is evident in leading modern European anarchists like William Godwin, Michael Bakunin, Pierre-Joseph Proudhon, Peter Kropotkin and Leo Tolstoy, as well as in the three Indian anarchists chosen for analysis here, Vivekananda, Aurobindo and Gandhi. The intent of this paper, however, is not to argue an identity of European and Indian conceptions of anarchism. On the contrary, the main purpose here is to trace the development and analyze the content of the modern Indian theory of anarchism, and in so doing, to illustrate the extent to which the Indian anarchists drew upon select elements of their own religious tradition. Perhaps, though, it will help at the outset to clarify the distinctiveness of the Indian idea of anarchism by contrasting it very briefly with the European anarchists just mentioned.

The key characteristic of Godwin's thought was his belief in the supremacy of reason. Man was rational and therefore perfectible, for "the phalanx of reason" was invulnerable and irresistable.[3] Such rationalism was typical of the Europcan Englightenment, but it is alien to the Indian theory of anarchism. Among the Indians it is not man's rational but his spiritual nature which makes him perfectible. "Faith transcends reason," said Gandhi, and the method of action which he developed rested far more on the power of faith, intuition, and moral example than on reason.[4]

While Godwin clung to his vision of the irrepressibility of reason, Bakunin believed as fervently in the need for revolution through violence. In his emphasis upon violence Bakunin stands close to anarchist terrorism in India as well as in Europe, but the accent on violence sharply distinguishes him from the theory of anarchism set forth by Vivekananda, Aurobindo and Gandhi. Proudhon shared some of Godwin's faith in reason but little of Bakunin's enthusiasm for the barricades. The anarchist ideal for Proudhon

[2]Reliable summaries and analyses of the general principles of anarchist theory as set forth above, include: George Woodcock, *Anarchism*, 1963; James Joll, *The Anarchists*, 1964; *International Encyclopedia of the Social Sciences* (ed.) David L. Shils, Vol. I, "Anarchism" by Andrew Hacker, 1968.

[3]William Godwin, *An Enquiry Concerning Political Justice*, 2 vols. 1793, I, p. 203.

[4]Gandhi as quoted in D.G. Tendulkar, *Mahatma, Life of Mohandas Karamchand Gandhi*, 8 vols, Delhi, 1961, revised edition, II, p. 313.

could be realized not by violent confrontation with the government but through fundamental change in the economic relationships among men.[5] This stress upon the economic structure of society places Proudhon in line with a dominant stream of 19th century European social theorists. However, it serves only to separate him from the Indian theory of anarchism. Whatever attention the Indians gave to the economic reorganization of society, it was always regarded as secondary to the primary goal of a spiritual or moral awakening.

The two Western anarchists whom Gandhi read closest were Kropotkin and Tolstoy. It is instructive to note how each compares with the Indian version of anarchism. While Kropotkin enthused, like the Indians, over the inherent goodness of human nature and the natural cooperativeness of man in society, he nevertheless stands far apart from Indian anarchism because of the arguments he employed. Vivekananda, Aurobindo and Gandhi, responding to the impact of Western culture and profoundly affected by the Indian nationalist experience, sought to use the language, symbols and beliefs of their own tradition. Kropotkin was involved in a different dialogue: his reply was as a biologist and geographer to Malthus, Darwin and Huxley. He remains distinctly within the idiom of Western science.[6]

When we move, then, from the abstract and general cluster of anarchist ideas indicated above to a brief look at the differences between the European and Indian groups, it becomes evident that the similarities, while significant, are relatively few. This is clearly because of the historical context within which each group found itself. If, however, there is a Western anarchist who stands close to the Indian school, then it is Leo Tolstoy. *The Kingdom of God is Within You* presents countless parallels with Indian anarchism. Each rests squarely on a belief in the divine nature of man. Each argues, from this, that man's primary task is the realization of his highest nature, the divine consciousness within. For once realized, this truth becomes the purpose of his every action; he perceives the identity of his own Self with that of all mankind. The implications of this principle are manifold: violence is condemned; rever-

[5] Pierre-Joseph Proudhon, *The General Idea of the Revolution in the 19th Century*, trans. J.B. Robinson, 1923. See also George Woodcock, *Pierre-Joseph Proudhon; A Biography*, 1956, pp. 169-172.

[6] Kropotkin, *Mutual Aid*, 1910.

ence for mankind forbids it. Government, which is intrinsically coercive, only threatens individual realization and thwarts, with its obstructive legislation, the moral progress of society. Tolstoy, Aurobindo and Gandhi condemn Western Socialism for the same reason: it underwrites the rise of the Leviathan, and thus inevitably ushers in violence and oppression. Man's Self must not be stifled by institutions; his only imperative is to look within, and listen to the voice of his own conscience. Social change must not await the initiative of a political party; it must begin with the individual transforming his own life.[7]

In sum, then, anarchism in India rests upon a set of general assumptions about the nature of man and society which have been shared by leading anarchist theorists everywhere. But beyond this, Indian anarchism maintains, in contrast to Western anarchism, its own peculiar qualities. It is not, for example, given to the rationalism of the European enlightenment or the scientific method of the West. It rejects violence. It does not give economic forces a primary role in effecting social change. While it stands close to the Christian anarchism of Tolstoy, this similarity is not so much suggestive of direct influence as of the patterns of thought and conceptual themes which the Indians chose to develop. The crucial question of why the Indians pursued one theoretical line rather than another leads us to a discussion of the purpose and content of anarchism in India, and more particularly of its relation to elements of traditional Hindu thought.

However, before the Indian theory of anarchism is examined, two assumptions underlying the analysis should be stated clearly. First, it is assumed correct to apply the term "anarchist" to these three Indian thinkers. Second, it is thought appropriate to group these three together as a "school" of political thought, even though they admittedly differ in important respects.

In regard to the first, the term anarchist has been applied to Asian political thinkers before, most notably to the Chinese.[8] It

[7]L.N. Tolstoy, *The Kingdom of God Is Within You*, 1905, trans. by Leo Wiener. The relevant passages are: 100-102, 110, 260-261, 39-40, 104, 152-153, 222-223, 185-187, 262-263, 343-345, 351-352, 191, 360-361, 218-229, 236-237, 23-40, 343.

[8]For example, Martin Bernal, "The Triumph of Anarchism over Marxism, 1906-07," in Mary Wright (ed.), *China in Revolution: The First Phase, 1900-13*, New Haven, 1968, pp. 97-142. Bernal is perhaps the foremost writer on Chinese

has also been frequently used in reference to Indian thinkers, most often to Gandhi, both by European and Indian scholars. This usage is legitimate, for an examination of the thought of the Indians and Chinese concerned reveals that they share with many Western anarchists those assumptions or clusters of ideas that have been outlined above. The European tradition exercises no monopoly on the term "anarchist" or the theory of anarchism; and insights may be gained into seemingly divergent traditions of political thought by uncovering elements which are universally shared.

Yet the objection to the use of the term anarchist in the Indian context goes deeper than this. Although little argument arises over relatively unresearched thinkers like Vivekananda and Aurobindo, controversy does centre on Gandhi as an anarchist, for Gandhi is a figure that, above all else, has come to mean many different things to many people. It is no surprise that to some, then, Gandhi does not mean "anarchist." He was neither careful, nor consistent, nor systematic in his thought, and statements may be cited from his immense writings that would seem to refute the assertion that he is an anarchist. It is said, for example, that Gandhi would have sanctioned, in his ideal society, prisons and police. Could an anarchist tolerate these? Rather than attempt the impossibly tortuous task of making Gandhi consistent, I will simply state my reasons for regarding him as an anarchist. First, Gandhi stated clearly, "I myself am an anarchist."[9] The most perceptive Indian observer of Gandhi, Jawaharlal Nehru, fully agreed with this judgment, admitting that while Gandhi is "an extraordinary paradox," "he is more or less of a philosophical anarchist."[10] It might be objected

---

anarchism. But see also R.A. Scalapino and G.T. Yu, *The Chinese Anarchist Movement*, Berkeley, 1961.

[9]M.K. Gandhi, *The Collected Works*, Delhi, 1964, Vol. XIII, p. 214. This statement is from his famous speech at the Benaras Hindu University, 6 February 1916. Here he is seeking to reply to anarchists as well as to distinguish his anarchism from theirs: "...India of today in her impatience has produced an army of anarchists. I myself am an anarchist, but of another type." The most coherent exposition of Gandhi's anarchism as an ideology is found in his first important publication, *Hind Swaraj* (*The Collected Works*, Vol. X, pp. 6-68). Note that in the bibliography attached to this work, Gandhi lists twenty key books. Six of these are by Tolstoy, and two by Thoreau. His indebtedness to Western anarchism can also be found in his later references to Kropotkin.

[10]Jawaharlal Nehru, *Toward Freedom, An Autobiography*, Boston, 1961, p. 318.

here that Gandhi also called himself a socialist. Nehru dismisses this neatly when he writes, "Sometimes he calls himself a socialist, but he uses the word in a sense so peculiar to himself which has little or nothing to do with the economic framework of society which usually goes by the name of socialism."[11] Nehru found the term anarchist applicable to this contradictory figure because of what Gandhi himself emphasized as the essential elements of his thought, and because of how Gandhi behaved. Briefly, the fundamentals of his thought are these: a view of man as a perfectible being possessed of a spiritual nature; a belief that the freedom (*swaraj*) of the individual is necessarily attained within the structure of society and not the state; an intense suspicion of state power and the lust for power politics; a strong faith in the power of the spirit (i.e. of *satya* and *ahimsa*) and in the moral authority of the spiritually pure individual (*satyagrahi*); finally, a vision of an ideal society which he called an "enlightened anarchy"[12] (*sarvodaya*). In his conception of each of these key ideas (*swaraj, satya, ahimsa, satyagraha* and *sarvodaya*) there is a clear commitment to the anarchist scheme of ideas outlined above and elaborated throughout the rest of the paper.

Finally, Gandhi's anarchism can be seen in his behaviour as a political and social leader. Gandhi was admittedly a master of organization and a genius at manipulating the Congress. Some would argue that this quality disqualifies him as an anarchist. In fact, it only means that he was an anarchist with an exceptional capacity for organization. Like other anarchists, he was committed to voluntary associations, as opposed to the political agencies of the state, and to a method of change which relied primarily upon

---

Nehru also comments here that "Since then (South Africa) Gandhi has had a fixed basis for all his ideas, and his mind is hardly an open mind" (p. 319). This is a valid and critical poitn. For all the observations about Gandhi's "experimentations" and his inconsistency, it remains true that a fundamental constancy of purpose and thought characterizes Gandhi's ideology. The anarchism that he formulated in his early phase in South Africa, particularly between 1906-09, provided a "fixed basis for all his ideas" and stayed with him until the end.

[11] *Ibid.*, p. 318.

[12] M.K. Gandhi, *Young India*, 2 July 1931. Although Gandhi concedes that this ideal is "never fully realized in life," it nevertheless provides the standard (what Gandhi often called "Euclid's line") for right conduct and direction of social change.

moral example and action (*satyagraha*) rather than on political legislation or the coercive power of the state and the party. The bearing of these commitments on Gandhi's role as a leader is evident in the most successful and representative of his *satyagrahas*, the Dandi Salt March, and the Calcutta and Delhi fasts of 1947-48. Each of these instances reveals the nature and dynamics of Gandhi's leadership in their clearest forms. All begin as intensely individual acts of protest, confident that through the sheer force of a single *satyagrahi's* pure moral example, society may be effectively controlled or directed. In each, there is a dramatic and forceful call for large-scale social action. Notably in the Calcutta and Delhi fasts, when Gandhi might have called upon an Indian government, he spurns its agencies, relying instead upon the "moral forces of society."[13] In that period of violence and dreadful turmoil following India's independence, Gandhi placed his faith not in political action but in the force of *satyagraha*, dynamized by a single individual. He sought to turn the mobs of Calcutta and Delhi into organized units of responsible citizens that would do what the government could not: stop the riots. In Gandhi's final phase, then, acting within an independent India, we find in his moral leadership a superb example of an anarchist in action.

The second assumption of the paper, indicated above, is that there exists a fundamental unity in the anarchist thought of the three Indians analyzed here. This unity lies in their common response to questions concerning the nature of man and of the good society, and of a right method of social and political change. As we shall see in a moment there is complete consensus among them in the purpose of their thought: to reconstruct the meaning of their Hindu tradition, and provide India with a spirit of nationalism. The

[13]See the present writer's analysis of Gandhi's Calcutta fast of 1947: "Gandhi During Partition" in C.H. Philips and M.D. Wainwright (eds.), *The Partition of India*, 1970. For further analysis of Gandhi as an anarchist see Gopinath Dhawan, *The Political Philosophy of Mahatma Gandhi*, Ahmedabad, 1957, esp. pp. 282-283. See also p. 230. For brief Western refrences to Gandhi as an anarchist, see George Woodcock, *op. cit.*, esp. p. 218; James Joll, *op. cit.*, esp. pp. 277-278; and Irving L. Horowitz (ed.), *The Anarchists*, N.Y., 1964. The last offers a variety of commentary on Gandhi by Western anarchists. See esp. the remarks by Herbert Read, pp. 352-353; Karl Shapiro, pp. 574-581; and the introduction by Horowitz, pp. 52-55. There can be no doubt that contemporary Western anarchists regard Gandhi as one of them.

chief difference among them rests with the comparative levels of development of certain themes. Gandhi, for example, developed far more than the others a theory and technique of social change as seen in his conception of *satyagraha.* Yet, this technique remains in accord with the assumptions set forth by Vivekananda in his theory of *karmayoga*, and with Aurobindo's later political thought, seen especially in his key work, *The Ideal of Human Unity*. Aurobindo, of course, outlived Gandhi and could reflect upon their mutual contributions. Unlike Tagore, he seems not to have regarded Gandhi's thought and actions as a departure from his own teaching; rather he insists upon the complementary nature of their respective positions. Gandhi and Aurobindo both espoused the old Indian principle of "unity in diversity," and the principle would seem to apply well to the three Indians considered here. None seeks to develop a line of thought that would represent a basic departure from the other. Rather there is a far greater degree of harmony than one would find among any three European anarchists.

2. The Indian Idea of Anarchism

An understanding of the meaning of the Indian idea of anarchism involves some appreciation of the nature of the enterprise in which Vivekananda, Aurobindo and Gandhi all saw themselves engaged. For if the purpose of their thought is not taken seriously, then one misses the significance of their relationship to the Hindu tradition. In brief, the purpose of these thinkers was to reconstitute their tradition, and their relationship to that tradition was consequently not that of an historian, but of an ideologist. The intent of each was not to explain or criticize his tradition, but rather to use it, to make it serviceable for modern India, that an effective nationalist response might be made to the challenge of the Raj and all that the Raj had come to represent.

But there is nothing new or unique about this enterprise. As one analyst of Western thought has observed, the purpose of some of the major thinkers of 19th century Europe was to employ ideas about Christianity, history and science as "instruments of cultural change, to be used deliberately for the purpose of reconstituting Western man's attitudes toward his tradition and, hence, toward himself."[14] The writer was commenting on thinkers like Comte, Marx, and Nietzsche, but the analysis is equally applicable to the Western anarchists, and especially to Tolstoy. A treatise like *The Kingdom of God is Within You* cannot be seen as a straightforward presentation of orthodox Christian doctrine: it is clearly a radical reinterpretation of it. The extreme emphasis which Tolstoy places on non-violence, for example, is extraordinary. His vituperative indictment of the church, with his absolute denial of its role as a spiritual or social force, reinterprets much of the Christian tradition out of existence; it tries to offer a creative substitute for orthodoxy to the individual who wishes to defy established authority. Tolstoy's anarchist condemnation of government may lie latent in Christ's teachings, but it never received prominence there. Tolstoy's purpose was to reinterpret an established religious tradition by claiming that this reinterpretation was in fact consonant with the spirit of that tradition, and further to use this new gospel to support a modern version of anarchism.

The purpose of Vivekananda, Aurobindo, and Gandhi was to extract from Indian history and religion, ideas that could serve as "instruments of cultural change, to be used deliberately for the purpose of reconstituting man's attitudes (in India) toward his tradition and, hence, toward himself." In a manner similar to Tolstoy, Vivekananda, Aurobindo and Gandhi sought to reconstruct their religious tradition, and in so doing, disregarded or denounced much of that tradition as inconsistent with the essential spirit of the teaching. Just as Tolstoy claimed to have found the truth in Christ and St. Francis, rather than in Augustine or Aquinas, Vivekananda looked primarily to Buddha, the *Upanishads* and Ramakrishna rather than to many of the accepted tenets of orthodox Brahmanism. Aurobindo indicated his sense of purpose as well as his supreme indebtedness to Vivekananda when he wrote:

> And the riper form of the return to the past has taken as its principle a synthetical restatement: it has sought to arrive at the spirit of the ancient culture and, while respecting its forms and often preserving them to revivify, has yet not hesitated also to remould, to reject the outworn and to admit whatever new motive seemed assimilable to the old spirituality or apt to widen

[14]H.D. Aiken (ed.), *The Age of Ideology*, New York, 1963, p. 25.

> the channel of its larger evolution. Of this freer dealing with past and present, this preservation by reconstruction, Vivekananda was in his lifetime the leading exemplar and the most powerful exponent.[15]

One might examine the meaning of Aurobindo's theme of "preservation by reconstruction" by analyzing the writings of Indian nationalists on the *Bhagvat Gita*. Perhaps Vivekananda's most significant contribution to Indian nationalist ideology can be found in his reinterpretation of the *Gita's* theory of *karmayoga*, and Aurobindo followed suit a decade later with an extensive re-examination of the *Gita*. But few examples illustrate better the meaning of "preservation by reconstruction" than the approach taken to the *Gita* by Gandhi.

> What, however, I have done [wrote Gandhi] is to put a new but natural and logical interpretation upon the whole teaching of the Gita and the spirit of Hinduism. Hinduism, not to speak of other religions, is ever evolving. It has not one scripture like the Quran or the Bible. Its scriptures are also evolving and suffering addition. The Gita itself is an instance in point. It has given a new meaning to *karma*, *sannyasa*, *yajna*, etc. It has breathed new life into Hinduism.
>
> The Gita is not an aphoristic work; it is a great religious poem. The deeper you dive into it, the richer the meanings you get. With every age the important words will carry new and expanding meanings. But its central teaching will never vary. The seeker is at liberty to extract from this treasure any meaning he likes so as to enable to enforce in his life the central teaching.[16]

"The seeker is at liberty to extract from this treasure any meaning he likes...": Gandhi's words bear repetition, for they underline the nature of the purpose that he shared with Vivekananda and Aurobindo. These men went to their tradition to uncover ideas which would meet the demands of a modern India. They were engaged in a consciously eclectic effort, and no one was more aware than they of the extent of their eclecticism. Historically, it can be argued

[15] Sri Aurobindo, *The Renaissance in India*, Calcutta, 1937, p. 46.

[16] M.K. Gandhi, *Harijan*, 3 October 1936, and Mahadev Desai, *The Gita According to Gandhi*, Ahmedabad, 1956, pp. 133-134.

that efforts of this sort are not only common but inescapable in periods of crisis, when men seek to renew their intellectual traditions. How else, we may ask, may one begin to forge a nationalist ideology, or restore an outmoded religious symbolism, or preserve a great culture subjected to an overwhelming external challenge?

3. The Nature of Man and the Individual's Relation to Society

At the core of the Indian theory of anarchism lies a main theme: belief in the divine nature of man. This view of human nature is as central to Indian anarchism as it was to Christian anarchism, and it may be seen in similar terms, as a belief that the "kingdom of God," or the "divine spark," is within each individual. It is this belief, moreover, that directs the Indian response to each of the major problems that it confronts: the problem of the right relationship of the individual to his society and polity, the problem of the nature of the ideal social order, and the problem of the right method of social and political change. These general concerns encompass many of the classic questions posed by political and social philosophy, such as those about freedom and order, authority and leadership, reform and revolution. It is not claimed that the Indian thinkers examined here offer grand solutions for long unresolved issues. It is only assumed that the underlying assumptions of the Indian anarchists may be best understood by examining their perceptions of man, society, and change against the background of their own tradition.

> The only God to worship [Vivekananda declared] is the human body. The moment I have realised God sitting in the temple of every human body, the moment I stand in reverence before every human being and see God in him—that moment I am free from bondage...the Impersonal Being, our highest generalisation, is in ourselves, and we are That. 'O Svetaketu, thou art That.' You are that Impersonal Being; that God for whom you have been searching all over the universe is all the time yourself—yourself not in the personal sense but in the impersonal. The man we know now, the manifested, is personalised, but the reality of this is the Impersonal. To understand the personal we

> have to refer it to the Impersonal, the particular must be referred to the general, and that Impersonal is the Truth, and Self of man.[17]

Vivekananda's restatement of Hinduism, with its far-reaching consequences for social and political theory, begins with this single idea: the divine Self inherent in man's nature. And, from this idea, two crucial developments emerge which represent Vivekananda's theory of the right relation of the individual to society. First, knowledge of the Self brings awareness of the highest truth, the identity of all being. This idea was explicit in the *Upanishads*; but orthodox Hinduism never developed, from it, a dynamic doctrine of social service comparable to that taught by Christianity. Vivekananda, responding to the impact of Western culture, undertook precisely this task. Since the realized Self, the *sannyasin*, has discovered his identity with humanity, a sense of "cosmic sympathy" compels him to serve his fellow man.

Vivekananda instructed his disciples:

> Remember, for the salvation of one's own soul and for the good and happiness of the many, the Sannyasin is born in the world.
>
> To sacrifice his own life for others, to alleviate the misery of millions...to provide the ignorant and the depressed masses with the ways and means for the struggle for existence and make them stand on their own feet, to preach broadcast the teachings of the Shastras to one and all without distinction, for their material and spiritual welfare, to rouse the sleeping lion of Brahman in the hearts of all beings by the diffusion of the light of Knowledge—the Sannyasin is born in the world.[18]

Vivekananda's contribution to modern Indian thought rests largely with this gospel of social service set forth to meet the demands

[17]Swami Vivekananda, *The Complete Works of Swami Vivekananda*, 8 vols, Mayavati, Almora, 1948, II, pp. 319, 332. It should be noted that for Vivekananda, Aurobindo, and Gandhi, God is a moral principle, not a person, a term that becomes easily synonymous with Truth and "The Moral Law," as well as with the individual Self (N.K. Bose, Selections from Gandhi, pp. 4, 6; and V.P. Varma, *Political Philosophy of Gandhi*, p. 67).

[18]Eastern and Western Disciples, *The Life of Swami Vivekananda*, Calcutta, 1960, pp. 498-499.

of a new India. He was the first Hindu to tell all India and the West: "You are a part of the Infinite. This is your nature. Hence you are your brother's keeper."[19]

This first development establishes man's duty to society; the second, a belief in individual freedom, asserts the individual's right to seek self-realization. "Liberty is the first condition of growth," Vivekananda insisted. Liberty allows growth of individual self-awareness, and beyond that it leads to a realization of human solidarity and social harmony. Supression of the Self by an alien state, an oppressive social order, or an organized religion is without exception unjustifiable:

> Every attempt at control which is not voluntary, not within the controller's own mind, is not only disastrous, but it defeats the end. The goal of each soul is freedom, mastery—freedom from the slavery of matter and thought, mastery of external and internal nature.[20]
>
> Freedom in all matters, i.e., advance towards *mukti*, is the worthiest gain of man. To advance oneself towards freedom, physical, mental, and spiritual, and help others to do so, is the supreme prize of man. Those social rules which stand in the way of the unfoldment of this freedom are injurious and steps should be taken to destroy them speedily.[21]

The twin concern for individual freedom and social responsibility outlined in the above assessment of Vivekananda was a common concern of both Indian and Western anarchists. But in an important respect Vivekananda's contribution indicates the distinctiveness of the Indian school, for it makes clear the relationship which Vivekananda attempted to form with elements of his tradition. The significance of the developments made by Vivekananda, then, is that they signal not only the line of theoretical development followed later by Aurobindo and Gandhi, but also the manner in which they all related traditional concepts and symbols to their own nationalist experience.

India has produced, in Aurobindo Ghose, an outstanding philosopher of anarchism. From his writings emerges one of the most

[19] Swami Vivekananda, *Complete Works*, IV, p. 49.
[20] *Ibid.*, III, p. 246, and I, 4th edition, pp. 172-173.
[21] *Ibid.*, V, p. 142.

sophisticated statements of anarchist theory set forth in this century. The passage from his writing that will be quoted at considerable length here was composed during the first decade of his Pondicherry residence. It indicates the striking change which occurred in his thought from his early phase as a Bengali terrorist. While the fundamental anarchist concern for freedom and self-realization occurs in both the early and later phases, it is only after Aurobindo's retirement from politics that he develops in some depth a response to the classic anarchist question of the right relation of the individual to society. The following passage indicates Aurobindo's closeness to Vivekananda's thought and also how he elaborated, in depth and power, arguments that remained half-said in Vivekananda:

> The individual as spirit or being is not confined within his humanity; he has been less than human, he can become more than human. The universe finds itself through him even as he finds himself in the universe, but he is capable of becoming more than the universe, since he can surpass it and enter into something in himself and in it and beyond it that is absolute. He is not confined within the community; although his mind and life are, in a way, part of the communal mind and life, there is something in him that can go beyond them. The community exists by the individual, for its mind and life and body are constituted by the mind and life and body of its composing individuals; if that were abolished or disaggregated, its own existence would be abolished or disaggregated, though some spirit or power of it might form again in other individuals; but the individual is not a mere cell of the collective existence; he would not cease to exist if separated or expelled from the collective mass...he can affirm himself in another communal life, or, if he is strong enough, in a nomad existence or in an eremite solitude where, if he cannot pursue or achieve a complete material living, he can spiritually exist and find his own reality and indwelling self of being....The individual is indeed the key of the evolutionary movement; for it is the individual who finds himself, who becomes conscious of the Reality....The individual does not owe his ultimate allegiance either to the State which is a machine or to the community which is a part of life and not the whole of life: his allegiance must be to the Truth, the Self, the

Spirit, the Divine which is in him and in all; not to subordinate or lose himself in the mass, but to find and express that truth of being in himself and help the community and humanity in its seeking for its own truth and fullness of being must be his real object of existence....As he develops, he moves towards a spiritual freedom, but this freedom is not something entirely separate from all existence; it has a solidarity with it because that too is the self, the same spirit. As he moves towards spiritual freedom, he moves also towards spiritual oneness. The spiritually realised, the liberated man is pre-occupied, says the Gita, with the good of all beings; Buddha discovering the way of Nirvana must turn back to open that way to those who are still under the delusion of their constructive instead of their real being—or non-being; Vivekananda, drawn by the Absolute, feels also the call of the disguised Godhead in humanity and most the call of the fallen and the suffering, the call of the self to the self in the obscure body of the universe. Foı the awakened individual the realisation of his truth of being and his inner liberation and perfection must be his primary seeking—first, because that is the call of the Spirit within him, but also because it is only by liberation and perfection and realization of the truth of being that man can arrive at truth in living. A perfected community also can exist only by the perfection of its individuals, and perfection can come only by the discovery and affirmation in life by each of his own spiritual being and the discovery by all of their spiritual unity and a resultant life unity.[22]

Aurobindo's argument, here, is crucial since the passage contains the essence of his reasoning on the reconciliation of individual freedom with social unity. The primacy of the individual becomes axiomatic: while society depends for its very existence upon its separate members, the individual can not only exist outside society, but may achieve, in solitude, the highest spirituality. The individual's loyalty, moreover, must not be to the community, but to the Absolute. Yet once he attains realization, to "help the community and humanity in its seeking for its own truth and fullness of being must be his ıeal object of existence." This, because "as he moves towards spiritual freedom, he moves also towards spiritual oneness": he comes to know, and revere, the identity of all being.

[22]Sri Aurobindo, *The Life Divine*, Calcutta, 1940, III, p. 1153-1156.

And the path—a path of service to man—has already been indicated: by the Buddha, the *Gita,* and Vivekananda. Finally, Aurobindo emphasizes that the path he has shown is the sole way to a spiritual unity of mankind: "A perfected community can exist only by the perfection of its individuals, and perfection can come only by...the discovery by all of their spiritual unity and a resultant life unity."

This statement represents the fullest development of Vivekananda's and Aurobindo's common attempt to deal with the problem of the right relation of the individual to society: to achieve full expression of individual freedom within a harmonious social order. They emphasized, moreover, that even with the emergence of the perfect society the individual must continue to enjoy complete liberty: mass uniformity of thought and behaviour, even among the morally perfect, is neither demanded nor expected. An Absolute Truth exists, but not an absolute interpretation of it: there must be no mass submission to a General Will. Truth, Vivekananda believed, may be expressed in "a hundred thousand ways, and each of these ways is true as far as it goes. We must learn that the same thing can be viewed from a hundred different standpoints and yet be the same thing."[23] He saw clearly that if absolute equality were demanded of any society then individual differences must be abolished and a system of external control imposed. Not equality but harmony must be achieved; not difference but privilege must be eliminated. The sense of privilege rests upon an attitude of superiority, which leads to a rationale for tyranny.[24] Once the psychology behind privilege is changed, the ideal of "unity in variety"[25] can be achieved.

Classical Indian thought held in some respects, that social institutions exist as a means to further the end of individual salvation,[26] that:

> The ultimate aim of all valid and worthy human activity is salvation, which cannot be achieved by corporate entities such

[23]Vivekananda, *op. cit.*, II, p. 380.

[24]Vivekananda, *op. cit.*, 4th edition, I, p. 334. Spiritual equality is considered axiomatic.

[25]Vivekananda, *op. cit.*, p. 379.

[26]R.C. Majumdar (ed.), *The History and Culture of the Indian People,* 1951, p. 308.

> as peoples, castes, and families, but only by individual human beings. Government exists to serve society, and, on final analysis, society exists to serve the individual. This latter proposition is hardly to be found in implicit form, but it is a necessary corollary of the fundamental presuppositions on which all Hindu thought was based.[27]

Vivekananda and Aurobindo are in complete agreement with this principle: the good society rests on the purity of its individual members. The function of any social order is to render "the highest truths practical," and thus provide an atmosphere conducive to the development of the Self. There is thus a close parallel here between classical and modern Indian thought. They share a belief in the divine nature of man as well as the conviction that the supreme goal for the individual is the realization of his higher nature; society, as the framework within which the individual achieves his realization, exists to foster and never to obstruct this end.

The radical individualism fundamental to Indian traditional thought which Vivekananda and Aurobindo fully developed, was solidly reinforced by Gandhi. He, too, interpreted the *advaitist* principle of man's unity with the absolute as a command to serve mankind, and he likewise stressed that the aim of social service is self-realization.

> I am here in the villages to serve no one else but myself, to find my own self-realization through the service of these village folk. Man's ultimate aim is the realization of God, and all his activities, political, social and religious, have to be guided by the ultimate aim of the vision of God. The immediate service of all human beings becomes a necessary part of the endeavour simply because the only way to find God is to see Him in His creation and be one with it. This can only be done by service of all. And this cannot be done except through one's country. I am a part and parcel of the whole, and I cannot find Him apart from the rest of humanity. My countrymen are my nearest neighbours. They have become so helpless, resourceless and inert that I must concentrate on serving them. If I could persuade myself that I should find Him in a Himalayan cave, I would

[27] A.L. Basham, "Some Fundamental Political Ideas of Ancient India," C.H. Philips (ed.), *Politics and Society in India*, 1963, pp. 21-22.

> proceed there immediately. But I know that I cannot find Him apart from humanity.[28]

Gandhi's unequivocal individualism emanating from his belief in the goodness of human nature became the cornerstone of his anarchism. It explains his insistence on absolute individual freedom and his faith that such freedom would produce a strong sense of social duty as well as his belief in the supreme power of individual action in the instigation of social change—or civil disobedience. "The individual," he often said, "is the one supreme consideration."[29]

4. THE NATURE AND FUNCTION OF THE GOOD SOCIETY: THE CLASSICAL IDEA OF VARNASRAMADHARMA AS OPPOSED TO A THEORY OF THE STATE

One historian of ancient India makes this observation on the concept of the state in classical Indian political thought:

> Many modern scholars, perhaps motivated by the idea that the concept of the state is a *sine qua non* of a civilized system of political thought, have tried to find evidence of such a concept in ancient Indian political writings. Though they have usually succeeded to their own satisfaction, it seems doubtful whether there was any clear idea of the state in pre-Muslim times. As used in the West the term seems to imply a corporate entity and continues to exist, irrespective of changes in the governing personnel. In the writings of the more doctrinaire theorists the state seems to take on the character of a living entity, greater than the sum of its parts. In India such political mysticism was discouraged by the doctrine of Dharma, which concerned society and not the state, and by the fundamental individualism of all the metaphysical systems.[30]

The theory of *varnaśramadharma* rather than any notion of the

[28] Tendulkar, *op. cit.*, IV, p. 88.

[29] *Selections from Gandhi*, p. 27.

[30] Basham, *op. cit.*, p. 21. See also U.N. Ghoshal, *A History of Indian Political Ideas; the Ancient Period and the Period of Transition to the Middle Ages*, Oxford, 1959, p. 553.

state served as the philosophical framework of the traditional Indian social order.[31] This idea, which embraced the three integrating concepts of Indian life—*dharma*, caste, and the *aśramas*—envisioned society as an organic growth, divinely created, as part of a grand design over man and the universe.[32] Government existed to preserve *varnaśramadharma*; it should not remain aloof and apart from society as an end in itself.[33] Professor Gonda argues that, "we should never forget that the *Arthaśāstra* means by the "state" an order of society which is not created by the king or the people, but which they exist to secure. These authors regarded the "state"—if the word might be used—as essentially a beneficial institution for protection of human life and welfare and for the better realization of the ideals of humanity."[34] Paramount among these ideals was *dharma*, the overriding aim of Indian life.[35] *Dharma* was seen, first, in the *Ṛg Veda*, as a cosmic law which regulated the universe and sustained society. Eventually the idea assumed social and moral implications: society should pattern itself after this model of cosmic harmony for only then would the people prosper. The moral meaning of *dharma* became explicit in a verse from the *Brhad Aranyaka Upanisad*. The passage begins with a description of the divine creation of the four orders of society. Brahman, the first cause, manifested itself successively in each of the four varnas; but, finding the social structure lacking in order, Brahman created the eternal law:

> That brahman brought forth an excellent form, dharma (law). This dharma is the sovereign power ruling over kshatra itself. Therefore, there is nothing higher than dharma. Thereby, even the weak can overcome the strong with the help of a king. Verily, that which is dharma is truth (*satya*). Therefore, they say of a man who speaks dharma, that he speaks the truth, for,

[31]Basham, *ibid.*, p. 13.

[32]W.T. de Bary, *Sources of Indian Tradition*, N.Y., 1958, p. 17. Also Ghoshal, pp. 19-20.

[33]Basham, *op. cit.*, pp. 13, 23.

[34]J. Gonda, "Ancient Indian Kingship from the Religious Point of View," *Numen*, International Review for the History of Religions, IV, Leiden, 1957, p. 159.

[35] Basham, *op. cit.*, p. 12.

verily, these two are one and the same.[36]

This passage is highly significant for Indian political theory since the social structure and the cosmic law which governs it are seen as divine creations to which the king owes his allegiance. *Dharma* itself becomes, in the words of Ghoshal, "the crown of the social structure completing and perfecting the divine purpose of its creation." Equally important, *dharma* is seen as identical with Truth.[37] Basham's argument, then, that the development of a mystical concept of a state was discouraged by the idea of *dharma* is substantiated. India, early in her history, conceived a transcendent moral law but it became the law of a society and never of a nation-state.

Traditional Indian thought conceived of government as subordinate to the divine creations of society and *dharma*; but beyond this there is a deep conviction that government is no more than a necessary evil. Basham, in setting forth those fundamental political ideas on which the three schools of ancient India—Brahmanical Hinduism, Buddhism, and Jainism—agree, writes:

> Again there would be general agreement that government is an unfortunate necessity in an age of universal decay. In former times, when the world was closer to perfection, society functioned without the need of government; but as the world degenerated, evil and crime became rife among men, and government appeared, whether on divine initiative, through a corporate act of human will, or in the natural course of events, in order to preserve the social order as far as possible, and to arrest for a while the inevitable ruin of all things. In twentieth-century terms the corollary of this is that society is prior to government and that government is the servant of society, which it exists to preserve.[38]

5. Implications of the Theory of Varnasramadharma for the Indian Idea of Anarchism

Society and never the state serves for Vivekananda, Aurobindo and

[36]de Bary, *op. cit.*, p. 241.
[37]Ghoshal, *op. cit.*, p. 23.
[38]Basham, *op. cit.*, p. 12.

Gandhi as the framework in which the individual achieves liberation. They share a profound distrust of politics and they refuse to assign a leading role to political machinery as an agent of individual or social change. Vivekananda had imagined a gradual social awakening, begun with the individual and carried to its fullest consummation by the example and service of moral men. He derided any suggestion that his speeches, so overtly nationalistic, carried any political implications. Political organization must not be encouraged, for it inevitably stifles individual liberty. Society could conceivably exist to promote man's self-realization, but the state seemed to him alien: an abstract entity that only threatened the supremacy of the individual.

Gandhi viewed "an increase in the power of the State with the greatest fear, because...it does the greatest harm by destroying individuality which lies at the root of all progress....The state represents violence in a concentrated and organized form. The individual has a soul, but as the state is a soulless machine, it can never be weaned from violence to which it owes its very existence."[39] The ideal society would be one of "enlightened anarchy," where "everyone is his own ruler, and...there is no political power because there is no State."[40] This idea of anarchy he saw as consistent with the classical concept of *varnaśramadharma*. Indeed, he remained adamant in his devotion to the *varnaśramadharma* ideal.[41]

Aurobindo found his ideal in ancient Indian society where *dharma* had governed social, economic, and political activity and "the full attainment of the spiritual life was left as a supreme aim to the effort of the individual."[42] In his *Spirit and Form of Indian Polity,* Aurobindo envisages a state of "spiritual anarchism" in the mythical age of *Satya Yuga*:

> The right order of human life as of the universe is preserved according to the ancient Indian idea by each individual being following faithfully his swadharma, the true law and norm of

[39]M.K. Gandhi, *Democracy: Real and Deceptive*, Ahmedabad, 1961, pp. 28-29.

[40]*Ibid.*, p. 28.

[41]Tendulkar, *op. cit.*, III, p. 193. Also, B.B. Majumdar (ed.), *The Gandhian Concept of State*, Calcutta, 1957, pp. 29-30; and Dennis Dalton, "The Gandhian Idea of Caste," P. Mason (ed.), *India and Ceylon: Unity and Diversity*, O.U.P., 1967.

[42]Sri Aurobindo, *The Spirit and Form of Indian Polity*, Calcutta, 1947, p. 22.

> his nature and the nature of his kind and by the group being, the organic collective life, doing likewise. The ancient theory supposed that in an entirely right and sound condition of man, individual and collective—a condition typified by the legendary golden Age, Satya Yuga, Age of Truth—there is no need of any political government or State or artificial construction of society, because all then live freely according to the truth of their enlightened self and God-inhabited being and therefore spontaneously, according to the inner divine Dharma. The self-determining individual and self-determining community living according to the right and free law of his and its being is therefore the ideal. But in the actual condition of humanity, its ignorant and devious nature subject to perversion and violations of the true individual and the true social Dharma, there has to be super-imposed on the natural life of society, a State, sovereign power, a king or governing body, whose business is not to interfere unduly with the life of the society, which must be allowed to function for the most part according to its natural law and custom and spontaneous development, but to superintend and assist its right process and see that the Dharma is observed and in vigour and, negatively, to punish and repress and, as far as may be, prevent offences against the Dharma.[43]

Several important assumptions are made here: first, "the right order of human life" occurs when each individual follows his own *swadharma*. Ancient Indian political theory saw this as the "Age of Truth." Second, the individual's *swadharma* is a natural part of his being, and it is only when "perversions and violations of the true individual" occur that an unnatural institution, "a State, king or governing body," must be superimposed to maintain *dharma*. In the present state of humanity that government is best which governs least; but in the ideal society there is no need for government at all.[44] The way by which man returns to his real Self, and discovers his natural *swadharma,* must be inward. Government

[43] *Ibid.*, pp. 30-31.

[44] Sri Aurobindo, *The Human Cycle*, Pondicherry, 1962, p. 292. "...the more the outer law is replaced by an inner law, the nearer man will draw to his true and natural perfection. And the perfect social State must be one in which governmental compulsion is abolished and man is able to live with his fellowman by free agreement and co-operation."

may render support, but even at its best it cannot give insight into that of which it has no knowledge, the moral nature of man.

For Vivekananda, Aurobindo, and Gandhi *dharma* means a standard of truth against which man may measure his conduct. It represents an ideal which is in fact a manifestation as well as a creation of the Impersonal Absolute. The individual Self is a part of the Absolute. When man realizes the Impersonal within he achieves moral perfection and lives in accordance with *dharma*. The corollary of this conception of *dharma* is that only moral men—great souls that have gained realization through one of the yogas—may discern the Absolute. Vivekananda argued that his hero was that of ancient India as well, that is, the Brahmin:

> Our ideal of high birth, therefore, is different from that of others. Our ideal is the Brahmin of spiritual culture and renunciation. I mean that ideal Brahminness in which worldliness is altogether absent and true wisdom is abundantly present. That is the ideal of the Hindu race...understand it in the light of the true and original Vedantic conception. If the Brahmin is he who has killed all selfishness and who lives and works to acquire and propagate wisdom and the power of love—if a country is altogether inhabited by such Brahmins, by men and women who are spiritual and moral and good, is it strange to think of that country as being above and beyond all law? What police, what military are necessary to govern them? Why should anyone govern them at all? Why should they live under a government? They are good and noble, and they are the men of God; these are our ideal Brahmins....[45]

Gandhi, too, shared this ideal of the Brahmins "who have given up their all in search of knowledge, that is, Truth. I know of no system other than Hinduism under which a class has been set apart from generation to generation for the exclusive pursuit of divine knowledge and consigned to voluntary poverty."[46] But Gandhi, with Vivekananda, insisted, in the words of Buddha, that "a Brahmin is such by his deeds."[47] The ideal of Brahminhood is only significant for what it symbolizes, the traditional conception ex-

[45]Vivekananda, *op. cit.*, III, p. 197.

[46]Tendulkar, *op. cit.*, III, p. 195.

[47]de Bary, *op. cit.*, p. 143. (Quoted from *Sutta Nipāta*, verse 136.)

plicit in Manu[48] of a moral elite. Thus, the ideal Brahmin became identified by Vivekananda with the *sannyasin*, by Aurobindo with the "gnostic being,"[49] and by Gandhi with the *karmayogin*. Vivekananda's development of the classical theme is crucial for his political theory, for he extends the ideal of a moral elite into a vision of a community of Brahmins, selfless and self-governing. This is his image of spiritual anarchism, an ideal that without traditional Indian thought would have little meaning. For this is "the ideal of the Hindu race," and one must understand it "in the light of the true and original Vedantic conception."[50]

6. The Method: Gandhi's Satyagraha

Vivekananda, Aurobindo, and Gandhi all favoured radical social change for India. Like all anarchists they shared a deep suspicion of the normal political and institutional processes through which social change is often pursued.[51] They set forth a common ideal social order, an anarchic society embodying the principles of *varnaśramadharma*. Vivekananda vaguely envisioned as a means of realization a social revolution led by "thousands of single-minded, self-sacrificing Sannyasins."[52] Aurobindo sought further to develop a philosophy of method:

> The problem of thought therefore is to find out the right idea and the right way of harmony: to restate the ancient and eternal spiritual truth of the Self so that it shall re-embrace, permeate, dominate, transfigure the mental and physical life; to develop the most profound and vital methods of psychological self-dis-

[48]*Ordinances of Manu*, trans. A.C. Burnell, 1891, p. 13. "When a Brahmin is born, he is born above the world, the chief of all creatures, to guard the treasury of Dharma."

[49]Aurobindo's vision of the "gnostic community," presented in the concluding chapters of *The Life Divine*, offers the fullest philosophical development of this theme.

[50]Conversely, the importance of Vivekananda's interpretation and restatement must be seen, for without this the classical theme loses its relevance. Manu conceived of the Brahmin as a priest, not as a *bodhisattva* and the idea of anarchism in this age of universal decay would have horrified him. The traditional idea of a moral elite is crucial, but so is Vivekananda's reinterpretation of it.

> cipline and self-development so that the mental psychical life of man may express the spiritual life through the utmost possible expansion of its own richness, power and complexity; and to seek for the means and motive by which his external life, his society and his institutions may remould themselves progressively in the truth of the spirit and develop towards the utmost possible harmony of individual freedom and social unity. This is our ideal and our search. . . . The effort involves a quest for the Truth that underlies existence and the fundamental Law of its self-expression in the universe—the work of metaphysical philosophy and religious thought; the sounding and harmonising of the psychological methods of discipline by which man purifies and perfects himself—the work of psychology, not as it is understood in Europe, but the deeper practical psychology called in India Yoga and the application of our ideas to the problems of man's social and collective life.[53]

But it was left for Gandhi to direct the "application of our ideas to the problems of man's social and collective life." Gandhi followed the lines indicated by Aurobindo. His aim became "a quest for the Truth that underlies existence" and his method involved a development of "the psychological methods of discipline by which man purifies and perfects himself. . .the deeper practical psychology called in India Yoga. . . ." Gandhi was the *karmayogin par excellence*. Vivekananda and Aurobindo wrote extensively on *karmayoga,*[54] but they eschewed its direct application to politics. Gandhi did not: "If I seem to take part in politics, it is only because politics encircle us today like the coil of a snake from which one cannot get out, no matter how much one tried. I wish therefore to

[51]Vivekananda, *op. cit.*, III, p. 182.

[52]Vivekananda, *op. cit.*, IV, p. 309.

[53]Sri Aurobindo, *Ideals and Progress*, Pondicherry, 1951, pp. 68-69.

[54]Vivekananda, *op. cit.*, I, essay on *karmayoga*, Aurobindo, *The Ideal of the Karma Yogin*, Calcutta, 1945. The ideal of the *karmayogin* (yogin of action), first set forth in the *Gita* ("Therefore, without attachment, perform always the work that has to be done, for man attains to the highest by doing work without attachment") has become one of the most crucial themes in Indian political thought. Vivekananda was the first to develop its implications for modern India: "Karma Yoga teaches, do not give up the world, imbibe its influences as much as you can; but if it be for your own enjoyment's sake—work not at all." (Vivekananda, *op. cit.*, I, pp. 83-84). This ideal, of selfless performance of good works, done in a spirit of detachment for the benefit of mankind, is shared by Gandhi.

wrestle with the snake."[55] Not to be bitten—poisoned with a lust for power—but to work selflessly, purging politics of its impurities: this was the task Gandhi undertook. His approach was characteristically religious: "My politics, and all other activities of mine, are derived from my religion."[56] He condemned, like Vivekananda and Aurobindo, the immorality of Western democracy as well as of Communist totalitarianism. Unlike them, he conceived a significant method of political action. He called it *satyagraha* (truth-force.)

"*Satyagraha*," he said, "is like a banyan tree with innumerable branches."[57] Truth and non-violence are the trunk, civil disobedience and the constructive programme the main branches. Gandhi is perhaps best known to the West for his non-violent non-cooperation; but he himself placed far greater emphasis on the constructive programme. Real *swaraj*, he untiringly stressed, would come only with the abolition of untouchability, the creation of Hindu-Muslim unity, and the development of the villages. All this, he believed, rested ultimately with the moral example set by each individual. "For this [the creation of the ideal village], no speech-making is necessary, nor is there any need of legislative councils or legislation. One thing only is essential, and, that is a small number of selfless workers—men and women. They can by their example and spirit of service get the requisite improvements made."[58]

Perhaps the essence of *satyagraha* appears most clearly in Gandhi's struggle with communalism in the period surrounding the Partition. In this final phase, as Gandhi moved among the communal rioters, from Noakhali to New Delhi, one realizes how much more than mere national Independence he really sought. Almost forty years earlier he had written, "It is *Swaraj* when we learn to rule ourselves....Real home rule is self-rule or self-control." Indeed, nowhere does the nature of Gandhi's aim, motive, and method appear more clearly than in his Calcutta and Delhi fasts for Hindu-Muslim unity in the closing months of his life. The technique of the fast, of course, represents just one of *satyagraha's* innumerable

[55]Bose, *op. cit.*, p. 45.

[56]C.S. Shukla, *Gandhi's View of Life*, Bombay, 1956, p. 133. "Religion," like "God," is used by Gandhi in the broadest sense; he defines it as "self-realization or knowledge of self" (*Autobiography*, p. 31). Thus, when he speaks of introducing religion into politics, he means providing politics with a moral basis.

[57] Tendulkar, *op. cit.*, I, p. 318.

[58] *Ibid.*, I, p. 328.

branches. However, in this technique, and especially in the use of it in Delhi and Calcutta, the essence of *satyagraha* becomes transparently clear. For here one sees demonstrated the power of the individual will, through sheer force of example, to prevail over an entire community. This is a kind of power which anarchism has historically lacked, in its attempts to reduce its theory to action.

No method could have been more deeply indebted to the view of human nature which Gandhi shared with Vivekananda and Aurobindo.[59] Gandhi demanded, above all, that the *satyagrahi* "must believe in truth and non-violence as his creed and therefore have faith in the inherent goodness of human nature which he expects to evoke by his truth and love expressed through his suffering."[60]

> Socialism and Communism of the West [he declared] are based on certain conceptions which are fundamentally different from ours. One such conception is their belief in the essential selfishness of human nature. I do not subscribe to it for I know that the essential difference between man and the brute is that the former can respond to the call of the spirit in him, can rise superior to the passions that he owns in common with the brute, and, therefore, superior to selfishness and violence, which belong to the brute nature and not to the immortal spirit of man. That is the fundamental conception of Hinduism....[61]

Conclusion

In this era of nationalism, national claims to indigenous ideologies are legion. Many are merely confused negative protests by writers unsure of their own as well as of their countries' identity. It is noteworthy that *The Discovery of India*, an eloquent, if confused, proclamation of cultural independence by a new nation in this century, closes with an extensive quotation from Emerson, an

[59]Gopinath Dhawan, *op. cit.*, p. 110. "The whole conception of *satyagraha* rests on the psychological assumption that the innate goodness of the most brutal opponent can be aroused by the pure suffering of a truthful man."

[60]M.K. Gandhi, *Harijan*, 25 March 1939, in *India of My Dreams*, Ahmedabad, 1959, p. 148.

[61]M.K. Gandhi, *Socialism of My Conception*, Bombay, 1957, p. 270.

equally eloquent exponent of intellectual self-reliance from a new nation of the last century. But it is more significant that the writer of the former was a highly anglicized Indian, and the latter, an incurably anglicized American. Neither established a serious claim to an indigenous national ideology. The difference between Vivekananda and Ranade, between Aurobindo and Gokhale, between Gandhi and Nehru, between *Hind Swaraj* and *The Discovery of India*: this difference may be overemphasized, but it certainly exists: the first group is at home in India; the second, in the words of Nehru's own self-characterization, represents "a queer mixture of East and West, out of place everywhere, at home nowhere."[62]

But India in calling up images from yesteryear has a decided advantage over America: India has a past. And, as one of India's intellectual historians has observed,[63] anything can be found in it. The question is not whether this past provided the sole source of modern Indian thought: it most certainly did not. Yet it may be said that the fundamental presuppositions of the Indian theory of anarchism are rooted in select elements of the Hindu tradition. For in their tradition the anarchists found a common substratum of attitudes and assumptions which they reconstituted into a nationalist ideology. In the field of modern political thought and movements, the significance of this school was twofold: as Indians, they provided the nationalist movement with an effective ideology that, through Gandhi, underpinned a sophisticated technique of political action. As anarchists, they contributed this century's most strikingly successful example of the theory and practice of anarchism.

REFERENCES

Vivekananda. The exultant spirit, alone, of Vivekananda's *Complete Works* (especially volumes I-IV) makes the nationalism which he inspired understandable. Two adequate biographies exist: *The Life of Swami Vivekananda*, by his Eastern and Western Disciples, and Romain Rolland's two volumes, *Life of Ramakrishna* (with abundant references to Vivekananda), and *Life of Vivekananda*. These two volumes are also published in a combined form entitled *Prophets of New India*.

[62]Jawaharlal Nehru, *Toward Freedom*. Boston, 1961, p. 353.
[63]Ghoshal, *op. cit.*, pp. 6-7.

Aurobindo: This paper has analyzed only the latter phase of Aurobindo's thought. It is in this period that his philosophical development occurs, and he confronts the traditional problems of political theory. In its most concentrated form his political thought appears in these works: *The Life Divine* (final two chapters, "The Gnostic Being" and "The Divine Life"), *Ideals and Progress*, *The Ideal of the Karma Yogin*, *Renaissance in India*, *The Spirit and Form of Indian Polity*, *The Human Cycle*, and *The Ideal of Human Unity*. The last two are published together in one edition by the Sri Aurobindo Ashrama, Pondicherry, 1962.

Gandhi: The subject, here, is of course vast. First, his *Collected Works*, Pub. Division, Government of India 1958. The publication now covers over seventy volumes, it is near completion. For the later development of his ideas, see D.G. Tendulkar's *Mahatma*, 8 vols. This is much more than a biography: it consists largely of primary source material, so arranged as to give insight into the historical evolution of Gandhi's ideas. Finally, there are the numerous publications of *Harijan*, through which Gandhi voiced many of his most personal thoughts. Many selective compilations of Gandhi's thoughts exist, arranged according to key themes. Among the best are: N.K. Bose (ed.), *Selections from Gandhi; India of My Dreams; Democracy: Real and Deceptive; Socialism of My Conception*, and C.S. Shukla (ed.), *Gandhi's View of Life*. A good critical analysis is J. Bandyopadhyaya, *Social and Political Thought of Gandhi*, Bombay, 1969, (esp. pp. 101-116). See also Geoffrey Ostergaard and Melville Currell, *The Gentle Anarchists, A Study of the Leaders of the Sarvodaya Movement for Non-Violent Revolution in India*, Oxford, 1971 (esp. pp. 27-45).

12. Nationalism and Tradition in Orissa, with Special Reference to the Works of Phakirmohana Senapati

JOHN BOULTON

Much of this paper must remain tentative. In it I have tried to create a context in which to view Oriya nationalism. I have suggested that in South Asia tradition for the majority of people is synonymous with Hinduism; that within Hinduism there have always been two wings, an authoritarian right and a reforming left; that the tactics which characterized the confrontations between these two wings on the religious plane were later adopted on a political plane, both on an all-India and a regional scale; and that therefore the Oriya nationalist movement may be regarded as conforming to a traditional, South Asian pattern of protest. As illustrations, I have discussed Bankim Candra and regional nationalism; Gandhi and pan-Indian protest; and finally the Oriya nationalist movement. As regards Phakīrmohana Senāpati, I have attempted to show that since Hindu traditions are more aligned with enlightened feudalism than democracy, he was truer to tradition than most Oriya nationalists, for his outlook was that of an enlightened feudalist, not a democrat.

1. Tradition

A. Nationalism and Tradition Interrelated

Nationalist movements are largely a 19th and 20th century phenomenon. Their diffusion throughout Europe and Asia has coincided with the almost concomitant diffusion of the concept of democracy. They have been associated in both Europe and Asia with either the unification of geographic areas with a common linguistic or cultural heritage, or with the throwing-off of an alien yoke. In either case, the promotion of nationalism has been facilitated by appeals to the widest possible basis of common sentiment and unity; to things now popularly cherished, which are old and durable, such as a common language, literature, folklore, mythology, history or religion; that is, to some particular cultural tradition.

B. Tradition Virtually Synonymous with Hinduism in South Asia

In South Asia a good working definition of tradition would be "unity in diversity," which in turn is virtually synonymous with Hinduism. This "unity in diversity" has found expression in three interrelated forms: caste; temples; and literature.

Castes were unified as a whole by the acceptance of a common religion, Brahmanic authority and a particular place in the social hierarchy; and generally by a common function in the economy, residence in a particular quarter of the town or village, a common code of conduct enforcible on the individual by the combined authority of the Brahmins, the caste councils and heads of families. So much for the unity of caste. Its diversity is to be found in the diversity of racial and tribal origins of the various castes and the diversity of duties, occupations and behaviour of individual castes; for example, though slaughter is forbidden to the Brahmin, it is permissible to the Kṣatriya; though the cow is revered by Hindus, its carcass may be disposed of by certain untouchable castes.

Temples symbolize the political, cultural and economic unity of Hindu society. Temples were founded by kings and large landowners. Purī Jagannātha Temple, for example, is legally the property of the King of Khordha: it is cleared of all other visitors when he wishes to enter; he is the head of the temple servants and symbolically sweeps the road before Jagannātha's car; the temple records, the *Mādaḷa Pāñji,* are also a chronicle of Oriya kings. The political significance of temples is seen in the sacking of temples by neighbouring rulers, both Hindu and Muslim, and the removal of their images as trophies of conquest. The image of Kṛṣṇa in the village of Sāksī Gopala in Puri district is one such image that was carried into Orissa from a raid on the Dravidian south. Part of the cultural unity of Orissa is symbolized in the Purī Jagannātha temple, which combines the aboriginal, Buddhist and Hindu strands in Orissan culture. Amongst the reasons for saying this are: the site of the temple is either Buddhist or tribal, for caste is not distinguished there; the temple cooks are non-Brahmins; some of the temple servants are aboriginals; the wood for Jagannātha's car and probably for the images of Jagannātha and his brother and sister also come from tribal areas. Temples further advance cultural unity by attracting pilgrims and saints from the length and breadth of India. Temples acted as pumping stations drawing in ideas from all over India, filtering and disseminating them again via teachers and pilgrims. Caitanya was drawn to Purī; and when Hindu worship was resumed in Mathurā towards the close of the 15th century, sandalwood and sacred objects were taken from Purī as a guarantee of Hindu purity. As for economic unity this is seen in the variety of castes who serve the temple: Brahmins, *karanas,* potters, carpenters, pullers of the cars, stone-masons, and indirectly, tillers of the fields, for there are vast temple lands as endowments.

Temples also evidence the diversity of Hindu life and culture: the temple sculptures in Bhubaneśvara illustrate not only gods and goddesses, but also bathing, the suckling of babes, the mating of married couples, the lonely austerities of ascetics and the march of triumphant armies. The images of the main gods and goddesses, their mounts, the subsidiary shrines and ornamentation indicate the diversity of cults which have been fused together into a unity. The bull, the monkey, the snake, the lion, the eagle and elephant were probably totems of aboriginal cults; and the mother goddesses are Dravidian or pre-Aryan; as also are some of the male deities, such as Śiva.

Literature again indicates the unity and diversity of Indian tradition. Though Sanskrit and vernacular literature are diversified by language, they are unified by mutual borrowings. The Sanskrit epics, the *Rāmāyaṇa* and *Mahābhārata,* and the *purāṇas* were probably enriched by regional borrowings from folk literature, just as the regional literatures were enriched by borrowings from the same source and also from Sanskrit, mainly in vocabulary, rhetoric, themes, and philosophic and religious terminology and thought.

This tradition of unity in diversity can also be carried a stage further in that the caste system is theoretically justified in the literature; and stories and incidents from the literature find concrete expression in the temples.

C. Hinduism Essentially a Feudal Economy

Hinduism had three dominant aspects: political, economic and religious. The religious aspect is too well known to require further comment; the political and economic aspects are less often alluded to, and will therefore be discussed below.

Religions have generally had strong political aspects and were often used to bolster existing social orders, reinforcing the state against foreign intrusion: allegiance to the state religion being interpreted as allegiance to the state. Hinduism in particular had strong political aspects: in modern terminology the three upper castes controlled the church, the legislature and the main means of production and distribution in the economy. Thus to manifest itself fully, Hinduism required political independence. Indeed, Hinduism reached the peak of its classical development precisely when India was politically independent: the *Vedas,* the *Upaniṣads,* the six systems of philosophy, the *Vedānta,* the *Rāmāyaṇa* and *Mahābhārata* and the great temples of India are all of pre-Muslim origin.

The economic aspects of Hinduism are obvious. The main means of production were controlled by the three upper castes (where this was not so, owners contrived to raise their caste status). Hindu ideals were enforced on the Hindu community by economic sanctions. These operated like this: the king or landowner, Brahmins, caste councils and heads of families, each goaded the other to exert combined economic pressure to enforce Hindu codes of conduct; recalcitrant castes, families and individuals faced excommunication, loss of livelihood and inheritance, all of which constitute economic sanctions. The organization of the family into *ātmīya* (own) and *para* (stranger) was essentially economic; *ātmīya,* mainly sons, were the producers and inheritors of wealth, and *para*, mainly daughters, were drains on family property. Suttee and widow-remarriage were essentially economic issues; the questions of who was to maintain the widow, if she did not die with her husband; and who was to provide a dowry, if she remarried, being covert, yet important factors in these disputes. Castes and families were economic units: castes indulging in collective bargaining like modern trade unions or professional bodies; and families collectively owning property. Disputes and feuds between families and castes, as described in modern literature, used religious issues for economic motives: the raising or lowering of caste prestige and the aggrandizement of family property were often made possible through the peccadilloes and misdemeanours of opponents: sinners had to expiate sin and expiation was a drain on property.[1] The praise of the chaste wife and the conservation of family property were therefore interrelated. The veneration of the *sannyāsī* was also economic in origin: the *sannyāsī* had opted out of the economic system and was therefore immune to sanctions and potentially socially disruptive; he had therefore to be placated. The conversion of tribes and the absorption of indigenous cults was also economic, since their conversion increased demand for Brahmanic services.

Though the political and economic aspects have probably been known for some time, it has perhaps been insufficiently realized how closely interdependent all the various aspects of Hinduism were; that is, the survival of Hinduism as a whole depended upon its continuing to dovetail with its inherent economy, which was basically feudal. Though requiring independence to manifest itself fully, Hinduism managed to survive the loss of political independence, because the feudal economy was retained wholly by the Muslims and in part by the British in the retention of the zamindari system and in the institution of the principle of paramountcy. In certain areas of Muslim, Mughal and British India, Hindu rulers and chieftains remained in control of the means of production and were thus able to exert economic pressure on their subjects and tenants and thereby ensure the survival of Hinduism.[2]

D. *Pan-Indian Stratified Society*

In independent India as in medieval Europe, the feudal economy was reinforced by religious myths and a common intellectual tradition couched in classical languages. Under this system, throughout India and Europe there existed a stratified society, whose upper layers were unified by a common classical tradition and whose lower layers were diversified by a variety of languages and indigenous folk cultures. The unity amidst this diversity was maintained in India through Hinduism and in Europe through Christianity, both of which were partly imposed from above and partly impregnated

[1] Examples would be *Śāsti* by Kāhnucaraṇa Mahānti and *Denā-Paonā* by Sarat Candra Cattopādhyay.

[2] An example of how this same pressure was used to enforce political ideals, that is, the *svadeśī* movement, is supplied by Rabindranath's *Ghare Bāire.*

with indigenous beliefs and customs from below.

This stratification of society tended to continue under the Muslims, Mughals and British. Brahmins, Kṣatriyas and Kāyasthas continued to fulfil virtually the same functions, though increasingly through Persian and English. The upper layers of society continued to feel more in common with each other than with the lower castes.

E. *The Right and the Left in Hindu Society*

Hindu society has throughout recorded history been characterized by a right wing and a left. The right tend to be exclusive, Brahmanic, orthodox and authoritarian; violent, oppressive and xenophobic; with a predilection for Sanskrit and the codification of caste conduct.

The left tend to be constituted of the low caste or the fallen; inclusive, anti-Brahmin, anti-caste, unorthdox, and non-authoritarian; non-violent and non-oppressive; with a predilection for the vernaculars, for syncretism with alien beliefs, and for social reform. The left has a tendency to deify its reformers and to make appeals to the *Vedas, Upanisads* and the *Vedānta.* Its leaders tend to be the voluntary poor; that is, *sannyāsīs,* who nevertheless seek the support or patronage of the rich, especially merchants. That is, it depends for its initiative and support on those who can afford to opt out of the economic system and are therefore immune to sanctions. Chief among these movements from the left have been Buddhism, Jainism, Vaisnavism and the *Brāhma Samāj.* Many represent compromises with alien elements: Vaisnavism with the sufism of Islam; and the *Brāhma Samāj* with the monotheism of Islam and Christianity. In some respects they seem to represent developments of each other: Hindu Buddhist and Islamic elements seem to have produced Vaisnavism, and Vaisnavite, Islamic and Christian elements to have produced the *Brāhma Samāj.* The thought and imagery of the famous *Brāhma* poet Ravindranāth Tagore seems full of Buddhist, Vaisnavite and Islamic sentiment, which is why he is popular in Bangladesh.

The right has tended, if possible, to persecute or punish the left; or at least to satirize and debunk it. In Bengal Buddhists were persecuted: the Vaisnavites and *Brāhmas* were satirized and debunked. The life-stories of Caitanya reveal the hostile attitude of the orthodox of Navadvip towards the Vaisnavites there. In early youth Caitanya himself was not at all sympathetic to the Vaisnavite friends of his father; he mocked their East Bengali accent and refused to join their community. In Bengali a common epithet for Buddhists, Vaisnavites and Muslims is *neḍe*: "shavenheaded ones." It both abuses them and hints at a possible common origin: both Vaisnavites and Muslims were perhaps largely descended from the Buddhists, who were persecuted by the Hindu Sens and presumably converted to Vaisnavism and Islam, when their monasteries were sacked by the conquering Muslims. Bankim Candra satirizes Vaisnavites in a brief passage in *Debī Caudhurāṇī*; and Tarak Gaṇgopādhyāy satirizes *Brāhmas* in *Svarnalatā;* Rāmmohan Rāy was satirized by Bhabānicaraṇ Bandyopādhyāy; and his reforming successors, Vidyāsāgar and Akṣay Kumār Datta less successfully perhaps by Īśvar Candra Gupta. In Orissa Baḷarāma Dāsa, a Vaisnavite saint, was contemptuously ejected from Jagannātha's car by Brahmins; imprisoned for daring to expound the *Vedānta;* and also driven from the *Mukti Maṇḍapa* in Puri Jagannātha temple: his offense in each case was usurping the prerogatives of the Brahmins, due to his Vaisnavite belief in social equality.

On one occasion disguised as a Brahmin Baḷarāma Dāsa entered the *Mukti Maṇḍapa,* a place in Puri Jagannātha temple reserved for the most venerable Brahmins, and intervened in a discussion of the sacred syllable "om". He was severely censured for his impudence. His claims, as a non-Brahmin, to be able to expound the *Vedānta* infuriated the Brahmins who had him imprisoned by King Pratāparudra Deva. On proof of his being able to make even an illiterate expound the *Vedānta* merely by placing his hand on the man's head, he was released.

This story about Baḷarāma's supernatural powers is related in his own *Vedānta Sāra Gupta Gīta.* The story was obviously an allegory. Presumably by composing the *Vedānta* in Oriya, Baḷarāma Dāsa was able to disseminate amongst the illiterate masses an understanding of sacred texts which had until then been inaccessible to them. Because of his breaking the Brahmanic monopoly on such texts, orthodox society probably tried to get him into trouble with the authorities.

The second story of Baḷarāma's brush with the authorities comes in *Bhāva Samudra,* a text which, though attributed to Baḷarāma, is considered by an eminent Oriya scholar, Nīlakantha Dāsa, to be of doubtful authenticity. The story runs that Baḷarāma once tried to mount Jagannātha's car during the car festival and was contemptuously thrown down by King Pratāparudra's attendants.

Much incensed Baḷarāma retired to the beach where he built a car of sand and implored Jagannātha to mount it. Jagannātha did so, because, according to the tenets of Oriya Vaisnavism, the God is subordinate to his devotee and must do his devotee's bidding. Meanwhile Jagannātha's car became immobilized, and in a dream King Pratāparudra was advised by Jagannātha that the only way to restart it was to seek Baḷarāma's forgiveness, which he did.

There is a second version of this story in an 18th century work called *Dārdhyatā Bhakti Rasāmṛta* by Rāma Dāsa. In this version the details of Baḷarāma's personal life have been changed. He is no longer the son of a royal official, but an abbot. He is poor and lives by begging. Though deeply devoted to Jagannātha and courting the society of the good, he nevertheless has a failing: on the day of the car festival he consorts with a prostitute and, thus defiled, attempts to mount Jagannātha's car. The rest of the story conforms to that of *Bhāva Samudra.*

This story is again an allegory. Presumably as in entering the *Mukti Maṇḍapa,* Baḷarāma, in attempting to mount the car, was arrogating a Brahmanic right and for this he was punished. The reason why Jagannātha's car stopped is most probably that out of deference to Baḷarāma people refused to pull it. The second version of the story is interesting, because of the change in the reason for Baḷarāma's being expelled from the car. In Baḷarāma's lifetime, the rift between orthodox society and the unorthodox Vaisnavites was probably obvious. Presumably by the 18th century this rift had disappeared and a second reason had to be sought to explain how it was that such an obvious saint as Baḷarāma could have been so grossly insulted. Hence the story of the prostitute.

I have described these incidents in detail because they illustrate several points that will be important to our theme: the right, here represented by the Brahmins, use their influence with the king to preserve their prerogatives; the left, here represented by Baḷarāma Dāsa, uses its influence on the masses to compel the king to recognize its rights; the prestige of the Brahmins in the king's eyes derived from their monopoly of the most highly respected cultural medium of the time, namely Sanskrit; the influence of the left on the masses derives from their use of the vernacular. In later sections of this paper we shall see that these same basic conditions obtained, even when the political power was no longer Hindu, but British; the cultural medium no longer Sanskrit, but English; and the arena no longer a centre of pilgrimage, but of administration.

2. Nationalism

A. Baṅkim Candra Chatterjee (1838-94) and Regional Bengali Nationalism

At least in north India, the Muslims and the Mughals prepared the ground for the development of regional nationalism: they undermined the intellectual dominance of Sanskrit and the Brahmins by commissioning translations from Sanskrit into Persian and the vernaculars; they reduced the sources of patronage and income to Brahmins by deposing Hindu kings and converting low caste Hindus, thus making it profitable for Brahmins to serve and cultivate indigenous cults; and they severely discouraged Hindu pilgrimage by destroying temples and imposing pilgrim tax, thereby further decreasing Brahmanic income. Thus two of the cohesive elements fostering pan-Indian culture, Sanskrit and pilgrimage, were weakened: the Hindu ruling classes therefore began to seek out sources of sympathy between themselves and their subjects via the cultivation of various left-wing devotional movements and the recreation in the regional languages of the Sanskrit epics, the *Rāmāyaṇa* and *Mahābhārata*. The foundations of the later regional literatures began to be laid.

In pre-Muslim times vernacular folk literature had probably been the concern of the low castes alone: its language had been simple, direct and Prākritic in character. Owing to increasing Brahmanic, and in Orissa aristocratic, cultivation, during the Muslim and Mughal periods, the language grew more Sanskritic and ornate. Perso-Arabic diction crept into Hindu literature, though only to create verisimilitude in Muslim contexts. The predominant tendency, even with Muslim court poets like Ālāol, was towards sanskritization in spelling, vocabulary, rhetoric, sentiment and theme.

This sanskritization may at first have had no particular religious or political significance: it may have been the natural consequence of increasing Brahmanic authorship, but after 1800 it began to assume the form of Hindu purism. Perso-Arabic diction and anglicized syntax were severely criticized by Hindus. Fort William College, instituted by the British, gave a tacit sanction to this

Hindu linguistic bigotry.

Actually Bengal had not, and now probably never will have, a truly national literature: it had merely a collection of communal literatures: Śaivite, Vaisnavite, Tantric, indigenous cult, Christian, Muslim, and folk. No community read and enjoyed all the available literature. The first vernacular translations of the *Rāmāyaṇa* and *Mahābhārata,* for example, were condemned by the Brahmins. This communalism continued into modern times via the newly emerging press. Christians condemned the literature of all other communities as "offensive," "idolatrous" and "indecent." Serampore literature was condemned on linguistic grounds by Hindus; and the writings of Rāmmohan Rāy were condemned by orthodox Hindus and Christians alike. For many young Western-educated Bengalis, Bengal possessed no literature at all: they virtually opted out of Bengali nationality and, considering themselves European, tried to write in English in the manner of Byron and Scott.

It was probably Īśvar Candra Gupta who laid the foundations of patriotism in Bengal: he collected and published medieval poets such as Rāmprasād Sen and Bhārat Candra; encouraged the younger generation to compose in Bengali; and probably under the inspiration of Rāmprasād, who as a wayward son had sung to his fickle mother Kālī, first addressed his native land as Mother, calling himself her *santān* or child. Baṅkim Candra had been one of the protégés of Īśvar Candra Gupta: he had at first tended to belittle his master and to write in English, but it was he who was to elaborate Īśvar Candra's theme, uniting the idea of Mother India and Mother Kālī in his *Bande Mātaraṁ* and infusing into *santān* the sense of patriot. By delving back to Bengal's roots, producing heroines reminiscent of early Bengali Buddhist literature and imparting to his historical novels a *paurāṇic* flavour, Baṅkim was able, as he had intended, to unify the Hindu community of Bengal, bringing together the urban English-educated and the rural Bengali-Hindu masses in a common pride in their literature and land, but he did so at the expense of the alienation of the Muslims.

All that I have so far said of Bengal was previously known and realized: what was not realized, however, was that the period 1800-65 was important in Bengal as a period of struggle between the conservative right and the reforming left. The right, as I have said, had been satirizing and ridiculing the left, but it had also been edging nearer to government. Īśvar Candra Gupta marks the transitional point. He had been satirizing the left, but during the Sepoy Mutiny he had begun satirizing the Muslim and Hindu mutineers and proclaiming his allegiance to the British "king." Here is where the link between Hindu tactics on a religious and political plane begins to be forged. Loyalty to the "king" was part of Hindu *dharma*, because it was from that loyalty that the right's power had derived. Here once again Īśvar Candra Gupta instinctively proclaims that loyalty and, strengthened by it, launches into an attack on Muslims and Hindus "blinded by irreligiousness." Baṅkim Candra follows suit. He, too, in *Ānanda Maṭh* (1882) welcomes the coming of the British and attacks the Muslims. His nervousness about his novels being taken seriously by Hindus derived, I would suggest, from his desire not to jeopardize Hindu loyalty in the eyes of the British, because it was that loyalty which was to enable Hindus to regain their social, economic and political ascendancy in Bengal.

B. Pan-Indian Nationalism—Gandhi and Indian Tradition

In order to unify the diverse races and peoples of India, Gandhi built his nationalist movement largely of left-wing elements: like Caitanya, he lived apart from his wife; became a virtual *sannyasi:* travelled on foot as if on pilgrimage; dressed and appeared before mass audiences to give *darśan* like a Hindu saint; utilized devotional songs with mass, *bhakti* appeal; and sought the patronage of rich Bombay merchants. Like the Buddha and Rāmmohan Rāy, he was also a social reformer, in his case passionately devoted to the uplift of the low caste untouchables, whom he called the sons of God (*harijans*). Like typical left-wingers he also incorporated alien elements in his outlook: the Christian "Sermon on the Mount" and the concept of "turning the other cheek" having a strong influence on his thought and behaviour. His attitude to Muslims, like that of Rāmmohan before him, was also typically left-wing. His non-violence was also an age-old left-wing institution.

In a Western suit and a large limousine, Gandhi could never have swayed the Hindu masses, nor would he have gained much ground with them using Western economic reasoning. Instead he cleverly and perhaps instinctively utilized Indian traditions. His spinning wheel and his defiance of the salt laws were blows for two castes who had suffered under the British: the weavers and the salt-makers. His *svadeśī* movement and non-cooperation were typical Inaian economic manoeuvres: boycotting British goods and excommunicating a recalcitrant caste boil down to the same thing; and non-payment of taxes was a typical form of Hindu revolt in the Orissan *Gaḍa Jāta Māhāl,* as it was probably elsewhere in India. The *dharma-ghaṭa,* or the withdrawal of labour and services, was also a typical Hindu economic sanction. In fact, nothing Gandhi did was new: even the pan-Indian scale had been attempted before him by the Buddha and Caitanya. His immediate aim too—unity in diversity—was far from new. The only new element was his eventual purpose: political independence.

3. Oriya Nationalism

A. The origins of the movement

The Oriya Nationalist movement began as a typical tussle between the right and the left. The movement started in the 1860s. Orissa was then partitioned: part of south Orissa, mainly the district of Ganjam, was under the Madras Presidency; part of west Orissa, mainly Sambalpur, was under the Central Provinces; and the major part of Orissa, the coastal belt comprising the districts of Puri, Cuttack, Balasore and Medinipur, and the feudatory states in the hills, all came under the Bengal Presidency. Thus the right in this instance was constituted by the Telugus, Hindusthanis and Bengalis, who being allied to the government by virtue of their official positions enjoyed an ascendancy over the Oriya-speakers, who were to constitute the left.

I have no detailed knowledge of events in Ganjam or Sambalpur, but, as regards the Bengal Presidency, it would appear that Oriya-speakers were at first unaware of the dangers inherent in their position as virtually a linguistic minority in their native land. They appear to have made no protest against the number of Bengalis holding key positions in Orissa or to Bengali being the medium of instruction in government schools. They may have been aware of the arrogance of individual Bengalis, if they chanced to meet them, but on the whole they were probably relieved at first at being freed from the marauding Marathas.

Oriyas showed no enthusiasm for English education. Most of the pupils in English schools, when they eventually got started, were the children of Bengali officials stationed in Orissa; most of the teachers were also Bengali; as also were the deputy inspectors of education. In government schools teachers, textbooks and medium of instruction were all Bengali. In the 1850s there were two major examinations; the junior and senior scholarship. No tuition was available for the latter in Orissa. Students such as Gaurīśaṅkar Rāy, who desired to take it, had to study in Bengal. All this was a natural consequence of education being controlled from Calcutta.

The most advanced Oriya-speaking community in Orissa at that time were probably people of non-Oriya descent, whose ancestors had come to Orissa to assist in the first revenue assessment under Todar Malla after the loss of Orissa's independence in the 16th century. Most of these were Bengali *kāyasthas,* whose families had been domiciled in Orissa ever since and had continued to occupy posts in government service. Some Oriya *karaṇas* (the equivalent Oriya caste to *kāyasthas*) held official posts, though probably less than those held by the domiciled Bengalis.

Gaurīśaṅkar Rāy came of such a *kāyastha* family. After being educated at Hughli College in Bengal he returned to Orissa and a few years afterwards established the Cuttack Printing Company (July 1865) and launched a journal, the *Utkaḷa Dīpikā* (August 1865). His aim appears to have been to emulate Bengal's rapid cultural advance. Īśvar Candra Gupta had by then published his collections of old Bengali poets. Gaurīśaṅkar attempted to do the same for Orissa. He was much attracted by the works of Upendra Bhanja (1670-1720), the Oriya equivalent of Bhārat Candra. He used to hold literary soirées in his flat over the Cuttack Printing Company. Many Oriya aristocrats attended. His printing of old Oriya literature was both popular and lucrative. Phakīrmohana Senāpati and his associates tried to follow suit in Balasore, founding the Utkala Press (1868), launching a newspaper and literary journal, the *Bodhadāyinī ebam Bāleśvara Sambādabāhikā* (July 1868), and beginning to edit a popular classic, the *Rasakalloḷa,* an early 18th century work by Dīnakṛṣṇa Dāsa.

Meanwhile Gaurīśaṅkar, whilst still a full-time government servant, was campaigning for better educational facilities. The great Orissa famine of 1865 seems to have awakened government sympathies towards Orissa. Commissioner T. Ravenshaw, guilt-striken by what had probably been an avoidable holocaust, began improving educational facilities. Before the famine there were only three government schools in Orissa, Cuttack High School and the district schools of Balasore and Puri. After the famine in 1869, a new era commenced in Orissa. A medical school and a survey school were established in Cuttack, together with a normal school (later renamed the Training School) to prepare teachers for service in the primary schools, and a law class was opened in Cuttack High School. Immediately afterwards government prizes were announced for textbooks in Oriya on mathematics, science, geography, history, hygiene, biology and surveying.

The reaction of the new Bengalis in Orissa was perhaps predictable. Their erstwhile arrogance and superciliousness now turned to hostility. They found it irksome to teach Oriya alongside Bengali. In shops and offices resentment smouldered. Finally a controversy developed in the press, sparked off by a speech by Rājendralāl Mitra in the Cuttack Debating Society, in which he said:

> The first thing anyone would do who really desired to promote the well-being of Orissa would be to abolish the Oriya language and introduce Bengali; for, as long as Oriya remains, the progress of Orissa will be impossible.[3]

The controversy was waged mainly between two journals: Gaurīśaṅkar's *Utkaḷa Dīpikā* and Kālipada Bandyopādhyāy's *Utkaḷa Hitaisinī* (the "Orissa Patriot," from which the Bengalis were satirically alluded to by Oriya-speakers as "Orissa Patriots").[4] Prominent on the Bengali side were Rājendralāl Mitra, Umācaran Hāldār and Rājkṛṣṇa Mukhopādhyāy, M.A., Lecturer in Law at Cuttack College; on the Oriya side were Gaurīśaṅkar Rāy and Phakīrmohana Senāpati.

[3] Mṛtyuñjaya Ratha, *Karmayogī Gaurīśaṅkara*, Cuttack, 1925, p. 40.

[4] It is interesting to note at this point the role played in this early language dispute by the *Brāhma Samāj*. This became extremely popular in Orissa after the famine of 1865-66. It may have accounted for the fact that not all Bengalis who had served or were serving in Orissa were hostile to the Oriya cause. Both Phakīrmohana Senāpati and Gaurīśaṅkar Rāy were *Brāhmas*. *Utkala Hitaisinī*, however, was extremely right-wing and conservative: it carried an article condemning "Brahmos in a Brahmin Land." See Priyaranjan Sen, *Modern Oriya Literature*, Calcutta, 1947, p. 40.

Rājendralāl Mitra started the controversy with a disparaging comparison between the number of titles recently published in Bengali and those published in Oriya, concluding that the number of Oriya-speakers was insufficient to support a publishing industry. Gaurīśaṅkar countered this by challenging Rājendralāl's population figures and raising the question of the numbers of Oriya-speakers in such places as Ganjam and Sambalpur, now incorporated in other administrative zones. The next step, advanced by Umācaran Hāldār, was to suggest that Oriya ought at least to be written in the Bengali script, and the final step in the Bengali argument, advanced by Kānticandra Bhaṭṭācārya and fully supported by Rājendralāl Mitra, was that Oriya was not a separate language, but merely a dialect of Bengali.

The controversy was mainly local to Orissa, though some articles concerned with it were published in Calcutta in the *Indian Mirror*, the *Education Gazette* and the *Calcutta Review*,[5] as also was Kānticandra's pamphlet *uḍiā svatantra bhāṣā nahe* (Oriya is not a separate language). It was, however, essentially a group conflict between rival parties with a vested interest in Orissa, in official employment, property or publishing.[6] The Bengalis were eager to bring their opinions to the notice of government by articles in the press, public petitions and Kānticandra's pamphlet. The domiciled Bengalis and Oriyas did their best to counter these moves. Superficially the controversy therefore consisted in two rival parties competing for the advantages of government favour. Unlike similar previous confrontations between the right and left, this one was not concerned with a religious dispute, in which the left could mobilize mass support through the vernacular, but with the vernacular itself, and therefore gave to the Oriya-speakers not only a moral superiority in the eyes of the British, but also the possibility of even greater mass support in the future, when the full implications of the dispute eventually became apparent.

[5] It is interesting to see how the Bengalis were trying to gain direct access to government sympathies by publicizing their views in English at the seat of government.

[6] The textbook market was of course one of the big prizes at stake here.

B. Kānticandra Bhaṭṭācārya's Pamphlet, Uḍiyā Svatantra Bhāṣā Nahe

As a scholarly work on comparative philology, Kānticandra Bhaṭṭācārya's pamphlet is of no imporcance. Its importance is entirely political. Though couched in the form of a philological discussion of Bengali and Oriya, it was an attempt to suppress the Oriya language and deprive it of significant status. Because of its form, however, its opponents had no option but to refute it in philological terms, but for the purposes of this paper it is important that the pamphlet should be seen in economic terms, as Phakīrmohana saw it. It epitomized Bengali aspirations for the aggrandizement of Bengal. It envisaged the whole of the region that now comprises Assam, West Bengal, Bangladesh and Orissa as one geographic, cultural, linguistic and ethnic area;[7] that is, the Bengali language area. It was assumed that Assam was universally recognized as part of Bengal, and Assamese as a dialect of Bengali. In consequence, Assam was frequently referred to under the blanket-term "in the East"; that is in east Bengal as understood by Bhaṭṭācārya, namely Sylhet, Assam etc. Bhaṭṭācārya made similar assumptions about Orissa, to which he referred as "in the South," meaning in south Bengal; that is, south of the Subarṇarekhā, traditionally regarded as the boundary between Orissa and Bengal, and now regarded by Bhaṭṭācārya as a mere dividing line between north and south Bengal.

Such arrogant prejudice dressed up as scholarship could appeal to no one but the bigoted. It alienated everyone else. It attributed the differences between Oriya and Bengali to the former's contact with uncivilized tribes.[8] The implication that standard Oriya approximated to the speech of the uneducated, lower castes of Bengal[9] could hardly have been expected to win support for Kānticandra's

[7]Kānticandra Bhaṭṭācārya, *udiyā svatantra bhāṣā nahe,* Calcutta, 1870, pp. 5-6, *et passim.*

[8]*Ibid.*, p. 7.

[9]In such typical statements as: "Gentlefolk do not use the word *pāni* in place of *jal*, but the lower caste people of Bengal do," (*ibid*, p. 27). Incidentally, this statement would have antagonized the whole Bengali Muslim community, who to a man use *pāni* in preference to *jal*. Again, "Low caste people in various parts of Bengal pronounce 'panara' as 'pandara' (*ibid.*, p. 58). *Pani* (Bhaṭṭācārya does not distinguish between the retroflex and dental nasal) and pandara are, of course, standard Oriya forms.

thesis from Oiryas; and his attacks on the missionaries for trying to reflect the actual pronunciation of Assamese and Oriyas in dictionaries and textbooks on the grounds that they were deliberately "corrupting pure Bengali forms"[10] must also have aroused antagonism. His slur on the competence of Europeans generally to judge whether or not Oriya and Bengali were separate languages[11] can hardly have been calculated to win support in European circles. In short, it was a tactless book from start to finish and deserved the almost universal condemnation it received.

Gaurīśaṅkar had every justification in observing:

> We see no reason for being satisfied with the author's knowledge of philology. It seems to us that he has relied merely on the similarity between Oriya and Bengali and utilised the word 'philology' to give to his opinions an air of authority. . . . He has casually passed off Sanskrit, Persian and Hindi words as Bengali. ... Had the author attempted an impartial judgement, he would have realized that the excessive use of Sanskrit words in modern books in Bengali and Oriya has increased the similarity between the two, but the ignorant Bengali and Oriya is unable to understand this type of language. They cannot fathom it out without education, and neither can understand the other's spoken language.[12]

Bhūdevancandra Mukhopādhyāy, Inspector of Schools, Orissa Division, and editor of Calcutta's *Education Gazette,* also refuted Bhaṭṭācārya's thesis. The following extract from his journal reveals that he regarded Bhaṭṭācārya's reasoning as mere prejudice:

> Where the Bengali and Oriya are alike, he has called both Bengali; where they differ, he has called the Oriya a corruption of standard Bengali. This is no way to reason. What prevents one from calling them both Oriya in the places where the Bengali and Oriya are

[10] *Ibid.*, pp. 64-65.

[11] *Ibid.*, p. 20.

[12] *Utkaḷa Dīpikā*, 1870, quoted by Mṛtyuñjaya, *Karmayogī Gaurīśaṅkara*, pp. 59-61. Gaurīśaṅkara may have been straining to control anger here, for Kānticandra had quoted from him in his pamphlet: "Newspapers are written in pure vernacular. If Oriya is an independent language, then it is to be expected that the Oriya. . .in newspapers will be. . .different from Bengali. ...The few lines from *Utkaḷa Dīpikā*. . .indicate that it is all Bengali. Only a few words deviate from Bengali" (*op. cit.*, p. 18).

alike, and from calling the Bengali a corruption of the Oriya in the places where they differ? ...If the vocabulary of one language is to be described from the outset as a corruption of that of the other language, then what need was there for reasoning? One can reach any conclusion one likes by question begging of this sort.[13]

However, by far the most important condemnation came from the European community. The *Calcutta Review* wrote:

The book states in its preface that the Commissioner and the missionaries made a mistake in introducing Oriya into kacheris of Orissa in the place of Bengali, and that they considered Bengali and Oriya to be separate languages. The author has accordingly attempted to prove that Oriya is not a separate language, but merely a corruption of Bengali. In our opinion his attempt failed ....Even if Oriya were bad Bengali (and we do not admit the fact), the Government were nevertheless justified in making it the language of the lawcourts of Orissa, for despite being 'bad Bengali', it is good for Orissa. Not only do three crores of people in Orissa converse in the language, but there was also a considerable corpus of literature composed in it in the past, and this is continually being added to in the present. Consequently, had the Government forcibly taught the people of Orissa Bengali, they would have been guilty of the same injustice as Prussia was in imposing its high language on Holstein.[14]

This was by far the most pragmatic approach. It reveals that its author, by comparing the imposition of Bengali on Orissa with that of Prussian on Holstein, fully realized the political significance of Kānticandra's book. It was the end of the dispute. Some of the Bengalis involved in it were transferred: the outcry in Balasore raised by Phakīrmohana had won the support of John Beames,[15]

[13] This is a translation of the Oriya version which appeared in *Utkaḷa Dīpikā*, 30 April 1870, quoted in *Karmayogī Gaurīśaṅkara*, p. 64.

[14] *Calcutta Review*, July 1870; quoted in *Karmayogī Gaurīśaṅkara*, pp. 67-68. The above text is a translation from the Oriya.

[15] Bhaṭṭācārya claimed to have quoted from Beames' *Indian Philology*; see K.C. Bhaṭṭācārya, *op. cit.*, p. i. Beames did not, however, support Bhaṭṭācārya's thesis, for he writes elsewhere:

The legends of the Oriya race render it probable that they came into the province through the hills and down the Mahānadī, and the characteristics of

who soon had the Bengali Deputy Inspector for Balasore Śivadās Bhaṭṭācārya, replaced by Rādhānātha Rāya. In 1873 the post of joint inspector was created for the supervision of the Education Department in Orissa and Nandakiśora Dāsa was appointed. Thus a new era in education commenced in Orissa with Oriya-speakers in charge of their own destinies for the first time.

C. *The Uncoordinated Phase of the Oriya Nationalist Movement*

The controversy brought home to some Oriya-speakers the invidiousness of their position as linguistic minorities in large administrative zones, where for legal and educational reasons they were liable to be obliged to adopt the major language of their respective zone: Bengali, Hindi or Telugu. Though awareness of the position gradually diffused throughout Orissa, no concerted effort was made towards unification till 1903, when the *Utkaḷa Sammilanī* was formed by Madhusūdana Dāsa, Orissa's first and foremost barrister.

Meanwhile, however, scattered and spasmodic efforts were made to found presses, launch journals and cultivate literature. Finance for these ventures came mainly from Oriya kings in the Gaḍajāt Māhāl, and from zamindars and landed gentry. The journalists were unpaid, though prizes were sometimes awarded for stories, articles and poems. Contributors and journalists were in the main

---

their language lead me to believe that they broke away from the main stream of Aryan immigration somewhere about Shababad or Gya (Gaya). That they are not an offshoot of the Bengalis is proved by the fact that their language was already formed as we now have it at a period when Bangali had not attained a separate existence, and when the deltaic portion of Bengal was almost uninhabited. So that in fact they could not have sprung from the Bengalis, simply because there were then no Bengalis to spring from....

The similarity between the languages is not by any means as great as some Bengali writers have sought to make out, and what similarity there is, is due to the fact that they both are dialects of the eastern or Magadhi form of Prakrit.

John Beames, *Notes on the History of Orissa under the Muhammadan, Maratha and English Rule*, first published in 1882 in the *Journal of the Asiatic Society of Bengal*, Vol. 52, Part I, and reprinted as Ch. VIII, Vol. II, *A History of Orissa*, N.K. Sahu, Calcutta 1956, pp 292-293. In an introductory note Beames explains: "These notes were written as part of a manual on the district of Balasore of which I was Collector from 1869 to 1873. The work was completed...in 1873; but... was ton printed."

government servants and teachers. By their part-time efforts between 1865 and 1896 they launched no less than thirty-nine journals, though of these only seven survived. The failure of journals was due partly to finance, but partly to the transfer of contributors.

The diffusion of presses to some extent indicates the gradual diffusion of the sense of nationhood amongst Oriya-speakers. At the time of the language dispute there were only three indigenous presses in Orissa: two Oriya-owned, the Cuttack Printing Company and the *Utkaḷa* Press in Balasore; and one Bengali-owned, the *Utkaḷa Hitaiṣiṇi* Press in Cuttack founded in 1868. After the dispute presses began to be founded further and further afield: a press in Mayūrbhanj in 1881; the Puri Printing Company in 1882; and it is possible that presses were established in Balasore and Kendrāpaḍā in 1884 and 1886, for there are references to journals published from these places at these dates. There are also references to a Victoria Press, Cuttack, the earliest being 1886. Maharaja Sudhala Deba of Bamra also founded the Jagannātha Ballabha Press in 1889. We also read of the Rāya Press in Cuttack in 1894; and the Gajapati Press in Pārlākhemuṇḍi in 1896; and of a press in Tāḷcer in 1896; founded by the local Raja Kiśoracandra Birabara Haricandana.

D. *The History of Oriya Nationalism*

Though a detailed history of the Oriya nationalist movement has yet to be written, it is necessary for the purposes of this paper to hazard a few remarks upon the nature and development of the movement. The first thing that should be made clear is that it was primarily concerned with the independence of Orissa from non-Oriya domination, not with the independence of India from British rule.

Though many of its adherents, especially aristocrats such as Rājā Baikuṇṭhanātha De, were motivated by national pride, the majority of its supporters were probably concerned mainly with middle class employment prospects in "natural" (*prākrtika*) Orissa,[16] and, precisely for this reason, the chief opposition to the movement probably came from the middle class in contiguous regions, Bengal,

[16]The phrase used by *Utkaḷa Sammiḷanī* to denote the total geographic area in which Oriya was spoken.

Bihar, Central Provinces and Madras; since any gain by the Oriyas was a loss to the Bengalis, Biharis, Hindusthanis and Telugus, and *vice versa*.[17]

The British were probably indifferent to the fate of Orissa. It can have made little difference to them whether Orissa remained divided and parcelled out as parts of other administrative regions and zones, or whether it was united as one linguistic and cultural whole and administered as a separate region. To the Oriya-speakers and their neighbours, however, the difference was crucial, and influential Oriya-speakers, as well as influential people from contiguous regions, were probably continually lobbying British officials, though with conflicting aspirations, throughout the period from 1866 to 1936. As early as 1866, the secretary to the Government of India wrote to the chief secretary to the Government of Bengal, proposing that Orissa be severed from Bengal. The fact that it remained unsevered was presumably due to an opposing lobby in Bengal.[18] In 1903 Lord Curzon, then Viceroy of India, proposed that the coastal belt (the so-called Mogal Bandī) and the feudatory states (the Gadajāt Māhāl) of Orissa should be united. Home Secretary to the Indian government, H.H. Risley circulated the proposal to all regional governments concerned. The *Utkaḷa Sammiḷanī* welcomed the proposal, but it was rejected at the nineteenth session of the Indian Congress, where, presumably at the

[17]Until 1880, for example, when Madhusūdana Dāsa returned to Orissa, the Bengalis enjoyed a monopoly in the legal profession in Orissa. They did all they could to prevent him getting established. See Naba Kiśora Dāsa, *Utkaḷa Gauraba Madhusūdana*, Cuttack, 1951. Phakīrmohana also records that during the language dispute of the 1860's the Bengalis created "closed shops" in the Post Office and Public Works Department in Orissa; that "the Oriya who could land a job on the railway had not been born"; and that commerce was entirely in the hands of non-Oriyas. By refusing to permit the study of Oriya in the universities, Madrasis and Bengalis were effectively reducing the number of Oriya graduates. Madhusūdana Dāsa had difficulty in obtaining permission to write Sanskrit in Oriya characters in the University of Calcutta in 1869-70. See N.K. Dāsa, *op. cit.*, p. 25. Arrangements to teach Oriya were not made at Madras University till 1873 and at Calcutta till 1902; both these victories were gained only after prolonged agitation. See *ibid.*, p. 62. Similarly, the use of Oriya in official documents was not allowed in Madras till 1890. Thus until that date Telugu-speakers enjoyed an advantage over Oriyas, when seeking positions as solicitor's clerks.

[18]N.K. Dāsa, *op. cit.*, p. 61. In 1895 the commissioner of Orissa proposed in his administrative report that the Oriya-speaking tracts be unified.

instigation of Telugu delegates, a resolution was passed that Ganjām should never be severed from Madras and joined to Orissa.[19] As early as 1911, Britishers such as Lord Hardinge and even the Indian Congress had accepted the principle of linguistic states, on which Oriya aspirations for unification were based, but the government of Madras opposed the principle.[20]

Orissa's aspirations were finally fulfilled as a result of *Utkaḷa Sammiḷanī* defying the Indian Congress in 1921, when Gandhi declared non-cooperation. When the Simon Commission arrived in India (1928), Congress issued instructions that it should be boycotted, but *Utkaḷa Sammiḷanī* sent representatives to testify to the Commission. As a result the O'Donnell Committee came to Orissa in 1931 to determine the boundaries of the proposed new state of Orissa and in 1936 the state was established.[21]

It should be pointed out that though independence from British rule was not the immediate object of the Oriya nationalist movement, it nevertheless formed one of its ultimate objectives. As far as Orissa was concerned, it was a question of priorities.[22] Had India been granted independence before Orissa achieved the status of a separate state, Oriya-speakers would still have been faced with the prospect of either remaining second class citizens of India, in comparison to Telugus, Hindusthanis and Bengalis, or campaigning for the creation of a separate state on linguistic grounds. As future events have shown, *Utkaḷa Sammiḷanī* undoubtedly had its priorities right.

[19] *Ibid.*, p. 63.

[20] *Ibid.*, p. 64. The same page also records that in 1918 the Montagu-Chelmsford report expressed approval of the principle whereby states should be organized on a linguistic basis.

[21] *Ibid.*, pp. 67-68.

[22] *Ibid.*, p. 52. The proposal that Independence should form part of the programme of *Utkaḷa Sammiḷanī* was put forward in 1921, three years after Phakīrmohana's death, by Pandit Gopabandhu Dāsa, an ardent admirer of Gandhi. Gopabandhu seems to have followed a more extremist line than most of the members of *Utkaḷa Sammiḷanī;* for example, he initiated a non-cooperation movement in Siṁhabhūma in 1921, when the rest of the *Sammiḷanī* favoured cooperation. There seem to have been differences of opinion amongst the *Sammiḷanī* leaders on the future of Orissa also. Some wanted a separate state; some, like Madhusūdana Dāsa, wanted a continued association with Bengal; and others, like Gopālānanda Caudhurī, favoured association with the Central Provinces.

4. PHAKIRMOHANA SENAPATI

A. His Career

Phakīrmohana Senāpati was an Oriya by blood. "By blood" is a term to which some social scientists strongly object, but in an Oriya context it is meaningful and important. Indian society was then divided by language and religion into mutually-exclusive communities, which regarded pedigree as the supremely important factor in such things as marriage. Thus society was aware of who was and was not Oriya by blood and judged accordingly.

Of the three men who ushered in the modern age in Oriya literature, Rādhānātha Rāya (1848-1908), Madhusūdana Rāo (1853-1912) and Phakīrmohana Senāpati (1843-1918), Phakīrmohana alone is extolled for the purity of his language, since he alone was genuinely Oriya, the other two being respectively of Bengali and Maratha descent. The majority of modern authors in Oriya have tended to model themselves on Phakīrmohana for precisely this reason; and in consequence the literary age in which he lived is now almost unanimously acclaimed as the "Age of Phakīrmohana."

Thus Phakīrmohana was an influential figure in the Oriya nationalist movement, because both he and his style came eventually to symbolize genuine Oriyaness. His ideas, expressions, themes, language and humour appealed directly to Oriya emotions. His description of the trial of Maṅgarāja, an extortionist landowner, serialized in *Utkaḷa Sāhitya* in 1897, brought peasants to Cuttack in bullock-cart loads to witness it. He was the Charles Dickens of his day and could, and can, wring tears and laughter from Oriya hearts and eyes like no one else before him or since.

Phakīrmohana's life, too, symbolized that of the average middle class Oriya of his times. His family fortunes rose and fell with the rise and collapse of the shipping and salt industries in Balasore during British rule. With virtually nothing but a primary village education, he began his second career, after the collapse of his uncle's ship chandler's business, as a schoolmaster on Rs 2½ a month. Good luck, backed by his own native wit and persistence, improved his prospects till by his thirties he was earning Rs 100 a month as a dewan in the feudatory states of Orissa. But for him employment and unemployment alternated like the wind and the tide, and his days of affluence were comparatively few.

He was passionately devoted to Oriya language and culture; and even the friendships he formed with Westerners were probably sparked off by a mutual interest in, and affection for, the Oriya language. Hallam and Beames spring to mind in this connection. Phakīrmohana says little of Hallam as a man except that he spoke exceptionally fluent and faultless Oriya and spent many hours after school discussing Oriya literature with him. Beames, whom he met through Hallam, emerges as a more colourful and dogmatic personality, which tended in some measure to stimulate Phakīrmohana's satirical bent, but Phakīrmohana nonetheless felt indebted to him for the personal help he gave him in his career; but more important he both admired and respected him for the ardour with which he leapt to the defence of Oriya against the Bengalis.

Pride in his language and literature was the mainspring of Phakīrmohana's life. Most of his spare time in adult life was spent in cultivating literature with his colleagues: writing textbooks, editing the *Rasakalloḷa,* founding a press, editing a journal, translating the *Rāmāyaṇa* and *Mahābhārata* from Sanskrit, composing occasional verse, and finally launching in retirement into full-time production of prose fiction in Cuttack and Balasore. Literature was his refuge from life's ills. When his first son died he started his translation of the *Rāmāyaṇa* (1880). When his wife died, he composed his *Puṣpamālā* (Flower Garland) (1894) and *Upahāra* (Presentation) (1895). When unemployment hung over him after the revolt in Keūjhar, in which he nearly lost his life, he jogged mournfully along on elephant back and suddenly to console himself he began jotting down the first edition of his comic and satirical *Utkaḷa Bhramaṇaṁ* (Orissan Tour) (1892), which immediately upon his arrival in Ānandapura was set up and printed in the Royal press, page by page, as he completed its composition. He was then fifty-two years of age and it was his first really original work. His satirical bent had at last burst into literature.

Such then was his love for Oriya literature; and his wrath and spleen when that literature was threatened can easily be imagined. A Bengali Brāhmo with whom he enjoyed discussing religion lost his friendship the moment he disparaged Oriya. The Bengali community of Balasore conferred on him the title of "bastard ringleader" (*śālā* ringleader) during the language dispute. He attacked and derided Bengali aspirations in the press and at public meetings.

He mobilized the support of Oriyas from the upper and middle classes in Balasore. He exploited the economic angle in explaining the importance of the language issue in regard to employment. And he has left a permanent record of his lampooning of Kānticandra Bhaṭṭācārya, who dared to pen his opinion that Oriya was not a separate language.[23] The language dispute of 1869/70 was to rankle with Phakīrmohana all his life: his biography composed just prior to his death bears numerous allusions to it and the one or two speeches of his that have survived are impregnated with the intensified love of Oriya that stemmed from this early controversy. His literary style—and in consequence that of the whole Oriya nation—has been reshaped by it. Previously, increasingly Sanskritization had narrowed the gap between literary Oriya and Bengali to a "mere handful of suffixes and inflexions,"[24] but after it the language of the village street found its way via Phakīrmohana's pen into literature. Written Oriya now re-echoes the rhythmic patterns of spoken Oriya intonations as a result of Phakīrmohana having spoken onto the page and thereby enchanted the hearts of his fellow countrymen. Later, when in the 1930s as a result of nationalist agitations Oriya power and prestige increased in Orissa, prose styles began being modelled on the "pure household Oriya"[25] of Phakīrmohana, whose influence can be traced in all the best novels of the last thirty years, Kālindī Caraṇa Pānīgrāhī's *Matira Manisa,* Kāhnucarana Mahānti's *Hā Anna* and *Sāstī,* and his younger brother's, Gopīnātha Mahānti's Parajā.

B. His Views on Language

In regard to language,[26] Phakīrmohana's views were probably typical of the Oriya nationalist movement. He believed that nationa-

[23]Phakīrmohana Senāpati, *parisista*, an Appendix to his *Ātma Jībana Carita*, in *Phakīrmohana Granthūbālī*, Part I, Cuttack, 1957.

[24]Compare Kānticandra Bhaṭṭācārya, *op. cit.*, p. 21: "Bābu Phakīrmohana Senāpati says in his foreword to *jībana carita*, 'The truth is, the change of the verb forms alone turns Bengali into Oriya,."

[25]The phrase used by Gopāla Praharāja, an admirer of Phakīrmohana's, who attempted to follow his style in the 1930s.

[26]All the quotations in this section are taken from three speeches of Phakīrmohana's reprinted in Part I of his *granthābalī*. They are: *utkaḷa bhāsāra bhūtabhabisyata*, pp. 1045-49; *sabhāpati abhibhāsaṇa*, pp. 1092-1101; and *abhibhāsaṇa*, pp. 1105-1111.

lity was determined by language: "Nations identify themselves by the name of their mother-tongue." National prestige therefore depended upon the prestige of the nation's language and literature. There were three impediments to national and linguistic progress: the cultural, the political, and the financial.

(i) *The Cultural Impediment.* The predominance in Orissa of alien tongues was the main cause of the backwardness and low prestige of Oriya: "If only our fore-fathers had cultivated their mother-tongue as well as the official language (i.e. Persian)...." Phakīrmohana's contemporaries were making the same mistake in regard to English: "No nation ever progressed by losing its mother tongue.... Just glance at Bengali. See how far they have achieved prestige in the eyes of the civilised world...." Education in a foreign language impeded the diffusion of knowledge. If India was to progress, her farmers and craftsmen required education, but this would only be possible through Oriya, not English.

(ii) *The Political Impediment.* The dispersal of the Oriya-speaking tracts in the early days of British rule had impeded the development of the Oriya language. People of Oriya parentage were beginning to pass themselves off as Telugus, Hindusthanis and Bengalis. British officials could suddenly discontinue the use of Oriya for official purposes. The only remedy was to petition government for the reunification of the Oriya-speaking tracts.

(iii) *The Financial Impediment.* Educated Oriya were reluctant to buy Oriya books: "No Christian home is without its Bible, nor Muslim without its Koran, yet how many Oriya Hindu households can produce a copy of Jagannātha Dāsa's *Bhāgavata,* which is our equivalent?" The plight of Oriya periodicals indicated the backwardness of Oriya: "Orissa imports as many copies of Bengali periodicals as it buys copies of *Utkaḷa Dīpikā*....Oriya authors are poor. Much of their work lies unpublished for want of capital." Publishing in Orissa was badly organized. Authors had to publish and market their own works. Inadequate finances resulted in limited editions, which were expensive and difficult to sell: Bengali houses are full of books because in Bengal excellent books worth Rs 5/- sell at 8 annas a piece. The only way out was government aid:

> In order to encourage authors in Bengal, the Government buys up their works....Bengalis ... on the Lt Governor's staff...are thus in a position to lobby the support of Government. I hope that

> one day poor Orissa will be able to enjoy such official favour.... I read in the paper ... how Rs 50,000 were raised for the promotion of Bengali literature....I wondered...when, oh when, would all the leading people ... of Orissan society unite for the promotion of their mother tongue.

Phakīrmohana made appeals to the patriotism of the educated to induce them to buy books, if not for themselves, at least for their womenfolk. It was the language which bound the nation together. Thus they had a patriotic duty to cultivate it:

> The *purāṇas* state that language is *brahmamayī*, for it binds society together. Hence the study of one's mother tongue is an important act of merit (*punya kārya*)....

The patriotism of Madhusūdana Dāsa was an example to the whole nation: "How much merit (*puṇya*) accumulated over how many ages, has enabled Orissa to acquire such a son. Madhu Bābu is a god, driven to earth by a curse."

There were four ways of promoting "national literature": "read it; induce others to read it; write; and induce others to write."

Prose fiction, drama and lyrics were important in popularizing one's mother tongue: "The sudden rise to fame of Bengali is due to the novels of Baṅkim Candra, the plays of Dīnabandhu, and the songs of the world-renowned Rabindranāth."

Phakīrmohana expressed modesty in his own achievements: "I am merely preparing the ground for the educated authors of the future to write their novels on."

Literature was however capable of stimulating national sentiment:

> Every educated Indian had in his heart love of his motherland, but they were all separate; then a novelist showed them a picture and pronounced 'Bande Mātaraṁ'; from the Himalayas to Cape Comorin the cry arose in chorus 'Bande Mataram.'

C. *The Representativeness of Phakīrmohana's Other Views*

Other than in regard to language Phakīrmohana's views were probably not typical of the Oriya nationalist movement. The *Utkaḷa Sammilanī* under Madhusūdana Dāsa represented a training in democracy: Phakīrmohana believed in a kind of aristocratic socialism. Madhusūdana Dāsa was an eminent modern lawyer: Phakīrmohana satirized the British legal system and the rapacious lawyers bred by it. As a member of the Legislative Council, Madhusūdana Dāsa was committed to parliamentary government: as an ex-dewan in a number of feudatory states, Phakīrmohana thought more in terms of enlightened feudalism. Younger, fiery members of the movement believed in the ultimate attainment of full independence by India: to Phakīrmohana, though he sympathized with Congress and revered its leaders, their aspirations seemed a distant misty dream; he foresaw as feasible nothing more than the unification of Orissa.

It should be remembered that Phakīrmohana belonged to the older generation. He was largely untouched by Western education and was therefore the natural spokesman of the rural masses. Precisely because of this, however, his views have probably proved more influential after both Orissa's attainment of the status of a separate state and India's attainment of full independence; for Phakīrmohana spoke in terms of traditional Oriya values and institutions, which claimed, and still claim, the respect of the vast rural masses and must therefore be respected by any party wishing to gain power in a democracy.

D. *Phakīrmohana's Attitudes and Values*

Though Phakīrmohana had no religious objections to either Muslim or Christian rule in Orissa, he had economic, cultural and moral objections. Ultimately British and Muslim rule had harmed Orissa as much as Maratha rule. All three were alien, and under them Orissa had been impoverished to the enrichment of Murshidabad, Berar and Calcutta. Alien rule affected not only the economy, but also culture and morality. The predominance of Persian and English had inhibited the development of Oriya culture. At the same time alien thought had undermined Hindu morality: the young had taken up alien vices, and in some classes atheism was rife and parents no longer respected. To counteract these influences Phakīrmohana stressed the old Hindu virtues of respect for morality (*dharma*), the ruling classes (the *Kṣatriyas*) the elders (*gurujans*), caste councils and family life. In doing so, however, he advocated not a return to the old feudal system but the initiation of a new social order based on the same values, a kind of aristocratic socialism.

Judging by Sanskrit literature, Phakīrmohana concluded that in ancient India the forces of law and authority had rested on spiritual rather than economic values. A king needed the respect of his people and it would be accorded him only if his character were immaculate and his faith in God sincere. Similarly, fathers and husbands were worthy of respect only if they believed in, and adhered to, the principles of *dharma* as revealed in the *śāstras* and *purāṇas;* similarly also, a wife whose chastity did not conform to *paurānik* standards should be abandoned. In his prose fiction Phakīrmohana reaffirms these beliefs derived from Sanskrit literature. In *Lachamā* the rule of the Muslim and the Turk ends because both have forsaken their religions; and the coming of British rule is welcomed because the British adhere to the principles of their religion even in business, where dishonesty is to be expected.

In Phakīrmohana's pre-June 1913 prose fiction, husbands are invariably respected by their virtuous wives, whose merit protects the husbands from disaster, Maṅgarāja is kept alive by the power of his wife's *puṇya*: he dies only after her death. He had shared her *dharma,* for she was his *sahadharmiṇi,* and thus, though evil, he had lived by her virtue. In Phakīrmohana's post-June 1913 prose fiction, however, fathers and husbands who err from the path of *dharma,* are no longer respected by their daughters and wives: Kamalī steals from her avaricious father and Sulocanā beats her dissipated husband.

Thus in his prose fiction Phakīrmohana reaffirms the spiritual values of Hinduism in order to counteract the materialistic values imported into Orissan society from the West. Under Western influence, the spiritual values of Hinduism were being replaced by materialistic ones. Social status was beginning to be measured in financial rather than spiritual terms. In *Prāyaścitta* Phakīrmohana depicts a conflict for the leadership of *karaṇa* society between Sankarśana Mahāṇti, a rich, self-made man, and Vaiṣṇava Caraṇa Vidyadhara Mahāpātra, the hereditary head of the *śrī karaṇa* community. Attracted by Saṅkarśaṇa's money, even respectable *karaṇas* were prepared to connive at gaining him acceptance as the social equal of Vaiṣṇava Caraṇa, but Vaiṣṇava Caraṇa would not hear of it, for Saṅkarśaṇa's blood had been polluted by an inferior marriage some generations earlier. Though sympathizing with Vaiṣṇava Caraṇa to some extent, Phakīrmohana nevertheless shows that his pride itself is a fault. Pride in status, status-seeking and empty pomp are themselves sources of evil, for they engender materialistic cravings. A man should be admired for his humility and virtue, not for his possessions, as becomes clear in the *dénouement* when both Vaiṣṇava Caraṇa and Saṅkarśaṇa Mahānti renounce the world to practice *dharma* in Vṛndāvana.

Brahmins and abbots were exulting in the pride of their social positions and were more intent on enhancing their possessions and incomes than their wisdom and virtue, forgetting that the true prestige of a Brahmin derives from the latter not the former. By satire, Phakīrmohana sought to remind them of their true social function, the propagation of *dharma*.

Though opposed to materialism, Phakīrmohana was not unaware of the importance of economic factors in conditioning the formation of personality. As he points out, Maṅgarāja becomes vicious and aggressively anti-social and acquisitive because he was born poor. His initial poverty caused him to exaggerate the importance of wealth. Phakīrmohana's praise of the middle class is essentially praise of economic sufficiency. The middle class were rich enough to be free from economic stress; and provided they were not deluded by the desire for grandeur, they could lead happy and virtuous lives, for their incomes were sufficient to enable them to receive an adequate education and grounding in morality. It was the rich and the poor who were most likely to be deluded by materialistic cravings, for both were more or less conditioned to over-stress the importance of social status and prestige, and imagine that such things derive from possessions.

Accordingly in *Prāyaścitta,* where Phakīrmohana proclaims his vision of the ideal kingdom, the landowners place all their possessions in trust to the temple, and ensure that the income from it is used for the education and social welfare of their tenants. Thus in effect Phakīrmohana was advocating not a return to the old feudal system but a new type of religious socialism, whereby all the means of production would reside in the possession of the state, the landowners becoming mere trustees, and the tenants or subjects enjoying an equal share in the produce via social services. Presumably under this system everyone would enjoy more or less middle class status. Since all would be educated and grounded in morality, and since no one would possess sufficient personal wealth to indulge in extravagance or ostentation, crime would be eradicated, for there would be no luxurious displays of opulence and grandeur to engender materialistic cravings. All would dedicate themselves to the performance of *dharma*, either through the service of each other, or, when their physical powers failed, through worship in a religious retreat for ascetics.

E. Phakīrmohana's Aims and Intentions in Comparison with Those of Baṅkim Candra Chatterjee and Rāmmohan Rāy

Phakīrmohana's position is analoguous to that of both Baṅkim Candra and Rāmmohan Rāy in Bengal. Being Baṅkim's contemporary, Phakīrmohana was trying to do in Orissa what Baṅkim achieved in Bengal. He was trying to create a truly national literature by getting all classes of Orissan society to read and cultivate it; to achieve a sense of national unity; to reinvigorate his nation by reminding it of past glories; and to improve the moral climate of Orissa by reaffirming the traditional values of Oriya society.

Unlike Baṅkim Candra, however, Phakīrmohana was not trying to achieve his purpose by alienating the Muslims. In this respect, Phakīrmohana's position accords with that of Rāmmohan Rāy. For historical reasons Phakīrmohana's background and experience were similar to those of Rāmmohan. Like Rāmmohan, Phakīrmohana had learnt Persian in childhood, because at the time Persian, not English, was the official language of Orissa. This knowledge of Persian engendered in them sympathy for the Muslim community and respect for Islamic religion and culture, just as their later knowledge of English led to a similar respect for Christianity and Western culture. But, being later in time, Phakīrmohana had witnessed the waning of Islamic culture in India; and he could probably foresee a similar waning of Western culture in the distant future, when British power in India ceased. Consequently, it was, in his view, a mistake to concentrate on the acquisition of the trappings of Western culture in dress, behaviour and speech. Such concentration was a waste of effort on the part of the nation. One should respect the best in all cultures and seek to borrow and absorb the most admirable elements of alien culture into one's own. But it was foolish to abandon one's native culture root and branch in favour of a foreign one whose sojourn in India could never be permanent. This, as far as one can make out, was the essence of Phakīrmohana's thought on Orissa's cultural dilemma during British rule.

5. Conclusion

It seems to me that the movements I have discussed are basically similar: they were all utilizing Indian traditions, though different traditions and in different ways. In each case an opposition was set up which helped to unify support: Baṅkim set up an opposition between Hindus and Muslims. He then linked the Hindus in his historical novels with Hindu traditions and values; with Mother Kālī and the Kṛṣṇa of the *Bhāgavad Gītā;* with the ideal of the *sannyāsī;* and with heroines reminiscent of heroines from early Bengali Buddhist folk tales. His style was Sanskritic; his attitude was xenophobic; he was typically right-wing.

Gandhi set up an opposition between Indians and Europeans. His movement was a typical Indian revolt: the ruler was unjust and unworthy to rule. Gandhi assumed the attitude of immense moral superiority, typical of the Brahmin and *sannyāsī,* which compelled the respect of his fellow countrymen, who saw in him virtually a divine incarnation. He was in fact the living embodiment of a Baṅkim Candra hero: living in an *āśram* on virtually nothing and surrounded by his *santān*. Neither Rām in exile, nor Yuddiṣṭhir marching off to heaven after his victory in Kurukṣetra, could have commanded greater Indian support.

The Oriya nationalists set up an opposition between people who declared themselves to be Oriyas on the basis of language and birth-place and non-Oriyas, whose identity ranged from Telugus, Madrasis, and Hindusthanis to Bengalis. Oriyas were vying with these non-Oriyas for royal favour; that is, British support. The non-Oriyas were established in that favour; the Oriyas were seeking to oust them. They therefore always stressed their loyalty to the British and defied even Congress to gain British support for their cause. They drummed up public support throughout Orissa via the newspapers, the rostrum, and the school. The Oriya language and Oriya literature were two of the important symbols to which they appealed.

Before the 20th century, confrontations between the left and the right in Hindu society generally ended either with the suppression of the left or with its inclusion in the right; that is, the essentially feudal structure of society remained unaltered, merely a slight shift in power took place. However, unlike religious movements, which attempted to abolish caste and ended by conforming to it, the nationalist movements became tied to a democratic process:

the outcome was bound to be more or less egalitarian. For this reason, I would suggest that Phakīrmohana's vision was truer to Indian tradition than that of most leaders of the Oriya nationalist movement. His Utopian vision remained essentially feudal: there was still a king and a ruling class, whose position ultimately derived from their moral superiority, not their economic power, which was vested in God. Nevertheless, his vision was not democratic, but monarchic: it was *Rāma rājya* not *Rāma ganatantra*.

Index

Abul Fazl, 138, 141, 146, 148-149
Acton, H.B., 1, 4, 10
Agnikuṇḍa tradition, 113-114
Agnipurāṇa, 116
Ahmad Manzuruddin, 132
Ahmad, M.B., 146
Ahmed, Imtiaz, 28
Aiken, H.D., 207
Akbar, 102, 136-137, 143-145, 147-149, 152, 160-161, 163, 168
Al-Ghazali, 132
Ali, M. Mohar, 167
Alsdorf, L., 63
Altekar, A.S., 110
Andrews, C.F., 172, 179
Andhra, 53, 59
Arbuthnot, A.J., 162, 163, 165
Ariyapala, M.B., 119
Arthaśastra 47, 50, 55, 66, 77, 86-93, 95, 96-102, 116-117, 119-120, 123, 217. *See also śāstras, Kauṭilīya*
Ashraf Khan Saiyid, 148
Asoka, 104, 117, 125-126
Aśvamedha, horse sacrifice, 69-70, 75, 100-101
Aśvatthamān, 106, 107, 111-112
Aungier, Gerald, 153-154
Aurangzeb, 146-147, 149, 154 158, 168

Babur, 147
Badauni, Abdul Qadir, 140
Bagley, F. R. C., 132
Bahadur Shah, 1, 147
Bailey, F.G., 67, 111-112
Bakunin, Michael, 200
Bandyopadhyaya, J., 227
Bandyopadhyaya, Bhabanīcaran, 234
Bandhopadhyaya, Kalipada, 241
Banerji, K.M., 173
Banerji, R.D., 112
Bangladesh, 233, 243
Baqir, Mira Muhammad, 147
Barani, Ziya-al ud-din, 130-131
Bārhaspatya Arthaśāstra, 86
Barnett, L.D., 110
Barua, B., 119
Basak, R.G., 112
Basham, A.L., 117, 134, 215-218,
Basu, Rajnarain, 177, 186
Beaglehole, T.H., 163
Beames, John, 245-246
Bengal, 120-121, 151-160, 163-164, 166, 169, 170, 172-174, 179-185, 233, 237-254, 258-259
Bentinck, Lord William 164-166, 170
Bernal, Martin, 202-203
Béteille, A., 68
Bhagvat Gita, 188, 208, 212-214, 259
Bhagavata (s), 104
Bhakti, 15, 29, 93
Bhandarkar, D.R., 67
Bhanja, Upendra, 240
Bhāttācarya, Kanticandra, 242-245, 252
Bird, William Wilberforce, 164-165
Bloch, J., 125
Blochman, H., 138
Boisselier, J., 107
Bombay, 153-154
Bosch, F.D.K., 113
Bose, Ashish, 20
Bose, Deb Kumar, 19
Bose, N.K., 210, 224, 227
Boulton, John, 8, 15
Brahman (authority), 65-66, 68, 75, 78, 112, 217. *See also* Brahmin
Brāhmaṇas, 105-107, 120, 124
Brahma Samaj, 175-176, 186, 188, 233
Brahmin (bearer of authority, caste), 15, 46, 52, 65-66, 68-71, 78, 81-82, 92 94-97, 221-222, 235, 257. *See also* Brahman
Briggs, L.P., 108
Brihaspati, 47

Brodkin, E.I., 163
Buddha, 101, 178, 207, 213, 214, 221, 239
Buddhist traditions, 93-94, 96-97, 104, 125 113, 134, 151, 178, 229, 233, 259
Buhler, G., 113

Caitanya, 230, 238-239
Calcutta, 159, 163-164. *See also* Bengal
Cālukya dynasty, 109, 117
Cālukya dynasty of Kalyāṇi, 121-122
Cambodia, 107
Cānakya, 92, 97-98
Candra, Bhārat, 237, 240
Carnatic, 154, 168, 169
Caste, 3, 15, 26-27, 53-54, 57-59, 82-84, 195. *See also jāti, varna*
Caṭṭopādhyāy, Sarat Candra, 232
Caudhuri, Gopālānanda, 249
Ceylon, 102-103, 112, 114, 116, 119, 121, 124
Chand, Tara, 139, 145, 148
Chandra Bhan, 141
Chatterjee, Bankim Candra, 188, 228, 234, 236-238, 258-259
Chowdhury, A.M., 110
Christianity, 13-14, 24, 25, 165-167, 173-174, 186, 202, 206-210, 232, 237, 244, 255, 258
Clive, Robert, 155-156, 167
Coedès, G., 108
Coḷa, Rājendra, 102
Coleman, Samuel, 4-5, 10
Congress, Indian National, 85, 181-182, 196-197, 204, 248-249, 255-260
Cornwallis, Marquess, 159-161, 162, 167, 169, 170
Coupland, R., 165
Currell, M., 227
Curzon, Lord, 248

Dabke, C.K., 41,
Dai Kaus Ibn Sikander, 135
Darke, Hubert, 132
Dāsa, Balarāma, 234-235
Dāsa, Dinakṛṣṇa, 240
Dāsa, Jagannātha, 253
Dāsa, Madhūsudana Rao, 249
Dāsa, N.K., 248-249
Dāsa, Nandakisora, 246
Dāsa, Nilikanta, 234
Dāsa, Pandit Gopabandhu, 249
Dāsa, Rama, 235
Deb, Radhakanta, 175
de Bary, W.T., 217-218, 221
de Bussy, 154-155
De Casparis, J.G., 11, 78, 99
Deccan States, 110, 165
de Josselin de Jong, P.E., 70 ,72
Delhi, 131, 149, 155, 164
Derrett, J. Duncan M., 13-14, 61, 62, 100, 120
Desai, I.P., 29
Desai, Mahadev, 209
Deshpande, C.E., 57
Deva, Indra, 30
Devahuti, D., 117, 123
Devarāja, ritual, 83, 108
Dharma, 36, 62, 68, 93, 99, 114, 117, 125, 134, 217-221, 238, 255-258
Dharmaśāstra, 29, 50, 53-55, 59, 83, 86, 93-96, 99, 102, 120, 150. *See also Śāstras*
Dhavan, Rajeer, 54
Dhawan, Gopinath, 205, 225
Divine Light, 137-40
Divine Right, 50, 67, 74-75, 90, 94, 95, 132-134, 136
Duff, Grant, 173-174
Dumont, Louis, 30, 64-65, 67,73-74, 79, 81-82
Durkheim, E., 11
Dupleix, Joseph Francois, 154-155

East India Company, 145, 152,153-171, 173
Eisenstadt, S.H., 61
Ellawala, H., 122
Elphinstone, Mountstuart, 151, 163, 165
Epics, 91, 93, 104, 108, 110

Fakhr-i-Madabbir, 148

Fazl-bin-Rozbhan,148
Finot, L., 107
Fleet, J.F., 109,113
Forster, E.M., 74
Foster, Sir W., 152
Francis, Sir Philip, 159, 161
Freud, S., 12
Fyzee, 44

Galanter, Marc, 57
Gandhi, M.K., 3, 27, 85, 195, 197, 200-208, 221-227, 228, 238-239, 249, 259
Gaṅgopādhyāy, Tarak, 234
Geiger, W., 116-117, 119, 122
Gellner, E., 15
Ghose, Aurobindo, 188, 200-227
Ghoshal, A.N., 216, 218, 226
Gibb, H.A.R., 129
Gleig, G.R., 165
Gnanambal, K., 59
Godwin, William, 199-200,
Gokhale, G.K., 193, 226
Gonda, J., 74-75, 217
Gopalan, R., 106
Goyal, S.R., 124
Grant, Charles, 165-166
Griffiths, Percival, 136
Guha, Ranajit, 159
Gujarat, 103,
Gupta, Isvar Candra, 237-238, 240
Guptas, 66, 109-110, 117, 119-120, 122-123, 125

Habib, Muhammad, 131
Hacker, Andrew, 200
Hāldār, Umācaran, 242
Hamid ud din, Khan, 147
Hardy, P., 128
Harṣacarita, 123
Hasan, Amir, 130
Hastings, Lord, 168
Hastings, Warren, 157-159, 162, 167, 169, 170
Held, G.J., 71
Hindu College, Calcutta, 173, 176-177
Hocart, A.M., 75
Horowitz, Irving L., 205
Hoselitz, Bert, F., 2-3
Hinduism, 13-15, 33, 37, 45-46, 51, 84, 105, 136, 150, 153, 186, 188, 192-193, 205,-222, 229-235, 256. *See also* Law; śāstras; *Arthaśāstra*; *Dharmaśāstra*; Ghose, Aurobindo; Vivekananda; Gandhi
Hindus, relations with Muslims, 183-185, 194-196
Hunter, Sir W. W., 156
Hyderabad, 154-155, 167

Ibn-al-Faqih, 138
Ibn Hasan, 146
Ibn-i-Taymiyyah, 132
Indra, 74, 93
Ingalls, Professor 92
Islam, 15, 102, 129, 131-132, 145 146, 151, 234, 258-259. *See also* Law, Muslim; Muslim
Iyer, V.R. Krishna, 46

Jahangir, 138, 149
Jain, H.M., 54
Jains, 92, 98, 233
Jan Sangh, 26-28
Jātakas, 98-99 113-114
Jāti, 26, 83-84
Jayawardana, W.A., 122
Jhabvala, Ruth Prabwa, 57
Joll, James, 200, 205

Kachin, tribe of Burma, 72-73
Kadamba clan, 114-115, 118-120
Kādambarī, 99
Kaliṅga, 112, 119, 121
Kallar, caste, 74, 78-79
Kāmandaka, 91
Kane, P.V., 75
Kangle, R.P., 86, 116, 120
karman, 114, 117, 123, 208
Kashmir, 103, 104, 117,
Kauṭilya, 75, 77, 86-87, 98-99
Kauṭilīya Arthaśāstra, 87-91, 96-99. *See also* Kauṭilya
Kaye, J.W., 162, 165

Kerala, 47, 53
Keshabchandra, 186
Khan, A. Majed, 157
Kielhorn, F., 109
King, kingship. *See kṣatriya*; Royal Mystique; *devaraja*; Divine Right; *aśvamedha; rājasūya*
Kothari, Rajni, 3, 10, 26, 28
Kropotkin, Peter, 200-201, 203,
Kṣatra, 65-66, 78, 217
Kṣatriya, 65-66, 68-82, 94-102, 107, 235, 255. *See also* King
Kuhn, Thomas, 17
Kumar, Ravindar, 165

Leach, E.R., 67, 72-73
Lévi-Strauss, C., 72, 83
Law, Hindu, 11, 13, 14, 39, 41-43, 45-47, 55, 159, 170; Indian, 3, 35-59, 161, 170; Muslim, 41, 43-45, 139, 147 159, 161, 171. *See also Arthaśāstra; Dharmśāstra; Manu; Yama; Brihaspati*
Levy, Reuben, 135
Lunar dynasty, 105-106, 110, 115, 124, 126

Mackenzie. Holt, 152, 163-165
Madras, 45, 53, 59, 153-154, 161, 163, 243, 253-254
Māhabhārata, 77, 93, 97, 98, 105-106, 135, 230, 236-237, 251. *See also Epics*
Mahānti, Gopīnātha, 252
Mathānti, Kāhnucaran, 232, 258
Maharashtra, 110, 113, 145
Māhāvaṃsa, 114
Majumdar, B.B., 219
Majumdar, R.C., 118, 214
Malasekera, G.P., 113, 119
Maṇḍala theory, 77-78, 82, 123-124
Manu, 46, 50, 63, 74, 81-82, 94, 222
Marathas, 149, 151-153, 155, 162, 163, 250, 255
Marr, John, 102
Marriott, M., 61
Marx, Karl, 12, 27, 28
Marxism, 12, 26-27, 30, 195-196
Mauryans, 98, 122, 135
Mauss, M., 77, 83
Mayer, Kurt, B., 20
Megasthenes, 98
Mehta, Rama, 57
Metcalfe, Charles, 151, 162, 164-165,
Minangkabau of Java, 72
Minogue, K.R., 2, 7-8, 10
Mir Kasim, 155-156
Mirrors for Kings, 135
Mishra, B.B., 116, 118,
Mitra, Rājendralāl, 241-242
Mohammad Shah, 141, 147
Mohammad Tahir Sabzwari, 148
Morehouse, Ward, 29
Moreland, W.E., 170
Mughals, 135-150, 151-153, 155, 157, 166, 168-171, 233, 236
Muhammad Ali Walajah, Nawab, 154
Muhammad Reza Khan, 156-157
Mukhopādhyāy, Bhūderancandra, 244
Mukhopādhyāy, Rajkṛṣṇa, 241,
Munro, Sir Thomas, 151, 162-165
Muslim political theory, 128-136, 151. *See also* Islam; Mughals; Law; Muslim
Muslim, relations with Hindus, 183-185, 194-196
Mysore, 115, 152, 167

Naga, 106-108, 111, 113
Najmuddin Razi, 132, 133
Nanda empire, 98, 120
Nārada, 95
Nasiruddin Tusi, 132
Nayak, 78-79,
Neale, W.C., 61
Nehru, Jawaharlal, 195-197, 203, 226
Nepal, 124, 168
Nicholas, C.W., 118
Nilakanta Sastri, K.A., 115, 118, 121-122
Nisbet, Robert, 21
Nītisāra of Kāmandaka, 91-92
Nītivākyāmṛta of Somadeva, 92

Nizamul Mulk (Nizum-ul-Mulk), 132-133

Oakeshott, Michael, 5-7, 8
Orissa, 112, 119-121, 228-260
Oriya, 228-260
Ostergaard, G., 227
Oudh, 158, 162, 168
Ovington, T., 153

Pakistan, 43
Pal, B.C., 174
Pālas, 109, 120
Pallavas, 106, 107, 111, 115, 120
Pancaviṃsa Br., 74
Pandnamas, 135
Pānīgrāhī, Kālindī Carana, 252
Paranavitana, S., 119
Parrish, William L., 19
Parsons, Talcott, 23
Pāsupata (s), 104
Pathak, V.S., 114, 123
Perera, Lakshman, 114, 119
Persia, 98, 128, 130-131, 133-134, 138, 153, 170, 233-236, 255, 258
Philips, C.H., 137
Pocock, J.G.A., 14
Poissin, L. de la Vallée, 106
Porée-Maspéro, Év., 107
Praharāja, Gopāla, 252
Pratihāras, 111
Pringle, Robert, 165-166
Proudhon, Pierre-Joseph, 200-201
Przyluski, J., 107
Purāṇas, 104, 108, 110, 111, 115, 126, 230, 254, 256
Puri, B.N., 111
Puri temple, 229-230, 234

Qabusnama, 135
Quran, 128, 208
Qureshi, I.H., 142, 160

Radhakrishnan, Dr. S., 47
Rajasthan, 40, 113-114, 122, 145, 168
Rājasūya, 69-70, 75, 76
Rajput, 113, 145, 151, 168
Rāmāyaṇa, 98, 105, 230, 236-237, 251
Ranade, M.G., 193, 226
Ranking, G.S.A., 140
Ratha, Mṛtyunjaya, 241
Rau, W., 69
Rāy, Gaurīsaṇkar, 240-242, 244
Rāy, Rāmmohan, 172, 174-176, 177-178 185-186, 188, 234, 237-239, 258
Rāya, Rādhānātha, 250
Renou, L., 75, 78
Rg Veda, 217
Rolland, Romain, 227
Rosenthal, E.I.J., 129
Ross, C., 170
Ross, Denison, 131
Rothermund, Dietmar, 85
Rothermund, Indira, 195
Roy, P.C., 135
"Royal mystique," 99-102, 150
Rudolph, L.I. and S.H., 2-3, 8, 23, 26, 60, 84

Sabervallah, Satish, 28
Sahu, N.K., 246
Śailodbhavas, 112, 114-115
Salim, Afsar, 131
Śaṅgam texts, of Tamilnāḍu, 104
Sannyasi, 208, 210-211, 232, 233, 242, 265
Sanskrit, 233, 235-236, 251, 256, 259
Śāstras, 13, 27, 116, 121, 152, 161, 212, 256. *See also Arthaśāstra*; *Dharmaśāstra*
Sastri, Hirananda, 109
Sastri, H.K., 106
Sastri, Mr. Justice Patanjali, 46
Sastry, K.R.R., 51
Satapatha, 69, 73
Sathe, S.P., 54
Sati, 35, 53, 159, 165-166, 231-232
Satyagraha, 195, 204-206, 224-225
Scalapino, R.A., 202-203
Scharfe, H., 67, 69, 77
Sen, Priyaranjan, 241
Sen, Ramprasad, 237

Senāpati, Phakīrmohana, 228, 241, 243, 250-260
Senas, 110-111, 120
Shah Alam, 155-156
Shahjahan, 147
Sharma, J.P., 72
Sharma, R.S., 68
Shils, Edward, 9-10
Shore, Sir John, 160, 162
Shukla, C.S., 224, 227
Silāhāras, 113-115
Sinha, K.G., 119
Sinha, S., 70
Sircar, D.C. 109, 115-116, 118-119, 121-123, 126
Smith, V.A., 159, 161
Solar dynasty, 105-106, 110-111, 115, 124, 126
Somadeva, 92, 97
Sondhi, M.L., 28
Southall, A., 78
Spellman, J.W., 75
Srinivas, M.N., 64, 84, 111
Stephens, T.B., 56
Stokes, E., 164
Sukra, 87
Śukrantītsāra, 87
Symson, Capt. W., 153

Tagore, Dwarkanath, 176
Tagore, Debendranath, 172, 175-178, 185-186, 188
Tagore, Prasanna Kumar, 176
Tagore, Rabindranath, 172, 176-177, 178-185, 186-190, 232-233
Talmon, J.R., 67
Taittīrīya Saṃhitā, 73
Tendulkar, D.G., 216, 219, 221, 224, 227
Tilak, B.G. (Lokmanya), 188
Thomas, Dorothy S., 21
Tipu Sultan, 149, 162, 167
Tod, James, 67, 114
Tolstoy, Leo, 200-203, 207
Tradition, defined, 1-2, 7, 14, 32-34, 61-62, 86, 104, 229
Trautmann, Thomas T., 11

Unnithan, T.K.N., 29, 30
Upanishads, 178, 188, 207, 210, 217, 231, 233

Vaidya, M.S., 39
Vaisnavism, 93, 233-235, 237
Van Ossenbruggen, F., 70
Vansittart, Henry, 155
Varma, V.P., 211
Varṇa, 71-72, 76, 82-84, 120
Vedas, 62, 90, 152, 192, 231, 233
Vedānta, 194, 196, 220, 231, 233-234
Vencataramayya, N., 122
Vijayanagar, 151, 153
Vivekananda, Swami, 188, 192-193, 195, 200-201, 203, 206-215, 218, 221-227,
Von Grunebaum, G.E., 128

Wasaua, 135
Weber, Adna Ferrin, 19
Weber, Max, 3-4, 10, 23, 28
Wellesley, Marquess, 161, 167
Wertheim, W.F., 8
Whitting, C.E.J., 130
Wilberforce, William, 165
Winstedt, R.O., 107
Woodcock, George, 200-201, 205,

Yama, 46
Yazdani G., 109, 122
Yu, G.T., 202-203